IN GOD'S PRESENCE

In GOD'S Presence

DAILY DEVOTIONS WITH

J. I. Packer

Compiled and edited by Jean Watson

Harold Shaw Publishers
Wheaton, Illinois

ISBN-13: 978-0-877-88409-5

Cover design by David LaPlaca
Cover photo by Luci Shaw

Library of Congress Cataloging-in-Publication Data

Packer, J. I. (James Innell)
 [Your father loves you]
 In God's presence: daily devotions with J.I. Packer / compiled and edited by Jean Watson.
 p. cm.
 Originally published: Your Father loves you. Wheaton, Ill. : H. Shaw Publishers, c1986.
 Includes bibliographical references.
 ISBN 0-87788-409-9 (pbk.)
 1. Family--Prayer-books and devotions--English. 2. Devotional calendars. I. Watson, Jean. II. Title
BV255.P26 1998
242'.2--dc21   98-36013
CIP

Contents

To the reader

About this book

Acknowledgments

To the reader

"Curiouser and curiouser!" cried Alice as she grew from ten inches to nine feet tall. Her words, I confess, ran through my own mind as I gazed on these pieces of Packer that Jean Watson has selected so skillfully. Becoming the source of a daily devotional brackets me with giants like Oswald Chambers, David Watson, C.S. Lewis, J.B. Phillips, and Martyn Lloyd-Jones, and who would not feel nine feet tall at joining a club like that? Yet all books of daily readings from a single author seem to me to have their hazards, and as this compilation is not the one book I would choose to have with me on a desert island, along with the Bible and Shakespeare, I feel rather unnerved at the thought that someone else might treat the thoughts of Chairman Packer as their sole source of private spiritual help for twelve whole months. Ought any teacher's material to be used this way, when we are all so lopsided in our vision and clumsy in our coverage of God's truth? Is any of our stuff really good enough for the purpose? I have never been sure, and I am not sure now.

Of this, however, I am sure: that Jean Watson has done an outstanding job in drawing material, printed and taped, from a great miscellaneous mass; in arranging it around what to me is indeed central, namely knowledge of our Maker as our sovereignly gracious Father, ever to be adored with shining-eyed gratitude for his saving love in Christ; and in choosing texts and devotional suggestions to go with each day's quota of Packer paragraphs, edited for the purpose. I salute her; I certainly couldn't have done it! To be sure, the Packer I meet here is not all the Packer I know, just as the Packer I know is assuredly not all the Packer God knows. But everything offered here could, I think, help someone somewhere along the line to know God better, so I cheerfully let it go with the prayer that Jean Watson's brilliant picking and choosing will in fact be blessed in this way.

Supposing, then, that this book is now yours, what should you do with it? Don't, I beg you, treat it superstitiously, as if it were verbally inspired; it isn't. These droppings from my head and heart should be your starting point, not your resting place. Use them as a springboard or trampoline before the Lord. Bounce on them, bounce off them, and see how far and how high your heavenly Father lifts you and enables you to go.

James Packer

About this book

Most "through the year" books are like spiritual buffets serving light refreshments. James Packer's readings provide much more substantial though tasty meals to help wean new Christians and fortify those of longer standing. The main theme is life in the Christian family, and James Packer approaches this devotionally and doctrinally, wanting his readers to grasp with their minds as well as their hearts what being in God's family means and involves.

The main theme is explored under sixteen related topics: extending the family (outreach); family attitudes and lifestyle; family foundations (Christian basics); family provisions; family relationships; family standards; family wisdom; growing up in the family (Christian maturity); the family at prayer; the family book (the Bible); the family in danger (spiritual war); the family's future (heaven); the family unit (the church); the head of the family (God); the heart of the family (Jesus); the Spirit of the family (the Holy Spirit).

Four topics are covered each month, with seven readings each on the first three weeks and between seven and ten readings (depending on how many days there are in the month) on the fourth.

Each reading is preceded by its topic heading, subheading, and Bible verse(s), followed by a question or reflective study, idea, or action and a prayer or meditative thought.

Many Bible study suggestions are given throughout the book and the frequent references and index of themes open up other possibilities for groups or individuals wanting to dig deeper into Christian truths. Except where otherwise indicated, the *Revised Standard Version* has been the basis for all scriptural quotations.

The material has been gathered from seventy-six sources in the shape of books, articles, and taped talks.

We hope the book will prove useful for individuals in their private quiet times and for clergy or lay people giving talks or leading Bible studies or devotions in homes, and other public situations.

Jean Watson

Acknowledgments

Grateful acknowledgment is made to the publishers of the following magazines in which articles by James Packer, excerpted in this work by permission, first appeared:

The Alliance Witness, Nyack, NY
Banner of Truth, Edinburgh, Scotland
Bibliotheca Sacra, Dallas Seminary, Dallas, TX
The Bulletin of Westminster Theological Seminary, Philadelphia, PA
Christianity Today, Carol Stream, IL
Churchman, Church Society, London, England
Discovery Papers, Peninsula Bible Church, Palo Alto, CA
Regent Quarterly Bulletin, Regent College, Vancouver, British Columbia, Canada
Special Collection Journal, Spiritual Counterfeits Project, Berkeley, CA
Tenth, 10th Presbyterian Church, Philadelphia, PA
Tyndale Bulletin, Inter-Varsity Press, Leicester, England
UCCF (Inter-Varsity), Leicester, England
Viewpoint, Inter-Schools Christian Fellowship, London, England

Grateful acknowledgment is made to the publishers of the following books which have been excerpted by permission in this work:

Baker's Dictionary of Theology, ed. C.F.H. Henry, Baker Book House, © 1959; rev. to *Evangelical Dictionary of Theology*, ed. by Walter Elwell, © 1984 by Walter Elwell. Published by Baker Book House, Grand Rapids, Michigan 49506. Used by permission.

From *Beyond the Battle for the Bible* by J. I. Packer, © 1980. Used by permission of Good News Publishers/Crossway Books, Westchester, Illinois 60153.

Bible Characters and Doctrine, Volume 11. First published in 1974 by Scripture Union, London, England. Used by permission.

Taken from *Evangelism and the Sovereignty of God* by J. I. Packer, © 1961 by Inter-Varsity Fellowship, Leicester, England. Used by permission of InterVarsity Press, Downers Grove, Illinois 60515.

Fundamentalism and the Word of God by J. I. Packer, © 1958. Used by permission of Eerdman's Printing Company, Grand Rapids, Michigan 49503.

Taken from *God Has Spoken* by J. I. Packer, © 1979 by J. I. Packer. Used by permission of InterVarsity Press, Downers Grove, Illinois 60515.

From *Gospel and Culture*, ed. J. Stott, R. Coote, © 1979 by the Lausanne Committee for World Evangelization. Published by William Carey Press, Pasadena, California. Used by permission of the Lausanne Committee for World Evangelization.

From *Hard Questions*, ed. Frank Colquhoun, © 1967, Falcon Books, East Sussex, England. Used by permission of Frank Colquhoun.

From *I Want to Be a Christian* by J. I. Packer. Published by Tyndale House Publishers, Inc., © 1977. Used by permission.

From *Keep in Step With the Spirit* by J. I. Packer, © 1984 by J. I. Packer. Published by Fleming H. Revell Company, Old Tappan, New Jersey. Used by permission.

Taken from *Knowing God* by J. I. Packer, © 1973 by J. I. Packer. Used by permission of InterVarsity Press, Downers Grove, Illinois 60515.

In the beginning God created the heavens and the earth.
Genesis 1:1

The solution chapter in one of Dorothy Sayers's detective stories is called, "When You Know How, You Know Who." Genesis chapters 1 and 2 however tell us *who* without giving us many answers about *how*.

The message of these two chapters is this: You have seen the sea, the sky, the sun, moon, and stars. You have watched the birds and the fish. You have observed the landscape, the vegetation, the animals, the insects, all the big things and little things together. You have marveled at the wonderful complexity of human beings with all their powers and skills and the deep feelings of fascination, attraction, and affection that men and women arouse in each other. Fantastic, isn't it? Well now, meet the one who is behind it all. Now that you have enjoyed these works of art, you must shake hands with the artist; since you were thrilled by the music, we will introduce you to the composer.

In other words, these chapters, like Psalm 104 and Job chapters 38–41, were written to show us the Creator rather than the creation, and to teach us knowledge of God rather than physical science.

In creating, God was craftsman and more. Craftsmen shape and are limited by existing material, but no material existed at all until God said, "Let there be. . ." To make this point, theologians speak of creation out of nothing, not meaning that nothing was a sort of something, but that in creating God was absolutely free and unrestricted, and that there was nothing to determine or shape what he brought into being except his own idea of what he would like.

Meditate on the passages mentioned above.
Write and offer in praise to God a song, poem, or prayer arising out of your meditation. (If you have put your own best craftsmanship and effort into it, you might share it at a home group meeting or even at church.)

The head of the family
Creation's origin, sustainer, and goal

From him and through him and to him are all things.
Romans 11:36

God has revealed himself to be the origin, sustainer, and goal of all creation and of mankind in particular. Everything that he causes to exist is meant to return to him in honor and praise. Paul develops these foundational truths of theism in his sermon to the Athenian idolators about the unknown God (Acts 17:22–31).

First he speaks of God as our *origin*, the one who brought us into existence. "The God who made the world and everything in it...made from one every nation of men to live on all the face of the earth" (vv. 24,26).

Then Paul speaks of God as our *sustainer*, the one who "gives to all men life and breath and everything" so that "in him we live and move and have our being" (vv. 25,28). We depend upon God for every moment of our existence: creatures only remain in being through the constant exercise of his upholding power. He, God transcendent, above and beyond and apart from his world and entirely independent of it, is also God immanent: in the world as the one who is over it; permeating and upholding it as the one who orders its goings and controls its course.

Lastly Paul speaks of God as our *goal*. God made man, he says, "that they should seek God" (v. 27). Man exists for God, and godlessness is a denial of man's own nature. Humanity is only perfected in those who know God.

Meditate on Jeremiah 17:10 and Psalm 139:1–5.
Lord, keep the words of today's text in my thoughts throughout this day.

I the Lord do not change.
Malachi 3:6

Strain, shock, or a lobotomy can alter a human being's character, but nothing can alter the character of God. In the course of a human life, tastes and
outlook and temper may change radically: a kind, equable person may turn
bitter and crotchety; a person of good will may turn cynical and callous.
But nothing of this sort happens to the Creator. He never becomes less
truthful or merciful or just or good than he used to be. The character of
God is today, and always will be, exactly what it was in Bible times.

God announced his name to Moses as "I am who I am" (Exod. 3:14).
This name is not a description of God but simply a declaration of his self-
existence and his eternal changelessness—a reminder to mankind that he
has life in himself and that what he is now, he is eternally. In a later chapter,
however, he "proclaimed the name of the LORD" to Moses by listing the various facets of his holy character (Exod. 34:5-7). So from these two references we learn who God is and that he is forever all that three thousand
years ago he told Moses he was. God's moral character is changeless.

James, in a passage that deals with God's goodness and holiness, his generosity to men, and his hostility to sin, speaks of God as one "with whom
there is no variation or shadow due to change" (James 1:17).

"He cannot change for the better, for he is already perfect; and, being perfect, he
cannot change for the worse" (A.W. Pink).

*God's unchanging character would certainly not strike everyone as a comfortable
truth. How does it strike you? Turn your reaction into prayer.*

January 4

The head of the family
God's unchanging purposes

The Glory of Israel will not lie or repent; for he is not a man, that he should repent.
1 Samuel 15:29

Repenting means revising one's judgment and changing one's plan of action. God never does this; he never needs to, for his plans are made on the basis of a complete knowledge and control which extends to all things past, present, and future, so that there can be no sudden emergencies or unlooked-for developments to take him by surprise. "The counsel of the LORD stands for ever, the thoughts of his heart to all generations" (Ps. 33:11). What he does in time, he planned from eternity. And all that he planned in eternity, he carries out in time. And all that he has in his Word committed himself to do, will infallibly be done. Thus we read of the "unchangeable character of his purpose" to bring believers into full enjoyment of their promised inheritance, and of the immutable oath by which he confirmed his counsel to Abraham, the archetypal believer, both for Abraham's own assurance and also for others (Heb. 6:17–19). So it is with all God's announced intentions. They do not change. No part of his eternal plan changes.

It is true that there is a group of texts (Gen. 6:6–8; 1 Sam. 15:11; 2 Sam. 24:16; Joel 2:13–14; Jon. 3:10) which speak of God as repenting. The reference in each case is to a reversal of God's previous treatment of particular men, consequent upon their reaction to that treatment. But there is no suggestion that this reaction was not foreseen, or that it took God by surprise, and was not provided for in his eternal plan. No change in his eternal purpose is implied when he begins to deal with a person in a new way.

Study the references above and draw your own conclusions.
Father, how I praise you that you always purpose good for me.

To whom then will you compare me, that I should be like him? says the Holy One. . .why do you say, O Jacob, and speak, O Israel, "My way is hid from the LORD, and my right is disregarded by my God"? Have you not known? Have you not heard? The LORD is the everlasting God, the Creator of the ends of the earth. He does not faint or grow weary, his understanding is unsearchable.
Isaiah 40:25,27–28

The first question here rebukes *wrong thoughts about God.* "Your thoughts of God are too human," Luther said to Erasmus. This is where most of us go astray. Our thoughts of God are not great enough; we fail to reckon with the reality of his limitless wisdom and power. Put this mistake right, says God; learn to acknowledge the full majesty of your incomparable God and Savior.

The second question rebukes *wrong thoughts about ourselves.* God has not abandoned us anymore than he abandoned Jacob. He never abandons anyone on whom he has set his love. If you have been resigning yourself to the thought that God has left you high and dry, seek grace to be ashamed of yourself. Such unbelieving pessimism deeply dishonors our great God and Savior.

The next two questions and the statements which follow rebuke *our slowness of heart to believe in God's majesty.* God would shame us out of our unbelief. He asks: Have you been imagining that I, the Creator, have grown old and tired? The rebuke is well deserved by many of us.

Let Isaiah's questions search your heart and make you more aware of your own spiritual attitudes.
"Wait for the LORD" in meditation on his majesty until you find your strength renewed (Isa. 40:31).

God is love.
1 John 4:8

"God is love" is the complete truth about God *so far as the Christian is concerned*. To say "God *is* light" is to imply that God's holiness finds expression in everything that he says and does. Similarly, the statement "God *is* love" means that his love finds expression in everything that he says and does. The knowledge that this is true for each of us personally is our supreme comfort as Christians. As believers, we find in the Cross of Christ assurance that we, as individuals, are beloved of God. Each of us can say with truth, "The Son of God. . . loved me and give himself for me" (Gal. 2:20). Knowing this, he is able to apply to himself the promise that all things work together for good to those who love God and are called according to his purpose (Rom. 8:28). Not just *some* things, note, but *all* things!

Every single thing that happens to the Christian expresses God's love and furthers God's purpose for him. Thus, so far as he is concerned, God is love to him—holy, omnipotent love—at every moment and in every event of everyday life. Even when he cannot see the why and wherefore of God's dealings, he knows that there is love in and behind them and so he can rejoice always; even when, humanly speaking, things are going wrong, he knows that the true story of his life, when known, will prove to be "mercy from first to last"—and he is content.

Do you believe that every single thing that has happened in your life is an expression of God's love for you?
Talk to God about the things that you cannot yet see in that light.

. . . your Father. . .
Matthew 6:1

The key thought running through Matthew chapter 6 is: Life with God as our heavenly Father. Read it through with this context in mind. Jesus urges us to see ourselves as God's children and to see him, think of him, and pray to him as our Father. He says, in effect: As you live, think "Our Father"; when you pray, say "Our Father."

We know how important a person's self-image is; it programs his thoughts, expectations, and emotional attitudes. Jesus wants us to have the self-image of children who live with love and are loved by their father. To know God as our father—our almighty, loving Father—is the highest, richest, and most rewarding aspect of our whole relationship with him.

In his capacity as judge, God has already blessed us with the gift of justification through the atoning death of Jesus. But the judge who has acquitted the person on trial naturally would not have a continuing relationship with him. So we need to move from the thought of God as judge to the thought of God as father with all that it implies of goodness, generosity, care, sustained concern, and closeness, along with thinking of the inheritance which he has in store for those who are adopted into his family and made joint heirs with Christ.

We are, then, children in God's royal family; the law of God is our family code; the blessing of the happy man, set out in the Beatitudes (Matt. 5:3–12), is the blessing of the royal child. Many faithful Christian ministers seem to downplay this thought of God as our heavenly Father. Surely, though, it ought to be our central theme in all teaching and learning about discipleship.

Go through Matthew 6, noting what our perfect heavenly Father does for us. *Turn these thoughts into praise now and as you live with your Father throughout the day.*

To all who received him, who believed in his name, he gave power to become children of God; who were born, not of blood nor of the will of the flesh nor of the will of man, but of God.

John 1:12–13

What is a Christian? The question can be answered in many ways, but the richest answer I know is that a Christian is one who has God for his Father. The gift of sonship to God becomes ours, not through being born, but through being born again. It is a gift of grace since it is not a natural but an adoptive sonship. The apostles proclaim that God so loved those whom Christ redeemed on the cross that he has adopted them all as his heirs, to see and share the glory into which his only-begotten Son has already come.

The question is: Do I know my own identity? *I am a child of God. God is my Father; heaven is my home; every day is one day nearer to reaching it. My Savior is my brother; every Christian is my brother too.* Say that over and over to yourself first thing in the morning; last thing at night; as you wait for the bus; anytime when your mind is free; and ask that you may be enabled to live as one who knows that it is all utterly and completely true. Is this the Christian's secret of a happy life? Yes, certainly, but we have something higher and more profound to say. This is the Christian's secret of a *Christian, God-honoring* life: and these are the aspects of the situation that really matter.

Am I proud of my Father and of his family to which by his grace I belong? *Share with God your honest answers to this double-barreled question.*

How shall we escape if we neglect such a great salvation?
Hebrews 2:3

We find that in both Testaments salvation is the central theme. There are two constants in its presentation. First, God is always the rescuer. In both Testaments he is hailed as Savior. In both Testaments he appears as the one who saves through saviors, men like the judges in the Old Testament and Jesus his only-begotten Son in the New. He is the King, and in both Testaments we see his sovereign, victorious action. In both Testaments this is accompanied by what we would call miracles—works of the new creation leading men and women into a salvation which is truly newness of life.

The second constant is the people who are rescued. They are sinful people; more precisely, they are a particular class of sinful people; they are, in fact, the seed of Abraham, the company that is first narrowed down in the New Testament to Jesus Christ himself and then expanded in and through him to become an international company of believing Christians. In passages like Romans 4 and Galatians 3, Paul lays down the principle that those who are saved, both Jews and Gentiles, are saved with faithful Abraham. That is, they are saved in their character as the seed of faithful Abraham by sharing in Abraham's faith.

Salvation, for the people of God, has three tenses: past, present, and future. Believers look back to Christ's saving work on the cross, rescuing them from sin's guilt. They look forward to Christ's saving work on his return when he comes, bringing salvation to those who look for him, ridding them at last of sin's temptations (Heb. 9:28). And in the present they rejoice in salvation as a day-to-day experience of deliverance from sin's dominion.

Am I managing to hold together the three tenses of salvation?
Praise God on the basis of Titus 3:5,7 and 1 Corinthians 1:18.

If while we were enemies we were reconciled to God by the death of his Son, much more, now that we are reconciled, shall we be saved by his life.

Romans 5:10

We are reconciled to God through the death of his Son. This death redeems us and redemption carries the idea of liberation through the payment of a price. Jesus' death for our sins also defeated Satan. Paul speaks vividly of Christ conquering the devil and his hosts, shaking off the principalities and powers, triumphing publicly over them in the manner of a general leading a procession of prisoners and spoils after a victorious campaign—and all this, Paul tells us, happened on the cross (Col. 2:14-15). So God saves first of all by the event of the Cross and symbolizes his victory in the Resurrection.

Secondly, God saves by the continuing ministry of Christ who finds and keeps those for whom he died, brings them into grace, calls them into faith, intercedes for them so that they find grace to help in time of need (Heb. 4:16), protects them when world, flesh, and devil attack them, and finally transforms them into his likeness. He shall change the body of our lowly state so as to fashion it like his glorious body, says Paul (Phil. 3:21). That is part of the Christian hope: a body to match one's already renewed spirit.

Thirdly, God saves us by the ministry of the Holy Spirit whom the saved receive as God's seal set upon them to mark them as his and to bring them in experience the first installment of the salvation which is finally to be theirs with Christ in glory (Eph. 1:13-14).

If we ask for the motivation of God in working all this for us, it is sheer grace, undeserved and unsolicited pity, mercy contrary to deep demerit, love to the unlovely and seemingly unlovable. The New Testament says that again and again.

If saving us cost God so much, can we expect to help others to receive God's salvation easily, cheaply, casually?
Lord Jesus, save me today by your life in me.

Believe in the Lord Jesus, and you will be saved.
Acts 16:31

To the question, "What must I do to be saved?" the gospel replies, "Believe on the Lord Jesus Christ." To the further question, "What does it mean to believe on the Lord Jesus Christ?" the reply is, "It means knowing ourselves to be sinners and Christ to have died for sinners; abandoning all self-righteousness and self-confidence, and casting ourselves wholly upon him for pardon and peace; and exchanging our natural enmity and rebellion against God for a spirit of grateful submission to the will of Christ through the renewal of our hearts by the Holy Spirit."

To the further question, "How am I to go about believing on Christ and repenting if I have no natural ability to do these things?" the gospel answers, "Look to Christ, speak to Christ, cry to Christ, just as you are; confess your sin, your impenitence, your unbelief, and cast yourself on his mercy; ask him to give you a new heart, working in you true repentance and firm faith; ask him to take away your evil heart of unbelief and to write his law within you, that you may never henceforth stray from him. Turn to him and trust him as best you can, and pray for grace to turn and trust more thoroughly; use the means of grace expectantly, looking to Christ to draw near to you as you seek to draw near to him; watch, pray, read, and hear God's Word; worship and commune with God's people; and so continue till you know in yourself beyond doubt that you are indeed a changed being, a penitent believer, and that the new heart which you desired has been put within you."

Has anything changed to make this "old-fashioned" gospel irrelevant?
Lord Jesus, keep me centering my life on you.

I, I am the LORD, and besides me there is no savior.
Isaiah 43:11

The people of God in the Old Testament were saved first for fellowship with God their Savior who met them on Sinai and established himself as the Lord who henceforth would be with them always. "Let them make me a sanctuary, that I may dwell in their midst" (Exod. 25:8).

Secondly, they were saved for obedience to God—the God who at Sinai gave them his law. "Save me that I may observe thy testimonies" (Ps. 119:146). In the psalter salvation appears not indeed as the goal of obedience but rather as the presupposition of obedience—that from which obedience takes its rise.

Thirdly, they were saved for the enjoyment of *shalom:* peace and happiness from God in the land which God was to give to them. They were saved for holiness, wholeness, health, and harmony in their life together, for all of this is a part of what *shalom* means. And when God established the festival calendar for them in the Promised Land, all three main feasts (Unleavened Bread and Passover, the Feast of Weeks, and the Feast of Tabernacles) and also the offering of first-fruits from each man's land were explicitly linked with the Exodus and made into occasions of praise and expressions of thanks for God's salvation.

In the New Testament the typical elements of the old dispensation give way to their antitypes under the new. God rescues now from spiritual bondage, bondage to sin and Satan, and offers a heavenly life, the life of a new world, through Christ his appointed Savior.

Am I enjoying all I was saved for?
Lord I need your salvation in these areas...(Be as specific as you can.)

He is able for all time to save those who draw near to God through him.
Hebrews 7:25

What are we saved from? Paul gives several answers to the question in Romans:

We are saved from sin, that demonic dynamic of hostility to God. All people, says Paul, are under sin by nature, and it drives them into the way of disobedience so that "none is righteous, no, not one" (Rom. 3:10). This is a person's natural state in which he plays God by treating himself as the center of his world and fights God by refusing the claims of his own true maker.

We are saved from being under the Law which both irritates sin, stirring it into activity, and passes censure on it in all its forms and expressions. The Law is good in itself and promises life to any who keep it entirely, but for us human beings it is very bad because of its allergic effect on moral natures already infected and dominated by the sin principle.

We are saved from God's wrath which is not ill temper but divine righteousness in action: righteousness that will be shown fully in the final judgment but already is apparent in the way that sin begets sin and increases misery, moral corruption, and social disruption, person against person.

We are saved from death—the destructive principle that negates all God's intentions for a person's fulfillment by cutting us off from God's life. Death operates both spiritually and physically in the present and will be experienced increasingly in the future existence for which eternal death is the only proper name.

Salvation means that we are saved right out of the order of things in which sin, Law, wrath, and death are the dominant forces.

We are saved from all that—but for what? Paul's answer is that we are saved to be with the Lord and to be like the Lord.

Think through the above in non-theological language, as though speaking or writing to an unchurched person who was questioning you about it.
Lord, I long that everyone should be saved from all those dreadful things, especially these people for whom I care...

When the goodness and loving kindness of God our Savior appeared, he saved us, not because of deeds done by us in righteousness, but in virtue of his own mercy, by the washing of regeneration and renewal in the Holy Spirit.

Titus 3:4–5

Christianity has certain distinct features:

Other faiths assume our ability to secure and retain God's favor by right action and give us detailed guidance as to how to do it; but Christianity has said that sin has so ruined us that we cannot do this. It is beyond our power to keep the law of God as we should; we are guilty and helpless, wholly unable to save ourselves, and so must be saved, if at all, by the action of another.

Other faiths direct us to follow the teaching of their founders—famous men long deceased; but Christianity, identifying its founder as God incarnate, who died for our sins and rose again to bestow forgiveness, proclaims him as alive and calls on us to trust him and his atoning work, making him the object of our worship and service. Redemption through the love of the Son of God, who became man, bore his Father's judgment on our sins, and rose from death to reign forever, is a theme without parallel in the world's religions.

Christianity proclaims that those who repent of sin and trust in Jesus Christ are created anew at the heart of their being by the Holy Spirit. They are united to Jesus Christ in his risen life, their inner nature is changed, so that their deepest impulse is not now to disobey God and serve self, but to deny self and obey God. Thus they are born again into a new life of fellowship with Christ, assurance, forgiveness, and sonship to God and are given unconquerable hope and joy. There is nothing like this in any other religion.

Do I see Christianity and relay it to others as a kind of yoga or as the truth? *Lord, I acknowledge again that you are the final, ultimate truth.*

*Jesus said... "I am the way, and the truth, and the life; no one comes to the Father,
but by me."*
John 14:6

In John 14:6 it's as if Jesus said: Yes, a filial relationship to God is possible
through relating to me and my ministry of mediation—though not otherwise. For sonship of God, in the sense that guarantees mercy and glory, is
not a fact of natural life, but a gift of supernatural grace. "To all who received him, who believed in his name, he gave power to become children of
God" (John 1:12).

The doctrine of the bestowal of sonship is part of the proper exposition
of 1 Peter 3:18: "Christ... died for sins once for all, the righteous for the un-
righteous, that he might bring us to God." The only-begotten Son who died
for us presents us to his Father as his brothers and sisters; thus we are adopted. But to this privilege unbelievers remain strangers—to their own infinite
loss.

Just like the sub-contractors who gain no benefit from a pension scheme,
one who shrugs off the gospel gains nothing from the mediation of Jesus
Christ. "You refuse to come to me that you may have life" (John 5:40), says
Jesus. As unadopted roads are just pebbles and puddles, lacking a surface,
so the spiritually unadopted lack a God they can call Father, and their living, however hectic, is drab in consequence. However vivid their sense of
God may be, and however ardent their quest to know more of him, there is
only one way they can find him as Father and that is by coming to terms
with and accepting the terms already announced by God's Son, Jesus
Christ, the living Lord. As no other relation to God save sonship brings salvation, so apart from Jesus, who brings about our adoption, "there is no
other name under heaven given among men by which we must be saved"
(Acts 4:12).

Do I shy away from spelling out to others these truths, which so often cause people
to take offense and call me narrow-minded?
*Lord, if being called narrow-minded is part of bearing the offense of the cross, may I
be willing to bear it rather than keep silent when I should speak.*

The heart of the family
                                        Fully God, truly man

*The Word became flesh and dwelt among us, full of grace and truth; we have beheld
his glory, glory as of the only Son from the Father. . . The only Son, who is in the
bosom of the Father, he has made him known.*

                                                                    John 1:14,18

God the Son, without ceasing to be God, became man in order to reveal the
Father and save sinners: that is the message of the apostolic gospel. "The
saying is sure and worthy of full acceptance, that Christ Jesus came into the
world to save sinners" (1 Tim. 1:15). Jesus of Nazareth is Christ—the Messiah, God's anointed Savior-king promised in the Old Testament—and he is
our Lord, because he is both Christ and God.

The incarnation (the word comes from Latin and means literally "in-
fleshing") is a *mystery*—a divine fact which we know is real though we do
not know how it is possible. (The Trinity is a mystery in the same sense.)

The gospel presents Jesus as truly and in every sense human, and Paul
speaks of him as "the last Adam," "the second (representative) man," even
though he is at the same time "from heaven" (1 Cor. 15:45,47). Yet he remains the Son of God, as he was before. What he emptied himself of in the
incarnation was dignity, not deity (Phil. 2:7).

Becoming "more Christian" should make us more, not less, human. In the coming
weeks you might like to read and meditate on the life of Jesus, using the Bible and,
if available, one of the well-researched "life of Christ" type of books, to discover
God's model for true humanity.

*Jesus, help me to spend more time thinking and reading about you and talking to
you. Let me see you more clearly, love you more dearly, and follow you more
nearly.*

If any man would come after me, let him deny himself and take up his cross and follow me.
Mark 8:34

If anyone wants to learn what it means to go the way Jesus went, he must do three things. First he must give up all right to himself: that is, cease bothering about self-preservation, self-aggrandizement, and self-protection against ridicule, and abandon self-assertion as a way of life. This is how the world is crucified to me (Gal. 6:14). Second, he must take up his cross: that is, settle for a life into which the world's favor and esteem do not enter. Only criminals going to execution—people from whom the world's favor has been totally withdrawn—carried crosses in those days. This is how I am crucified to the world (Gal. 6:14). Third, the would-be disciple must follow Jesus by accepting as leader and guide one who was even then on his way to execution and who expected to involve his disciples in sufferings like his own. This, says Jesus, is the only path that leads to life.

Paul wrote: "I have been crucified with Christ; it is no longer I who live, but Christ who lives in me; and the life I now live in the flesh I live by faith in the Son of God, who loved me and gave himself for me (Gal. 2:20). This brings together both aspects of the Christian's identification with Christ: acceptance of Christ's cross as both the end of the old life and the pattern of the new one.

Do phrases about denying ourselves, being crucified with Christ, and having Christ living in us suggest that our human personalities are to be obliterated? If not, what do they mean?

Lord, I don't fully understand this teaching and I think I want to evade it. Clear my mind and take away my fear. (Pray this for someone else if not for yourself.)

The heart of the family
Unforgettable example

Jesus, knowing that the Father had given all things into his hands, and that he had come from God and was going to God, rose from supper, laid aside his garments, and girded himself with a towel.

John 13:3–4

As John 13:1–20 Jesus set us an unforgettable example. As the Son of God he knew he would soon return to his Father to reign; as searcher of hearts he knew which of his chosen disciples were "clean" (i.e., forgiven and accepted by God) and which one was not "clean" and would betray him. Also he knew that the road back to the Father led through the ultimate humiliation of the cross, the humiliation which he symbolized here by taking the role of a low-grade menial.

Jesus loved his own "to the end"—not only to the end of his earthly life and of his redeeming work, but also to the nth degree. A Jewish host normally had his guests' feet washed by an underling; Jesus, as host of the supper, did the job himself, first taking off his coat to reveal himself as a true servant in action. A modern equivalent of feet-washing would be shoe-shining. And the particular blessing which this task signified was daily cleansing within an already established relationship of acceptance.

As teacher, lord, and director of his disciples' lives, Jesus charged them to follow his example of loving service. The particular service which the feet-washing signified was unique (i.e., cleansing from sin) but the spirit of love and care which the action revealed was not to be unique; Christians must reproduce it. Rather than displaying particular outward behavior-patterns, Christians are called upon to imitate Christ by maintaining an attitude of self-humbling love.

Do I see and embrace my menial tasks as opportunities to imitate Jesus in loving service?
Lord, I bring these tasks to you... Change my attitude toward them and my way of doing them...

I can do nothing on my own authority; as I hear, I judge; and my judgment is just, because I seek not my own will but the will of him who sent me.
John 5:30

The Son appears in the gospels not as an independent divine person, but as a dependent one who thinks and acts only and wholly as the Father directs. "The Son can do nothing of his own accord" (John 5:19). "I have come down from heaven, not to do my own will, but the will of him who sent me" (John 6:38). "I do nothing on my own authority . . . I always do what is pleasing to him" (John 8:28–29).

It is the nature of the second person of the Trinity to acknowledge the authority and submit to the good pleasure of the first. That is why he declares himself to be the Son, and the first person to be his Father. Though coequal with the Father in eternity, power, and glory, it is natural to him to play the Son's part and find all his joy in doing his Father's will, just as it is natural to the first person of the Trinity to plan and initiate the works of the Godhead and natural to the third person to proceed from the Father and the Son to do their joint bidding.

Thus the obedience of the God-man to the Father while he was on earth was not a new relationship occasioned by the incarnation, but the continuation in time of the eternal relationship between the Son and the Father in heaven. Both in heaven and on earth, the Son was utterly dependent upon the Father's will. He only did what the Father willed him to do and knew what the Father willed him to know.

"A servant is not greater than his master" (John 15:20). Our master chose a life of complete dependency upon the will of his Father. Am I equally dependent on God's will?
Lord, is there any matter about which I need to be seeking your will now?

I am the vine, you are the branches. He who abides in me, and I in him, he it is that bears much fruit, for apart from me you can do nothing.

John 15:5

It's well worth studying and meditating on Jesus' parable about the vine (John 15:1-17). The main thoughts are:

God the Father has his hand on Christ's disciples. He wants them to fruit, i.e., to be Christlike in character, hard-working in God's service, and influential for good and godliness. Therefore he prunes fruitful branches to make them fruit better: he cuts them back through humbling and chastening providences, so improving their quality. Barren branches (professed Christians whose faith, being merely mental and not touching the heart, is dead—James 2:14-17) he cuts off entirely by adverse providences on earth or in judgment hereafter.

The condition of fruitfulness is to abide in Christ, as objects of his abiding love. "Abide" means "stay," and the way to stay is to obey. Christ's obedience to his Father (in loving those he calls his friends up to the point of dying for them) is the model here: Christ directs us to love in the same way. We shall not be able to stay steady in Christ without humility, self-distrust, sustained attention to Christ's command as we move among men, and total reliance on him for enabling grace.

Those who stay in Christ may pray confidently and successfully because their will and his coincide, and they may ask in his name, invoking his authority as the author of their right to pray, the authorizer of their particular requests, and the Father's agent in granting them.

The major task in petitionary prayer is getting from the Lord himself the requests to be made. How much time do I spend doing this?

Lord, I set my will to obey you. Please give me a mind and heart to match my intention.

Jesus increased in wisdom and in stature, and in favor with God and man.
Luke 2:52

Wisdom in the Bible embraces the thought of discerning the best thing to aim at and being able to choose the best means to that end. Jesus chose the best thing to aim at—namely his Father's will: that he should redeem men and bring a multitude of sinners to glory. Then he chose the best means to that end. His Father taught him from the Old Testament Scriptures what sort of person the Messiah, God's appointed Savior, must be. Jesus understood this; he knew that the way to his kingdom was via the cross and he went that way. This was an expression of his wisdom.

His wisdom was also shown in his teaching and in his dealings with people. Because he knew and understood what was wisdom for his own life, he was able to help others to know and understand wisdom in their own lives. It's generally true that one who understands how to follow God's will for his or her life is able to guide another person in this area. God's will for others won't necessarily be identical to God's will for me, but having worked out the next step of the way that God wants me to go, I can share the principles which will help others to find the overall strategy and the next step that is right for them.

Look at Jesus, then, as embodying the perfection of God's wisdom. This is one aspect of the total human maturity (emotional and ethical) which Jesus showed and which the Holy Spirit starts to bring about in us.

Am I increasing in wisdom? Is this a valid question to ask myself/ask others about myself? How may I know if I am wiser than I used to be?

Jesus, you are my wisdom. I need to look more closely at your life and teaching and experience your changing power through your Spirit more and more.

The Spirit of the family
Second birth

That which is born of the flesh is flesh, and that which is born of the Spirit is spirit.
Do not marvel that I said to you, "You must be born anew."

John 3:6-7

The new birth or regeneration is an inner recreating of fallen human nature by the Holy Spirit. It changes the disposition from lawless, godless self-seeking into one of trust and love, of repentance for past rebelliousness and unbelief, and loving compliance with God's law henceforth. It enlightens the blinded mind to discern spiritual realities and liberates and energizes the enslaved will for free obedience to God.

The use of the figure of new birth to describe this change emphasizes two facts about it. The first is its decisiveness. The regenerate man has forever ceased to be the man he was; his old life is over and a new life has begun; he is a new creature in Christ, buried with him out of reach of condemnation and raised with him into a new life of righteousness.

The second fact emphasized is that regeneration is due to the free, and to us, mysterious, exercise of divine power. Infants do not induce or cooperate in their own procreation and birth; no more can those who are dead in trespasses and sins prompt the quickening operation of God's Spirit within them.

How would you answer someone who said that he or she longed to be a Christian but God did not seem to have chosen to regenerate him/her?
Lord, I thank you that my longings for you and my desires for holiness mean that your Holy Spirit is at work. (Tell God about those longings and desires, and ask him to make them stronger.)

When we cry, "Abba! Father!" it is the Spirit himself bearing witness with our spirit that we are children of God.
Romans 8:15–16

The Spirit's witness is not ordinarily an experience in the sense in which orgasm or shock or bewilderment or being "sent" by beauty in music or nature or eating curry are experiences—datable, memorable, short-lived items in our flow of consciousness, standing out from what went before and what came afterward. Yet there are moments of experience in which the Spirit's witness becomes suddenly strong.

Such was the famous experience of Blaise Pascal on November 23, 1654, the record of which he began thus:

From about half-past ten in the evening till about half-past twelve

FIRE

God of Abraham, God of Isaac, God of Jacob, not of the philosophers and scholars *(savants).*

Certainty. Certainty *(certitude).* Feeling *(sentiment).* Joy. Peace.

Such too was Wesley's equally famous experience on May 24, 1738. While listening to Luther's preface to Romans, he felt his heart "strangely warmed. I felt I did trust in Christ, Christ alone, for salvation; and an assurance was given me that he had taken away *my* sins, even *mine,* and saved *me* from the law of sin and death."

Such experiences intensify a quality of experience that is real in some measure for every believer from the first. Paul speaks of the Spirit's witness in the present tense, implying that it is a continuous operation that imparts permanent confidence in God. Though not always vividly felt and sometimes overshadowed by feelings of doubt and despair, this confidence remains constant. The Spirit himself sees to that!

Can you echo what has been said above?
Thank God for your "datable, memorable" experiences and also for the less dramatic ones.

*When the Counselor comes, whom I shall send to you from the Father, even the
Spirit of truth, who proceeds from the Father, he will bear witness to me.*
John 15:26

In the New Testament the Holy Spirit is set forth as the third divine person,
linked with and yet distinct from the Father and the Son, just as the Father
and the Son are distinct from each other. He is the *paraclete* (John 14:16,25;
16:7)—a rich word for which there is no adequate English translation since
it means by turns comforter (strengthener), counselor, helper, supporter,
adviser, advocate, ally, senior friend—and only a person could fulfill such
roles. More precisely he is another paraclete, second in line (we may say) to
the Lord Jesus, continuing Jesus' own ministry—and only a person, one like
Jesus, could do that.

John underlines the point by repeatedly using a masculine pronoun to
render Jesus' reference to the Spirit when Greek grammar called for a neuter
one to agree with the neuter noun "Spirit." John wants his readers to be in no
doubt that the Spirit is *he* not *it.*

Again the Holy Spirit is said to hear, speak, witness, convince, glorify
Christ, lead, guide, teach, command, forbid, desire, give speech, give help,
and intercede for Christians with inarticulate groans, himself crying to God
in their prayers (John 14:26; 16:7-15; Acts 2:4; 8:29; 13:2; 16:6-7; Rom.
8:14, 16, 26-27; Gal. 4:6; 5:17-18). Also he can be lied to and grieved (Acts
5:3-4; Eph. 4:30). Such things could only be said of a person. The conclusion is that the Spirit is not just an influence; he, like the Father and the
Son, is an individual person.

What is your relationship with the third divine person? Are you allowing him to
be your counselor, adviser, and senior friend?
Put yourself and all that faces you today into the hands of God the Spirit.

You shall receive power when the Holy Spirit has come upon you.
Acts 1:8

The empowering from Christ through the Spirit is a momentous New Testament fact, one of the glories of the gospel and a mark of Christ's true followers everywhere. When the Spirit had been poured out at Pentecost, "with great power the apostles gave their testimony to the resurrection of the Lord Jesus" (Acts 4:33); "and Stephen, full of grace and power, did great wonders and signs among the people" (Acts 6:8; see also Acts 10:38).

Paul prays for the Romans "that by the power of the Holy Spirit you may abound in hope" (Rom. 15:13). Then he speaks of "what Christ has wrought through me . . . by word and deed, by the power of signs and wonders, by the power of the Holy Spirit" (Rom. 15:18–19). He reminds the Corinthians that he preached Christ crucified "in demonstration of the Spirit and power, that your faith might . . . rest . . . in the power of God" (1 Cor. 2:4–5).

He emphasizes to Timothy that God has given Christians "a spirit of power and love and self-control" and censures those who are "lovers of pleasure rather than lovers of God, holding the form of religion but denying the power of it" (2 Tim. 1:7; 3:4–5). There is no mistaking the thrust of all this. What we are being told is that supernatural living through supernatural empowering is at the very heart of New Testament Christianity, so that those who, while professing faith, do not show forth this empowering are suspect by New Testament standards. And the empowering is always the work of the Holy Spirit, even when Christ only is named as its source, for Christ is the Spirit giver (John 1:33, 20:22; Acts 2:33).

Study the New Testament references to power (with the help of a concordance), noticing what this power is for and what it is *not* for.
Lord, give me the power to speak and act in a way that pleases you.

The Spirit of the family
                                   The effect of the Spirit's work

*I will pray the Father, and he will give you another Counselor, to be with you for
ever, even the Spirit of truth. . .; you know him, for he dwells with you, and will be
in you.*

                                                                        John 14:16–17

The distinctive, constant, basic ministry of the Holy Spirit under the new
covenant is to mediate Christ's presence to believers so that three things
keep happening:

First, personal *fellowship* with Jesus (the to-and-fro of discipleship with
devotion which started in Palestine for Jesus' first followers before his passion) becomes a reality of experience, even though Jesus is not here on earth
in bodily form today but is enthroned in heaven's glory.

Second, *transformation* of character into Jesus' likeness starts to take
place as, looking to Jesus their model for strength, believers worship and
adore him and learn to lay out and, indeed, lay down their lives for him
and for others.

Third, the Spirit-given *certainty* of being loved, redeemed, and adopted
through Christ into the Father's family, so as to be "heirs of God and fellow
heirs with Christ" (Rom. 8:17), makes gratitude, delight, hope, and confidence—in a word, *assurance*—blossom in believers' hearts. This is the
proper way to understand many of the Christians' post-conversion moun-
taintop experiences. The inward coming of the Son and the Father that Jesus
promised (John 14:21–23) takes place through the Spirit and its effect is to
intensify assurance.

By these phenomena of experience, Spirit-given knowledge of Christ's
presence shows itself.

What effect is the Holy Spirit having on you?
Lord, I pray for more of your Spirit in this area of my life. . .(Focus on one.)

The Spirit is the witness, because the Spirit is truth.
1 John 5:7

I hold that the Spirit's way of witnessing to the truth that as believers we are sons and heirs of God (Rom. 8:5–17) is first to make us realize that as Christ on earth loved us and died for us, so in glory now he loves us and lives for us as the mediator whose endless life guarantees us endless glory with him. He also makes us see that through Christ, in Christ, and with Christ, we are now God's children; and hereby leads us spontaneously and instinctively— for there are spiritual instincts as well as natural ones—to think of God as Father and so to address him.

To know that God is your Father and that he loves you, his adopted child, no less than he loves his only-begotten Son and that enjoyment of God's love and glory for all eternity is pledged to you brings inward delight that is sometimes overwhelming; and this is also the Spirit's doing. For the "joy in the Holy Spirit" (Rom. 14:17) is the rejoicing in God spoken of earlier (Rom. 5:2,11), and it is the Spirit's witness of God's love for us that calls forth this joy.

I hold also that the Holy Spirit given to us is the "first fruits" (Rom. 8:23) because by enabling us to see Christ glorified and to live in fellowship with him as our mediator and with his Father as our father, he introduces us to the inmost essence of the life of heaven. To think of heaven as a place and a state cannot be wrong, for the Bible writers do it; nonetheless what makes heaven *heaven* and what must always be at the heart of our thoughts about heaven is the actual relationship with the Father and the Son that is perfected there. This is the first installment of the Spirit's present ministry to us.

Am I aware of the Spirit's inward witness? What is he telling me?
Lord, this is how I treasure my relationship with you. . .(Finish the sentence stating just how highly you do treasure your relationship with the Lord Jesus.)

The Spirit of the family
The agent and means of holiness

We all, with unveiled face, beholding the glory of the Lord, are being changed into his likeness from one degree of glory to another; for this comes from the Lord who is the Spirit.

2 Corinthians 3:18

It is by the Spirit's enabling that Christians resolve to do particular things that are right, and actually do them, and thus form habits of doing right things; and out of these habits come a character that is right.

What are the means which the Spirit uses? He uses the objective means of grace (biblical truth, prayer, fellowship, worship, and the Lord's Supper) and the subjective means of grace whereby we open ourselves to change (thinking, listening, questioning, admonishing and examining ourselves, sharing what is in our heart with others, and weighing any response they make). These are the Spirit's ordinary ways of leading us on in holiness. I believe visions, impressions, and prophecies come only rarely and to some believers not at all.

From one standpoint, the fruit of the Spirit is a series of habits formed by action and reaction. Love, joy, peace, patience, kindness, goodness, faithfulness, gentleness, self-control (Gal. 5:22–24) are all habitual dispositions: that is, accustomed ways of thinking, feeling, and behaving. We must remember however that these habits, though formed in a natural manner by self-discipline and effort, are not natural products. The discipline and effort must be blessed by the Holy Spirit or they would achieve nothing. So all our attempts to get our lives into shape need to be soaked in constant, humble, thankful prayer.

What's the difference between self-sanctification and cooperating with the Spirit's way of working?
Lord, help me not to discount either your ordinary or your extraordinary ways of working.

Anyone who does not have the Spirit of Christ does not belong to him.
Romans 8:9

If anyone does not have the Spirit of Christ, he does not belong to Christ and what he needs to do is not search for the Spirit but rather come to Christ in faith and repentance, whereupon the Spirit will be given to him (Acts 2:38).

The important question then is: Does the Holy Spirit have you? Does he have all of you or only some parts of you? Do you grieve him or are you led by him (Eph. 4:30; Rom. 8:12–14; Gal. 5:18–24)? Do you rely on him to enable you to respond to Christ when he prompts you? Do you reckon with the fact that "your body is a temple of the Holy Spirit within you, which you have from God" (1 Cor. 6:19)? Do you revere his work within you and cooperate with it or obstruct it by thoughtlessness and carelessness, indiscipline and self-indulgence?

The specific questions must be understood Christ-centeredly; in reality they are all ways of asking whether Christ your Savior is Lord of your life. But to ask them in relation to the Spirit is to give them a force and a concreteness that otherwise they might not have. In the world of projecting pictures on to screens, this would be called sharpening the focus.

The Spirit indwells us in order to transform us and works constantly in our hearts and minds to bring us closer to Christ and keep us there. As God resident within us, he himself is close to any foul thinking or behavior in which we allow ourselves to engage. This thought should weigh with us when temptation comes.

Spend time searching your heart along the lines suggested above.
Father, sharpen my focus on Jesus through the Holy Spirit today.

He (Jesus) breathed on them, and said to them, "Receive the Holy Spirit. If you for-
give the sins of any, they are forgiven; if you retain the sins of any, they are retained."
John 20:22

Jesus gave the Spirit to his people. In these days we need to remind ourselves of that. If we want the Spirit or more of the Spirit, we must seek Jesus
who gives him.

The Spirit's first work is to bring the Lord's people into communion with
their Savior. "He will glorify me, for he will take what is mine and will declare it to you" (John 16:14). "He will teach you all things, and bring to your
remembrance all that I have said to you" (John 14:26). In other words: He'll
make fellowship between you and the Lord—you as the needy one and the
Lord as risen, triumphant, and living—a happy reality.

As a result of that will come boldness. "They were all filled with the Holy
Spirit and spoke the word of God with boldness" (Acts 4:31). When the
Spirit of Christ is revealing to the Christian just how rich he is in Christ and
just how close Christ is to him, the inhibitions drop away, and the saint is
able to speak boldly and feelingly of what God has done for him.

Something else which flows from this is discernment and authority. The
people of God with the authority of Christ may and must tell the world
that everyone who repents and trusts the Savior will have his sins forgiven,
and that until they do, there is no forgiveness for them. As counselors and
helpers, it's the privilege of all Christians to say to people who are genuinely
repentant and genuinely believe in Jesus, "I tell you that for Christ's sake
your sins are forgiven. " On the other hand we may have to tell others that
since they have not yet repented, their sins are retained. It is the Spirit who
gives us the discernment to do this, as he did to Peter (see Acts 8:18–24),
along with giving us the authority for doing it.

Am I/Is my church behaving as though I/we had these resources?
Pray about the lacks in your own and your church's ministry.

If you then, who are evil, know how to give good gifts to your children, how much more will the heavenly Father give the Holy Spirit to those who ask him!
Luke 11:13

Just as notional knowledge may outrun spiritual experience, so a person's spiritual experience may be ahead of his notional knowledge. Bible believers have often so stressed (rightly) the need for correct notions that they have overlooked this. Eleven of the twelve disciples of Jesus were "made clean"—their sins were forgiven and their hearts renewed (John 15:3)—and others entered with them into Jesus' gift of pardon and peace (Luke 5:20–24; 7:47–50; 19:5–10) before a single one of them had any grasp at all of the doctrine of atonement for sin through Jesus' coming cross. The gift was given and their lives were changed first; the understanding of what had happened to them came after.

So, because God is gracious, he may deepen our life in the Spirit even when our ideas about this life are non-existent or quite wrong, provided that we are truly and wholeheartedly seeking his face and wanting to come closer to him. The formula that applies here is the promise: "You will seek me and find me; when you seek me with all your heart, I will be found by you" (Jer. 29:13–14). Then comes the task of understanding by the light of Scripture what the Lord has actually done for us and how his specific work in our personal experience, tailored lovingly to our particular temperamental and circumstantial needs at that time, should be related to the general biblical declarations of what he will do through the Spirit for all who are his.

Don't assume that because you have experienced something of the Spirit's work in your life you know all that matters about him. Were you in danger here?
Lord, add to my experience and knowledge, and also to my knowledge and experience of the Holy Spirit.

I will not leave you desolate; I will come to you. Yet a little while, and the world will see me no more, but you will see me; because I live, you will live also.

John 14:18–19

The Holy Spirit's distinctive role is to fulfill what we may call a floodlight ministry in relation to the Lord Jesus Christ. So far as this role was concerned, the Spirit "was not yet" (John 7:29, literal Greek) while Jesus was on earth; only when the Father had glorified him (John 17:1,5) could the Spirit's work of making men aware of Jesus' glory begin.

I remember walking to church one winter evening to preach on the words, "He will glorify me" (John 16:14), seeing the building floodlit as I turned a corner, and realizing that this was exactly the illustration my message needed. When floodlighting is well done, the floodlights are placed so that you do not see them; in fact, you are not supposed to see where the light is coming from; what you are meant to see is just the building on which the floodlights are trained. The intended effect is to make it visible when otherwise it would not be seen for the darkness, and to maximize its dignity by throwing all its details into relief so that you can see it properly. This perfectly illustrates the Spirit's new covenant role. He is, so to speak, the hidden floodlight shining on the Savior.

Or think of it this way. It is as if the Spirit stands behind us, throwing light over our shoulder on to Jesus who stands facing us. The Spirit's message to us is never, "Look at me; listen to me; come to me; get to know me," but always, "Look at him, and see his glory; listen to him and hear his word; go to him and have life; get to know him and taste his gift of joy and peace." The Spirit, we might say, is the matchmaker, the celestial marriage broker, whose role it is to bring us and Christ together and ensure that we stay together.

Do we, through the Spirit, floodlight Jesus for others?
Lord, your Spirit has so much to teach me. Keep me ready to learn and change.

He who did not spare his own Son but gave him up for us all, will he not also give us all things with him?
Romans 8:32

In Romans 8:1–30 Paul rhapsodizes about God's grace to us: about justification and our new life in the Spirit; about our adoption and our inheritance; about God's provision of help so that we need not fear our weaknesses or our circumstances. In verses 31–39 he spells out the implications of what he has been saying earlier.

First, he invites us to do a calculation. "If God is for us, who is against us?" (v. 31). Think it through, face up to it, work it out. That kind of realism is always good for the soul. Total up who and what stands against you and then remind yourself that one with God is a majority. Read 2 Kings 6:15–19 for an illustration of this truth.

Then Paul points out that if God didn't spare his own Son but gave him up to die for us while we were sinners, then he certainly will not withhold from us anything that's for our good, benefit, joy, or blessing. The gift of Christ on Calvary guarantees every other good gift that God can devise (v. 32).

Thirdly, Paul asks, "Who shall bring any charge against God's elect?" (Rom. 8:33). Christians sin and fail dreadfully and Satan is the accuser of the brethren, but the fact is that none of his accusations can ever succeed against us. We are secure in our acceptance by God through all eternity, for God justifies us and Jesus who died for us now intercedes (intervenes) with his Father on our behalf (v. 33–34).

Fourthly, Paul points out emphatically and lyrically that nothing anywhere, here or hereafter, can ever cut us off from God's almighty love (v. 35–39).

Which of these truths do I most urgently need to grasp?
Lord, I need to believe with all my mind, heart, and will in the truth that. . .

If God so clothes the grass of the field, which today is alive and tomorrow is thrown into the oven, will he not much more clothe you, O men of little faith?
Matthew 6:30

In Matthew 6:19–34 Jesus is speaking out against worldliness. On the positive side, what he is saying in these verses is: Live by faith. We tend to think that living by faith means operating in the Lord's service without any stated, visible means of support! But when Jesus spoke of living by faith, what he had in mind was acting as though God's promises were certainties, as the great heroes of faith did (Heb. 11:1–40). Abraham "looked forward to the city which has foundations, whose builder and maker is God" (Heb. 11:10). In other words, his eyes saw beyond the limits of this world and this life. He may not have known much about that future "city" but he treated God's promises concerning it as certainties. Moses chose "rather to share ill-treatment with the people of God than to enjoy the fleeting pleasures of sin" because "he considered the abuse suffered for the Christ greater wealth than the treasures of Egypt, for he looked to the reward" (Heb. 11:25–26). Looking to the reward, to the glory that was to be because God had promised it, he was prepared to endure the abuse which came his way because of his commitment to God's cause.

These and others lived in terms of the invisible realities which God had set before them by promise. Thus they modeled for us the life of faith.

Jesus called his disciples men of little faith because they worried about things in the future. By inference, men of mature faith would not be anxious about such matters. They would reason: God is our heavenly Father and has promised to provide for all our needs. We have complete confidence in that promise and determine our purposes, policies, and priorities accordingly.

What are the "things hoped for" and "things not seen" about which you have full "assurance" and "conviction" (Heb. 11:1)?
Praise God for these now.

Family provisions
Guidance

The Lord will guide you continually.
Isaiah 58:11

The basic form of divine guidance is the presentation of positive ideals as guidelines for all our living. "Be the kind of person Jesus was"; "seek this virtue and this one and practice them to the limit"; "know your responsibilities—husbands, to your wives; wives, to your husbands; parents, to your children; all of you, to your fellow Christians and all your fellow-men; know them and seek strength constantly to discharge them": this is how God guides us through the Bible, as any student of the Psalms, the Proverbs, the prophets, the Sermon on the Mount, and the ethical parts of the epistles will soon discover. "Depart from evil, and do good" (Ps. 34:14)—this is the highway along which the Bible leads us, and all its admonitions keep us on it. Note that the reference to being "led by the Spirit" (Rom. 8:14) relates not to inward voices or any such experiences, but to mortifying known sin and not living after the flesh!

Only within the limits of *this* guidance does God prompt us inwardly in matters of vocational decision. So never expect to be guided to marry an unbeliever, or elope with a married person (1 Cor. 7:39; Exod. 20:14). I have known divine guidance to be claimed for both courses of action. Inward inclinations were undoubtedly present, but they were quite certainly not from the Spirit of God, for they went against the Bible. The Spirit "leads me in the paths of righteousness" (Ps. 23:3)—but not anywhere else.

Do you find any conflict between what is said above and God's instructions to Hosea (Hos. 3:1)? Does God ever ask us to do things that are unconventional or even apparently wrong?

Lord, where I am not sure of your answers, help me to live with the questions.

To keep me from being too elated by the abundance of revelations, a thorn was given me in the flesh, a messenger of Satan to harass me, to keep me from being too elated.
2 Corinthians 12:7

Whatever Paul's "thorn" may have been, we know it was a distressing disability that went unhealed despite three solemn sessions of prayer during which Paul had asked Christ to remove it. He called it "a messenger of Satan to harass me" because it tempted him to think hard thoughts about the God who let him suffer (2 Cor. 12:7–10).

But in the end Paul perceived that the thorn was given not for his punishment but for his protection. The worst diseases are those of the spirit: pride, conceit, arrogance, bitterness; these damage us far more than any malfunctioning of our bodies. The thorn was a prophylactic against pride, says Paul, "to keep me from being too elated."

As he prayed, Christ said to him, "My grace is sufficient for you, for my power is made perfect in weakness." So Paul embraced his continuing disability as a kind of privilege. "I will all the more gladly boast of my weaknesses, that the power of Christ may rest upon me." The Corinthians, in typical Greek fashion, already despised him as a weakling. They did not consider him an elegant speaker or an impressive personality. I am weaker than you thought, says Paul, for I live with my thorn in the flesh. But I have learned to glory in my weakness, "for when I am weak, then I am strong." Now you Corinthians learn to praise God for my weakness too!

Has Paul's pattern of requesting, listening, accepting, and even rejoicing, anything to teach me?
Lord, let this limitation/affliction. . . lead to some expansion in my life/bring some benefit to others. Help me to glorify you in my distress.

Go and tell John what you hear and see: the blind receive their sight and the lame walk, lepers are cleansed and the deaf hear, and the dead are raised up, and the poor have good news preached to them. And blessed is he who takes no offense at me. Matthew 11:4-6

It is true: Christ's power is still what it was. *However,* we must remember that the healings he performed when he was on earth had a special significance. Besides being works of mercy, they were signs of his messianic identity. This comes out in the message he sent to John the Baptist. This, in effect, was: Let John match up my miracles with what God promised for the day of salvation (Isa. 35:5-6). He should then be left in no doubt that I am the Messiah, whatever there is about me that he does not yet understand (Matt. 11:2-6).

Anyone today who asks for miracles as an aid to faith should be referred to the above passage and told that if he will not believe in the face of the miracles recorded in the Gospels, then he would not believe if he saw a miracle in his own back yard. Jesus' recorded miracles are decisive evidence for all time of who he is and what power he has.

But in that case, supernatural healings in equal abundance to those worked in the days of Jesus' flesh may not be Jesus' will today. The question concerns not his power but his purpose. Can we guarantee that because he was pleased to heal all the sick brought to him then, he will act in the same way now? I do not think so.

Not all accept this viewpoint. Do you? Read widely on this matter and make up your own mind in due course, letting biblical reasons and the experience of the best Christians down the ages guide you.

Lord, I don't ask you to heal as a proof of anything, but I long for you to reach out in compassion to. . .

I do not cease to give thanks for you, remembering you in my prayers, that the God of our Lord Jesus Christ, the Father of glory, may give you a spirit of wisdom and of revelation in the knowledge of him.

Ephesians 1:16–17

It is worth reading the whole of this wonderful prayer (Eph. 1:15–23) many times. Paul asks the Father of the one Savior and the one family that his readers may know the wealth of their salvation and the greatness of Christ's love and that through this knowledge they may grow. As the knowing is a corporate destiny only happening in fellowship with all the saints, so is the growing. It takes all the saints together to become the mature new man who matches Christ's stature (Eph. 4:13). It requires the whole church to be Christ's fullness; he has more to give, and there is more in him to be embodied than any one of us can contain.

The realities which Paul wants Christians to know better than they do at present make a striking list:

First, he wants them to know the *hope* belonging to those whom God has called, that is, the prospect of being filled up to God's fullness through enjoyment of grace here and glory hereafter. Second, they are to know the rich *inheritance* that God bestows on the saints—a bequest mostly still future that constitutes immeasurable personal wealth. Third, they need to know the greatness of God's *power* toward believers here and now—power that may be estimated in part from the raising and exalting of Jesus and the spiritual resurrection and re-creation which believers have already undergone.

Another reality which Paul wants Christians to know comes in a second wonderful prayer (Eph. 3:14–21). It is the reality of God's *love* in Jesus Christ—the love revealed in Christ's suffering for worthless wrongdoers and God's consequent quickening of them.

How much am I experiencing these realities of hope, inheritance, power, and love? *Lord, I can only know spiritual realities and grow spiritually through your Spirit; may he have more of me.*

All scripture is inspired by God.
2 Timothy 3:16

It is very important that we approach Scripture as the Word of God, not just as a mixed bag of human reflections and testimonies, some of which are likely to be more right-minded and some less, so that our main job is to pick out which are which. This is very inhibiting to fruitful dealing with the Scriptures.

As I look around the churches I see a broad division between pastoral leaders whose attitude to the Bible is generally one of trust because they take the Bible as coming from God, and those whose attitude is fundamentally one of mistrust because they see it only as a very mixed collection of human testimonies. Some of these people have been stumbled by what they've learned in seminary—or, as speakers of British and Canadian English say, in theological college—because it has been fashionable for a long time in these institutions to highlight the human aspects of Scripture and spend time dwelling on the differences, real or fancied, between the viewpoint of one writer and another. The effect of this can be to leave students adrift in a sea of pluralistic relativism, with a bewildering sense that the Bible offers a lot of different points of view and who can say which is right?

I am not questioning the value of these studies of the human side of Scripture but I see a need to balance them in a way that not all institutions do. I would balance them by saying to all Bible students, "Remember, all Scripture proceeds from a single source, a single mind, the mind of God the Holy Spirit, and you have not taken its measure until you can see its divine unity underlying its human variety."

For meditation or learning: Scripture is the Word of God in the form of human words, giving God's point of view on everything we need to know.
Lord, help me continually to discover your point of view on life.

*All scripture is inspired by God and profitable for teaching, for reproof, for correc-
tion, and for training in righteousness.*

2 *Timothy 3:16*

If while looking at you I should take my glasses off, I should reduce you to
a smudge. I should still know you were there; I might still be able to tell
whether you were male or female; I could probably manage to avoid
bumping into you. But you would have become so indistinct at the edges
and your features would be so blurred that adequate description of you,
save from memory, would be quite beyond me. Should a stranger enter the
room while my glasses were off, I could point to him, no doubt, but his
face would be a blob and I would never know the expression on it. You and
he would be right out of focus, so far as I was concerned, until I was be-
spectacled again.

One of Calvin's rare illustrations compares the way purblind persons like
me need glasses to put print and people in focus with the way we all need
Scripture to bring into focus our genuine sense of the divine. Though
Calvin stated this comparison in general terms only, he clearly had in mind
specific biblical truths as the lens whereby clear focus is achieved. Everyone, Calvin thought, has inklings of the reality of God, but they are vague
and smudged. Getting God in focus means thinking correctly about his
character, his sovereignty, his salvation, his love, his Son, his Spirit, and all
the realities of his work and ways; it also means thinking rightly about our
relationship to him as creatures either under sin or under grace, either living
the responsive life of faith, hope, and love or living unresponsively in barrenness and gloom of heart. How can we learn to think correctly about
these things? By learning of them from Scripture.

How do I make sure that I am spiritually in focus?
*Lord, as I read Scripture I pray that I may be open enough to allow it to shape my
thinking and my way of perceiving everything.*

Do your best to present yourself to God as one approved, a workman who has no need to be ashamed, rightly handling the word of truth.
2 Timothy 2:15

There are two different ways of reading the Bible which seem to me fundamental for anyone wanting to get the most out of it for himself or to lead others in spiritual things. One is to read it straight through, over and over again, to get an overall perspective. The other is to study particular passages in detail—taking a few verses, setting them in context and digging into them. You could call these the *macrocosmic* and *microcosmic* ways of reading Scripture.

For both ways, it's helpful to have a scheme of questions to apply to the text. I have found the following sequence of questions helpful:

What does the passage show me about God? The wise man will always start here.

What does the passage show me about living? This question opens my eyes to notice the right and wrong ways of living, the different sorts of situations in which people find themselves, the way of faith with all its difficulties and delights, the different emotional states and temptations that overtake people, and the many and various realities of human existence that each passage presents.

What does all this mean for me in my own life here and now? At this point I begin to meditate and pray as I bring to the Scripture the particular tasks or pressures that lie ahead that day and relate them to the knowledge of God and his will and ways that the passage has given me.

Review your methods of Bible reading in light of the above.
Lord, make me willing to learn and change.

I will meditate on thy precepts, and fix my eyes on thy ways.
Psalm 119:15

How does a leader (or anyone else) learn to apply Scripture to his life? It is easy to find ourselves at the end of a time of Bible study feeling that it all has to do with God and with people who lived two, three, or four thousand years ago, and isn't in any way related to us.

At this point we may pull down the commentaries. But a lot of these are the reverse of helpful when it comes to making the application. They concentrate on the technical side of exegesis, historically conceived: telling you what Scripture *meant.*

But what we need to know is what it *means* for us—in other words, how it applies today. Here the commentaries are not so strong.

Martin Luther said, "Prayer, meditation, and temptation make the theologian." By "theologian," he meant someone who could take and apply Scripture; and I take temptation to mean the discipline of living for God even when contrary pressures of all sorts come.

Luther is right, I believe. Those three things will enable us to perceive the application. While the commentaries tell us what the passage meant historically, only the Spirit of God really shows us what it is saying to ourselves and others today. That is his own ministry of enlightenment. Historical study of what the text meant when it was first produced does not answer the question of its application, and until that question is answered the Bible is not properly understood.

If you are a preacher, do you need to start writing "So what?" right across your notes to remind you to work out the application of everything you say?
Lord, slow me down, if necessary, so that meditation (thinking things through unhurriedly before you) becomes truly possible.

Sanctify them in the truth; thy word is truth.
John 17:17

The Bible is a library—two distinct collections, one made up of thirty-nine books written over more than a millenium, the other containing twenty-seven that were all produced in less than half a century. Some of these books are historical narratives, some sermons, some poems, some visions, and one is a hymn and prayer book containing 150 separate items. Yet we bind up this mass of literary allsorts within two covers and treat it as one book, and rightly so. Why?

First, all the books tell the same story; the coherence of their contents as they proclaim the Creator in redemptive action is quite stunning.

Secondly, they all mediate the God of their story; it is standard Christian experience that God steps out of the pages of these books into our lives.

Thirdly, as Jesus and the apostles believed and taught, Scripture is God's own instruction, given by the Holy Spirit to lead us to Christ and through him to eternal life. This is what we mean when we call Scripture inspired (2 Tim. 3:15-17).

Why should we believe the Bible? Because it is not only man's witness to God, but also equally, and indeed primarily, God's witness to himself in and through the testimony of his servants; and we may be certain that what God tells us is true. This is the faith we confess when we call Scripture inerrant.

Try writing in your own words the central story of the whole Bible as though answering the question: What, in a nutshell, is this book all about?

Lord, show me where my grasp of your story is weak and help me to take steps to remedy this.

Men moved by the Holy Spirit spoke from God.
2 Peter 1:21

Scripture is more sure than any other source of knowledge, just because it is directly and essentially the testimony, word, or witness of God. "I have put my words in your mouth" (Jer. 1:9)—this was not only a promise to Jeremiah but also an explanation of divine inspiration. And in the New Testament it is acknowledged that God put his words into the mouths of, for instance, David and Isaiah (Acts 4:25; 28:25; Mark 12:36).

This view of Scripture is not the instrumental view of inspiration which some hold: the view that Scripture is essentially human witness (albeit God-aided) to God and his grace, through which God somehow speaks to us a word that is not fully identical with what the Bible says. Peter and the others regarded Scripture rather as the human form of God's own witness. Just as in the person of Jesus we see the Son of God taking on human nature while his essential identity remains divine, so in the Scriptures we see the human form which God's word took while its essential identity as God's Word remained constant.

Men, borne along by the Holy Spirit, spoke from God. Their word is the Word of God because it is divine in origin. And because the Bible is the Word (communication, instruction, message) of God, it is utterly trustworthy and utterly authoritative for our lives—not just relatively so as being the best source that we have, but absolutely so as being God's pure word of address which stands for all eternity.

How much do I appreciate, treasure, and share God's Word for the world?
Lord, I pray for those who would give a great deal to have even a small portion of the Bible, and here I am with so many copies and versions of the whole Bible around me...

Give me understanding that I may learn thy commandments.
Psalm 119:73

There are basically three rules for interpreting the Bible.

We must interpret Scripture *historically* in terms of what each writer wanted his own first readers to gather from his words. This means seeing each book in its own historical and cultural setting and putting ourselves in both the writer's and the reader's shoes. Each book was written as a message to the writer's contemporaries, and only as we see what it was meant to tell them shall we discern what it has to say to us. For the way into the mind of the Holy Spirit is through the meaning expressed by the men he inspired.

We must also interpret Scripture *organically*, as a complex unity proceeding from one mind, that of God the Spirit, the primary author of it all. The sixty-six books of Scripture—a library of great literary diversity by more than forty writers put together over more than a thousand years—express that one mind, telling one story about one God, one Savior, one covenant, one church, and teaching one way of serving God: the way of faith, hope, and love, of repentance, obedience, praise, prayer, work, and joy.

We must interpret Scripture *practically* too, always seeking from the text God's message to us today. As we study Scripture, we stand in the presence of the living God. Each time it is as if he has handed us a letter from himself and stays with us while we read it to hear what our answer will be.

Do I read the Bible expecting Father, Son, and Spirit to meet, teach, question, challenge, humble, heal, forgive, strengthen, and restore me?
Lord, give me understanding of your Word as I use my mind, seeking to interpret it rightly.

Pray to your Father who is in secret.
Matthew 6:6

By suggesting that we pray, give, and fast in secret (Matt. 6:1–28), Jesus is not attacking the ideal of public worship or suggesting that there's no place for supportive Christian fellowship and testimony. What he's saying is that the heart of our personal discipleship must be our inward, secret, one-to-one relationship with our heavenly Father. The way to ensure that the relationship is as it should be is to spend time with God on our own so that he and you or I can concentrate on one another, and we shall not be distracted by the thing that ruins the hypocrite: the sideways glance to see if he's being noticed and applauded.

A child who has something important to say to his father will often whisper it, or else say, "Daddy, can we go into a corner on our own? There's something I want to tell you." Jesus is saying that "the pure in heart" (Matt. 5:8) will often be found doing that with God. And we need to do it because, being fallen human beings, we are prone to hanker after the applause and approval of other people more than the praise given by God. This is a chronic problem for preachers to live with, but all who minister in any way to others or serve as role models for them in any sense must be aware of this very natural tendency. Jesus however wants us all regularly to get away from people and be alone with the God who probes the depths of our hearts and knows not only how we appear to others, but also what we're like when we're on our own.

An English one-liner that has always amused me is: "A gentleman is one who uses the butter knife when he is alone." In other words, it's what someone does when no one's watching that indicates the true person. Now God is the one who watches when no one else is watching, and hence knows us as we really are.

Think about this saying: "What a man is alone on his knees before God, that he is and no more."
How much of a priority in my life is one-to-one time with God?

Through him we both have access in one Spirit to the Father.
Ephesians 2:18

I believe that praying in the Spirit includes four elements.

First, it is a matter of seeking, claiming, and making use of access to God through Christ. Then the Christian adores and thanks God for his acceptance through Christ and for the knowledge that through Christ his prayers are heard. Third, he asks for the Spirit's help to see and do what brings glory to Christ, knowing that both the Spirit and Christ himself intercede for him as he struggles to pray for rightness in his own life (Rom. 8:26–27, 34). Finally, the Spirit leads the believer to concentrate on God and his glory in Christ with a sustained, single-minded simplicity of attention and intensity of desire that no one ever knows unless it is spiritually wrought.

Prayer in the Spirit is prayer from the heart, springing from awareness of God, self, others, needs, and Christ. Whether it comes forth verbalized, as in the prayers and praises recorded in Scripture, or unverbalized, as when the contemplative gazes God-ward in love or the charismatic slips into glossolalia, is immaterial. He or she whose heart seeks God through Christ prays in the Spirit.

How would you define praying in the Spirit? What is the biblical teaching about this?
Use the prayer in Ephesians 3:14–19, adapted as necessary, to pray for.yourself, your church family, and a Christian friend.

Ask, and it will be given you; seek, and you will find; knock, and it will be opened to you. For everyone who asks receives, and he who seeks finds, and to him who knocks it will be opened.

Matthew 7:7-8

Jesus urges his disciples to ask God for their needs and expect him to meet them (Matt. 7:7–11). Even flawed parents know how to give good gifts to their children, so if we don't ask and don't expect God to give good things to us, we are suggesting that he doesn't behave as well as faulty human parents do. What an insult to God!

Of course we have to remember that if we ask for something that is not for our best, God may answer the prayer we *should* have made rather than the prayer we *did* make. To gratify one's children when what they ask for would be bad for them is not the mark of a loving parent, and experience shows that God who loves us will not act like that. Again and again, for instance, we ask for circumstances to be changed, as with Paul and his thorn in the flesh, but God gives us instead new strength and resourcefulness in the unchanged situation.

When Jesus says that everyone who asks will receive, he is assuming that those who pray will be disciples who are right with God and not cherishing iniquity in their hearts (Ps. 66:18). Everyone is required to remember that God is a perfect father and believe that if we pray seriously for his help, it will come to us in one way or another.

Jesus tells us to ask, ask, ask! Because God is the perfect father, he will not fail to hear us and respond. So we should pray for what we need and then start looking for his answers.

Have you been treating God as though he were less loving and good than an earthly father?
Ask forgiveness for any wrong attitudes and pray for the development of new right ones.

*To thee, O LORD, I lift up my soul. O my God, in thee I trust. . .Redeem Israel, O
God, out of all his troubles.*
Psalm 25:1,22

Read the whole psalm and see its five layers: prayer (vv. 1-7); meditation
(vv. 8-10); prayer (v. 11); meditation (vv. 12-15); prayer (vv.16-22). In our
Christian lives there should be a balance between prayer (talking to God in
God's presence) and meditation (thinking about God in God's presence).

Verse 11 is central to the prayer: "For thy name's sake, O LORD, pardon
my guilt, for it is great," the psalmist says. He invokes God's nature, for that
is the reality to which God's name is pointing, and asks that God will be
who he is—namely, a merciful God: one who will forgive his sins.

The prayer is repetitive. I am not always happy when I hear leaders say
in prayer meetings, "Keep the prayers short because we want to let everyone
have a turn" (or words to that effect). It isn't always or even usually the biblical pattern that prayers are short. Repetition in prayer is not something to
be ashamed of or embarrassed by: only if we think there is some magic in
repetition does it become "empty" (Matt. 6:7). When we're talking to one
another, we often repeat ourselves in order to emphasize something; so
when we're talking to God we can do the same. See how often the psalmist
repeats himself. He tells God twice that he's waiting on him (vv. 5,21); he
asks for pardon three times (vv. 7,11,18).

The prayer is basically a cry for help, interspersed with praise: praise to
God for being the sort of God who helps those in trouble. Breaking it down
a little, we could say that first the psalmist waits for guidance (vv. 1-7),
then he thinks of God's goodness (vv. 8-10, 12-15), and then he pleads for
grace (vv. 16-22).

What has this psalm to teach me about prayer, the pray-er, and his God?
To thee, O Lord, I lift up my soul. . .

The family at prayer
                                      Praying to a generous God

All the paths of the LORD are steadfast love and faithfulness, for those who
keep his covenant and his testimonies.

                                                        Psalm 25:10

The God to whom we pray is a generous God (Ps. 25:5–7,14). He is a God
who shows people his covenant and invites them to keep it and so enter into
his blessings.

What is God's covenant? It is the bond by which God first binds himself
to us, pledging to make all his resources available to us for our blessing. The
Bible illustration for God's covenant is the marriage relationship, which
starts with the husband giving himself to the bride, pledging himself to be
her husband and to love, cherish, and look after her. So God promises good
things to his people and over and above that he also gives himself to his
people; this committed relationship in and of itself guarantees that God will
bless us. Every time the psalmist says "LORD" (Hebrew *Yahweh*, God's covenant name) or "*my* God" he is using covenant language and is invoking the
covenant relationship between God and his people. Only those to whom
our Maker has first said "my people" have any right to say to him "my God."

So the psalmist is remembering that the one to whom he prays is a God
who loves us and gives first himself and then his blessings—a God who forgives (vv. 7,11), guides (vv. 8–9), guards and delivers (vv. 20,22), enriches
and befriends his people (v. 14).

The New Testament (that is, the book of the new covenant) picks up all
these blessings of the old covenant: forgiveness (1 John 1:9), guidance
(Rom. 8:15), protection (1 Pet. 1:5), enrichment (Eph. 1:3), and friendship
(John 15:14–15). All these, it says, are ours through Christ in a richer way
than Old Testament believers ever knew.

Is there a difference between the Old Testament and New Testament blessings mentioned above? If so, what and why?
Lord, I thank you with all my heart that you are a generous, good, kind, concerned,
and caring God, as you have shown me . . .

For thee I wait all the day long.
Psalm 25:5

___

There won't be any real prayer unless there is longing and desire in our hearts. Prayer has been defined as the offering up of our desires to God. What does the psalmist long for in Psalm 25? He longs for protection (vv. 2,20), direction (vv. 4–5), preservation (v. 21), forgiveness (vv. 11,18); and over and above all these things which he wants for himself, he wants blessing for the church (v. 22).

Every healthy Christian will have this dual concern—for himself and for others. We shouldn't be ashamed of being concerned for ourselves. If we are concerned about the relationship between us and God, we have to be concerned for ourselves, lest we spoil the relationship. We will have personal needs which we will want to bring to God. At the same time, though, we are, or should be, well aware that we are not the only pebbles on God's beach. God is building a family and his purposes are for this family unit as well as for its individual members.

Self-absorption is not a Christian virtue, and if the Spirit of God is teaching a Christian, he will find in his heart a concern for the blessing of others, just as he finds in his heart a concern for his own blessing. He will long to see God glorified in the blessing of the church, just as he longs to find his own relationship to God deepened and enriched through God's blessing on him. So he'll be praying and longing for blessing both for himself and for others.

What are the longings of my heart for myself and for my church family?
Put these longings into prayer, regularly. (Writing them down might be helpful.)

We are told to pray at all times. That means we're to pray at every significant moment, making the most of every opportunity. Just as police need to
keep in constant touch with their headquarters in order to receive fresh orders and pass on information, so the Christian needs to be in constant
touch with his Lord so that when the moment of opportunity or crisis
arises, he can immediately fire off an "arrow prayer," just as Nehemiah did
(Neh. 1:4–2:8).

Nehemiah had been praying that something might be done concerning
the walls of Jerusalem and that he might be involved. But he was a high-
grade slave in the Persian royal palace, and he couldn't ask to be released
from the king's service. Then one day the king looked at him and said,
"You're sad. What's the trouble?" So Nehemiah explained and the king
asked what he wanted done about it. "So I prayed to the God of heaven,"
wrote Nehemiah (2:4). Then he spoke up and the king gave him permission
to go to Jerusalem to rebuild the walls.

Nehemiah certainly didn't know that the imperial policy of King Arta-
xerxes was to allow subject cities to regain their self-respect by having as
much autonomy as possible. As far as the king was concerned, what Nehemiah had requested fitted in with his policy, and that presumably was
why he agreed at once to Nehemiah's request. But as far as Nehemiah was
concerned, this was a wonderful answer to a prayer that he had made over
a three-month period (see the dates in 1:1 and 2:1) before shooting off that
"arrow prayer" at the crucial moment.

How would you explain what is meant by the instruction to "pray at all times"?
*Lord, every moment is significant. Help me to be in tune and touch with you—ready
for that sudden temptation or momentous opportunity.*

*What is man that thou art mindful of him, and the son of man that thou dost care
for him?*
Psalm 8:4

Man is a cosmic amphibian, having a body which links him with animals
below him, but being in himself a thinking, loving, choosing, creative, active person like God and the angels above him.

I am a man; what, then, am I? Not, as philosophers and gnostics ancient
and modern would tell me, a soul that would do better without a body, but
a complex psycho-physical organism, a personal unit describable as an en-
souled body no less than an embodied soul. I am at once the highest of animals, since no other animal shares my kind of mental life, and the lowest of
rational creatures, for no angel is bounded by physical limitations as I am.
Yet I, as a man, can enjoy the richest life of all God's creatures. Mental and
physical awareness meet and blend in me fearfully, wonderfully, and fasci-
natingly. My task is not to dizzy myself by introspecting or speculating to
find (if I can) what lies at the outer reaches of consciousness, nor to pursue
endless, exquisite stimulation in the hope of new, exotic ecstasies. It is,
rather, to know and keep my place in God's cosmic hierarchy, and in that
place to spend my strength in serving God and men.

I can all too easily lose my cosmic balance, so to speak, and lapse into
incoherent oscillation between seeing myself as no less than God, a spirit
having absolute value in myself and settling the value of everything by its
relation to me, and seeing myself as no more than an animal, whose true
life consists wholly of eating, drinking, and seeking pleasures for mind and
body until I die. Such is life in a fallen world.

Many characters in modern novels operate at a "driven" level. Do you? Should
you? How is it possible not to live at this level?
*Lord, thank you that growing more Christian means growing more truly human,
like Jesus. That's the way I want to grow, through your continual help.*

God created man in his own image.
Genesis 1:27

The image of God in which man was and is made has been variously explained in detail. Although scholars may differ on the nuances of the phrase, there is general agreement that it has to do with dignity, destiny, and freedom.

The assertion that man is made in God's image shows each man his true *dignity* and *worth*. As God's image-bearer, he merits infinite respect. God's claims on us must be taken with total seriousness. No human being should ever be thought of as simply a cog in a machine, a mere means to an end.

The assertion points also to each man's true *destiny*. Our Maker so designed us that our nature finds final satisfaction and fulfillment only in a relationship of responsive Godlikeness—which means, precisely, that state of correspondence between our acts and God's will which we call *obedience*. Living that is obedient will thus be teleological—progressively realizing our *telos* (Greek for "end" or "goal").

Also the assertion confirms the genuineness of each man's *freedom*. Experience tells us that we are free, in the sense that we make real choices between alternatives and could have chosen differently, and theology agrees. Self-determining freedom of choice is what sets God and his rational creatures apart from, say, birds and bees, as *moral* beings.

Do I take too little or too much account of the predisposing factors that influence my choices? Do I take myself seriously as a decision-maker in the sight of God? *Lord, thank you that you chose to create and redeem. Restore your image in me, your child, so that I am in no doubt about my dignity. May I enter more fully into my destiny and exercise with greater joy and responsibility my freedom of choice.*

Your adversary the devil prowls around like a roaring lion, seeking someone to devour.
1 Peter 5:8

God is not the source of sin; he neither commits nor wills nor prompts it (James 1:13). God made rational creatures who were capable of loving him freely and by choice and that meant they could freely choose not to love him—which is what some angels and all our race have done. How such disobedience is possible, while God is Lord of this world, we cannot conceive; that it is possible, however, is undeniable, for it has happened.

How did sin enter the cosmos? Scripture tells us that Satan and his angels rebelled against the Creator before man was made (2 Pet. 2:4; Jude 6), so that when the first human beings appeared "that ancient serpent, who is the Devil and Satan" (Rev. 20:2) was there to trip them up (Gen. 3). And "the tempter," the "ruler" and "god of this world" (1 Thess. 3:5; John 14:30; 2 Cor. 4:4) still marauds with serpentine cunning and lion-like savagery. It is right to trace moral evil back to Satan as its patron, promoter, producer, director, and instigatory cause.

Where do the inclinations to evil which I find in myself, and so often yield to, come from? The Bible says their source is my own heart (James 1:13–15; Mark 7:21–23). Just as a cripple's twisted leg makes him walk lame, so the motivational twist of my fallen heart—anti-God, anti-other, self-absorbed—constantly induces wrong attitudes and actions.

Have you ever thought of your Christian life in terms of God straightening you out?
Lord, I pray for your victory this day over the enemy without and the enemy within.

I will greatly multiply your pain in childbearing. . . Cursed is the ground because of you; in toil you shall eat of it all the days of your life.

Genesis 3:16–17

Four things must be borne in mind if we are going to make any sense of our experiences of suffering. First, the whole cosmos is cursed and out of joint. The curse is part of God's judgment on human sin (Gen. 3; Rom. 3:19–23). The creation has been subjected to "futility" (i.e., non-achievement of its end, and failure to achieve anything at all—Rom. 8:20, 22). We are not told in detail what this subjection involved, but it is natural to suppose that just as physical death in the form in which we know it belongs to the curse, so death-dealers like cancer would not be as they are, were it not for the curse. The curse then is one source of pain and sickness, and for those who are not Christians there is no final remedy.

Second, Christians follow Jesus "who endured from sinners such hostility against himself" (Heb. 12:3). Active hostility against them, as against their master, springs from the adverse reaction of sin-twisted nature to godliness in others—a reaction which is regularly destructive in intent. Here is a second source of suffering in this world.

Third, God is training all his children to enjoy a future life in which it is promised that tears and tribulation will be a thing of the past (Rev. 17:14–17; Heb. 12:2). Meanwhile through what we experience, God is teaching us patience, courage, humility, faithfulness, and similar lessons as part of his plan for our sanctification (Heb. 12:5–11).

Fourth, Jesus endured and by enduring overcame evil in all its forms, including pain and distress, and God means us to do the same in Jesus' power.

Am I willing to let explanations wait and simply focus on God's power to transform suffering and overcome evil with good?

Jesus, you endured hostility, pain, and other forms of suffering. Help . . .

Sin again, Christian?

We know that our old self was crucified with him so that the sinful body might be destroyed, and we might no longer be enslaved to sin.
Romans 6:6

Through union with Christ in his death, says Paul, our old self was put to death with him so that our sinful body might be brought to nothing and cease to be the decisive controlling factor of our lives. This is one aspect of the change in us that is called regeneration.

Here, speaking of the sinful body, Paul is not referring to the physical frame; he means a person's total self, a human individual. "Body," like "soul," can signify the whole person in Scripture, and there are traces of this broadened meaning in our ordinary speech. Perhaps you know the word *boss* derives from the words *body master*—the title given to a person in charge of a slave gang. And when we speak colloquially of so many "bods" (or bodies), we mean so many people.

So when Paul speaks of the sinful body, he means the sinful self—the sinful person I was in my natural, fallen state with my God-dishonoring, self-serving, sin-dominated disposition. That, says Paul, was brought to an end by my union with Christ in his death. The person I used to be was crucified with Christ so that my sinful self (disposition, character) might be brought to nothing, so that from now on I would no longer be sin's slave, living under sin's dominion. I am a new person now, for Christ's inclination and instinct to love and serve and honor his heavenly Father has also become the core of my character through my union with him in his risen life.

It is important to understand that this is the work of God. We are to consider ourselves "dead to sin and alive to God in Christ Jesus" (Rom. 6:11) because God has made us so, and this radical change that he has worked in us now has to be lived out. So henceforth we must crucify and mortify each sinful habit that once held us captive (Rom. 8:13), and use all our liberated powers to serve God in righteousness (Rom. 6:12-13; 12:1-2)—something that we could not do before.

Have I really accepted what God has already done in me?
Lord, help me to grasp what you have done in me so that I see my life in terms of living out my new nature.

Where sin increased, grace abounded all the more.
Romans 5:20

In Romans chapter 6 Paul deals with two questions which he feels might naturally arise in the minds of his readers as a result of his statement that where sin increased, grace abounded all the more.

The first question (v. 1) is: Should we go on sinning as before in order that grace may continue to abound? Paul's answer in brief is: You can't! You mustn't for a moment think that the right way to behave, for God has made it impossible. He spends the first half of the chapter explaining that God has so changed us believers that obedience is now our only natural response (vv. 3–11), and summoning us to live out the new life that God has given us in Christ (vv. 12–14). That means righteousness, not sin, as our way of life.

A second question follows (v. 15): Would it matter if we continued to sin, since the more sin, the more grace? Paul answers: Yes, it would matter very much because anyone who serves sin must expect to receive sin's wages: death. Should you spend your life on the road which leads to spiritual death, you would miss God's gift of spiritual life. Paul does not expect that any real Christian will actually do this—indeed, he explained in the first half of the chapter that it is not possible—but he wants to make his readers realize the link that exists between man's direction and man's destination.

Certainly we are justified through God's grace. But we are justified for a life of holiness. Grace comes to us in our sin in order to save us from our sin—from its power and control as well as from its guilt and penalty. Born-again believers become "slaves of righteousness" (v. 18). Their feet are taken off the way of sin and set on the path of obedience. Then they lay hold of eternal life in its fullness by following that path. This is a matter not of meriting life, but of entering it.

Study Romans 6 and try to think out the implications. What light does it throw on the question of whether the end justifies the means, for example?
Lord, help me to use my mind in thinking out the practical applications of your truth.

The dust returns to the earth as it was, and the spirit returns to God who gave it.
Ecclesiastes 12:7

What is death? It is a dissolving of the union between spirit and body. As in the beginning God made man by breathing life into a thing of dust, so now in death he partly unmakes him, severing the two realities which he originally joined together. This disintegration is to man unnatural in the highest degree.

Does death mean personal annihilation? Indeed no. Death is an unclothing of a person by dismantling his earthly tent but it is not the end of his personal life. The Bible everywhere takes personal survival for granted. The Old Testament pictures the dead as going down to the place which it calls *Sheol* (*Hades* in the Septuagint and Greek New Testament).

Sheol, however, is not the ultimate abode of the dead. Scripture looks forward to an emptying of Hades when the dead are raised bodily for judgment at Christ's return (John 5:28–29; Rev. 20:12–15). Those whose names are written in the Book of Life will then be welcomed into endless bliss but the rest will undergo the extremest manifestation of divine displeasure. This is described in various ways throughout the New Testament. From these texts it seems plain that those whose names are not written in the Book of Life face the prospect of an endless awareness of God's just and holy displeasure. That is why physical death (the first death) is so fearful a prospect for Christless people; not because it means extinction but precisely because it does *not* mean extinction—only the unending pain of the second, eternal death.

What are your feelings when you think about your own death?
Talk to God about your feelings.

Why be holy?

Thanks be to God, that you who were once slaves of sin have become obedient from the heart to the standard of teaching to which you were committed, and, having been set free from sin, have become slaves of righteousness.

Romans 6:17–18

Why should Christians seek to live holy lives? Not because they still have to do so in order to earn their final acceptance with God. The gift of God's righteousness in their justification is God's final judgment on their status and will never be revoked; they are already accepted. So they don't have to work *for* it; rather they will work *from* it, not for gain, but from gratitude.

Again, the proper motive for living holy lives is not that it makes us feel good and happy. It's certainly true that those who don't set themselves each day to live in the way that pleases God don't feel good or happy: God in his grace will see to that. In order to bring us to our senses, he will chasten us one way or another if we lapse into sin, and we will only know inward peace and joy in their fullness, and have a sense of our Father smiling on us, as we wholeheartedly obey him. But to practice godliness simply because it makes us feel good or happy is to fall short of the highest motive.

The two right reasons for seeking to please God by doing his will are: First, gratitude for grace received, and second, the discovery that he has so changed our nature that nothing else is fully natural to us. We seek to lead holy lives because we know that God is working in us "to will and to work for his good pleasure" (Phil. 2:13), and knowing this we more and more willingly cooperate with him.

If you are troubled by conflicting desires, don't despair: this was Paul's experience too (Rom. 7:14–25).

Lord, show me now any area of my life in which I act unnaturally by failing to co-operate with your ongoing work of grace.

All who believed were together and had all things in common; and they sold their possessions and goods and distributed them to all, as any had need.
Acts 2:44-45

Pentecost loosed into the world a new quality of corporate life marked by exuberant caring, sharing, and joy (Acts 2:43-47; 4:32-37). As praise is both a Christian instinct and duty, so is togetherness. Today mutual ministry and meetings are duties but in the Bible togetherness in worship, at the table, and at other times is simply recorded as fact: Christians saw and treated each other as friends in those days of spiritual vigor, and friends do not usually need to be told to get together!

The ancient world was by and large callous towards poverty but the first practical expression of Christian fellowship was to pool resources for poor relief. For the first time ever Marx's maxim, "From each according to his ability; to each according to his need," became the rule of action. The maxim, which came to Marx from Christian sources, is profoundly right but only where Christ is Lord can there be motive force enough to live it out.

The poverty of the Jerusalem saints twenty-five years later (Rom. 15:25-27) may suggest that from one standpoint this experiment in communal Christianity was injudicious: it may have reflected an incautious assumption that because Jesus' return was certain, therefore it had to be soon. Paul's charge to the rich (1 Tim. 6:17-19) shows that there is another way of being a faithful steward of property rather than selling everything. But the Christian goodheartedness of Barnabas, who sold his entire estate for charity, is not to be faulted; it is a model for us all.

Is there sufficient incentive for us to come together as Christians? Do we go away from such gatherings feeling closer to God, uplifted, clearer in our thinking, more committed and joyful? If not, why not?
Lord, show me what I can do to bring about exuberant sharing, caring, and giving.

March 2
Family attitudes and lifestyle
Sharing lives

They devoted themselves to the apostles' teaching and fellowship, to the breaking of bread and the prayers.

Acts 2:42

What is meant by fellowship in this verse? Gossip? Cups of tea? Tours? No. What is being referred to is something of a quite different order and on a quite different level. "They met constantly to hear the apostles teach, and to *share the common life,* and to break bread and to pray. A sense of awe was everywhere. All whose faith had drawn them together held everything in common. With one mind they kept up their daily attendance at the temple, and, breaking bread in private houses, shared their meals with unaffected joy as they praised God" (Acts 2:42–47, *NEW ENGLISH BIBLE*). That is fellowship as the New Testament understands it, and there is clearly a world of difference between that and mere social activities.

The Greek word for fellowship comes from a root meaning *common* or *shared.* So fellowship means common participation in something either by giving what you have to the other person or receiving what he or she has. Give and take is the essence of fellowship, and give and take must be the way of fellowship in the common life of the body of Christ.

Christian fellowship is *two-dimensional,* and it has to be vertical before it can be horizontal. We must know the reality of fellowship with the Father and with his Son Jesus Christ before we can know the reality of fellowship with each other in our common relationship to God (1 John 1:3). The person who is not in fellowship with the Father and the Son is no Christian at all, and so cannot share with Christians the realities of their fellowship.

Fellowship corresponds to the circulation of blood in the human body. How healthy is the body of Christ where you are?
Think out before God what the "giving and taking" is like in your fellowship, starting with what you yourself give and receive.

Through love be servants of one another.
Galatians 5:13

"Servant" in our English New Testament usually represents the Greek *doulos* (bondslave). Sometimes it means *diakonos* (deacon or minister); this is strictly accurate, for *doulos* and *diakonos* are synonyms. Both words denote a man who is not at his own disposal, but is his master's purchased property. Bought to serve his master's needs, to be at his beck and call every moment, the slave's sole business is to do as he is told. Christian service therefore means, first and foremost, living out a slave-relationship to one's Savior (1 Cor. 6:19–20).

What work does Christ set his servants to do? The way that they serve him, he tells them, is by becoming the slaves of their fellow-servants and being willing to do literally anything, however costly, irksome, or undignified, in order to help them. This is what love means, as he himself showed at the Last Supper when he played the slave's part and washed the disciples' feet.

When the New Testament speaks of ministering to the saints, it means not primarily preaching to them but devoting time, trouble, and substance to giving them all the practical help possible. The essence of Christian service is loyalty to the king expressing itself in care for his servants (Matt. 25:31–46).

Only the Holy Spirit can create in us the kind of love toward our Savior that will overflow in imaginative sympathy and practical helpfulness towards his people. Unless the Spirit is training us in love, we are not fit persons to go to college or a training class to learn the know-how of particular branches of Christian work. Gifted leaders who are self-centered and loveless are a blight in the church rather than a blessing.

How is it possible to serve without being subservient or "martyred"?

Lord, may your Holy Spirit be equipping people for Christian service, and when they are ready, may their gifts, qualities, and calling be recognized so that they can be trained, commissioned, and set to work.

Let us consider how to stir up one another to love and good works, not neglecting to meet together, as is the habit of some, but encouraging one another, and all the more as you see the Day drawing near.

Hebrews 10:24–25

The fellowship of sharing with one another what we have received from the Lord is a *spiritual necessity*, for God has not made us self-sufficient. We are not made so we can keep going on our own. This is often illustrated from the coals of a fire. Put the coals together and the fire burns. Separate them one from another, and each goes out quite quickly. So it is with the body of Christ. We are not made for isolated and self-sufficient living but for togetherness in dependence on each other.

Christian fellowship is also the *family activity* of God's children. In a good family there is plenty of sharing among the siblings. In the family of God that is also the way it is meant to be. Like fellowship with the Father and the Son, it is two-way traffic: you give and you receive. So Christian fellowship is *seeking to share with others* what God has made known to you, while letting them share with you what they know of him, as a means of finding strength, refreshment, and instruction for your own soul.

Paul, writing to the Romans, says, "For I long to see you, that I may impart some spiritual gift to strengthen you," and then adds, lest he should give the impression that he thinks the fellowship between him and them is one-way traffic only, "that is, that we may be *mutually encouraged* by each other's faith, both yours and mine" (Rom. 1:11–12). Those who preach must be open to receive whatever ministry comes back to them from those to whom they have spoken. The attitude of, "I'm the one who gives, but I don't need to take," has ruined the ministry of more pastors than I can number.

Are there opportunities in your church family for members to be mutually encouraged through one another's faith?
Lord, show us how to stir up one another to love and good works.

Bear one another's burdens, and so fulfill the law of Christ.
Galatians 6:2

In Galatians chapter 5 Paul tells us to walk in the Spirit and serve one another in love, and in Galatians 6:1–6 he explains what that will mean. The law of Christ, he says, is precisely this: to bear others' burdens, accepting involvement in their troubles and laying ourselves out to help, support, and restore. It pleases God more that I should carry someone else's burden and let him carry mine than that we should each carry our own. The latter is the way of lonely isolation, one aspect of the fallen human condition; the former is the way of Christian fellowship.

Fellowship means sharing burdens as well as benefits: we carry each other's luggage, both material and spiritual, and find relief and strength in doing so. This path of exchange—problem-sharing and burden-bearing—is Christ's image in our lives for it reflects his loving substitution for us under judgment on the cross. Paul summons his readers to burden-bearing as brothers in Christ and as spiritual men.

With the call to burden-bearing goes a warning against complacent conceit (6:3). Psychologically this is shrewd: those who seek to do good especially in counseling and rescue work are always tempted to feel they are a cut above those they are helping. Gentleness is called for here, since "there but for the grace of God go I."

The "load" which "each man will have to bear" (6:5) has nothing to do with burden-bearing; it's his responsibility for his own life for which he must answer to God and reap what he has sown. Each of us, then, will be wise to test our own work and not rest in the thought that some are a lot worse than we are (6:4)! Verse 6, so comforting to preachers, is not as isolated from Paul's theme as it looks. How else when pastors are impoverished (and they often are) should the rule of burden-bearing be applied?

Am I bearing anyone else's burdens? How am I doing so?
Thank you for those you have given me to help me with my burdens, especially...

*May the Lord make you increase and abound in love to one another and to all men
. . .so that he may establish your hearts unblamable in holiness before our God and
Father, at the coming of our Lord Jesus with all his saints.*
1 Thessalonians 3:12–13

In the passage 1 Thessalonians 3:11–4:12, the apostle Paul has some practical things to say about holiness and sanctification—the former meaning a state of being set apart for God, the latter the event or process whereby this apartness comes about.

Holiness is *not optional.* Sanctification is God's will for all Christians. It is a matter of obeying instructions which come with God's call to salvation; it starts with the heart and is then expressed in conduct.

Holiness entails *avoiding sexual immorality.* The right course is to marry "in holiness and honor," respecting my partner as a person made in God's image and the marriage relationship as God's own ordinance of a lifelong bond. Using myself to please myself rather than my partner, clandestine adultery, and overt wife-swapping are among the things that Paul condemns.

Holiness involves *loving action toward both Christians and non-Christians.* Holiness is more than abstaining from all evil; Christian love is the way separation to the Christian God must show itself.

Holiness requires *willingness to work,* so as to be independent. Sponging and scrounging have no place in the true life of faith.

Holiness involves *minding my own business,* and not being a nosey gossip. How down-to-earth Paul is!

How do I stand in relation to these tests of practical holiness?
Lord, search me and show me where my attitude and conduct are not reflecting your image. . .

Beloved... beware lest you be carried away with the error of lawless men and lose your own stability.
2 Peter 3:17

In 2 Peter chapter 3, Peter deals with the perplexity and disappointment of his readers over what seemed to them unexpected delay in the Lord's return. Peter assures them that nothing is surer than Christ's return and gives them advice on how in the interim they (and we) should play the waiting game.

First, he urges acceptance of the actual situation, without lapsing into rancor or despair. Often in the Christian life expectations are disappointed. If we then lapse into bitterness and bear a grudge against God, our growth in grace and joy in discipleship will be badly hindered. God knows what he's doing. We must accept the way things are, knowing that he shapes our circumstances, and wait patiently for him.

Second, Peter urges avoidance of lawlessness. Peter wrote at a time when immorality, representing itself as a higher form of morality, was invading the Christian church (2 Pet. 2). "Beware lest you be carried away with the error of lawless men," Peter writes. The problem of lawlessness is still with us. There are those, for example, who want to get homosexuality accepted as a valid lifestyle for Christians and their ministers. There are no ethical delusions, it seems, too great and grievous to invade the Christian church. We must discern all forms of the so-called new morality, the permissive way, and set ourselves against it.

Third, by implication, Peter directs his readers to the Scriptures and tells them to assimilate their food (2 Pet. 3:15, 16; 1 Pet. 2:2). We are to take large doses of spiritual nourishment by reading and studying the Scriptures.

Fourth, we are to affirm our fellow Christians. "Beloved," Peter's address to his readers four times in this chapter, is not a formality for him. He really loves and values his fellow Christians. Do we?

Can you honestly echo the words of Psalm 119:27?
Lord, help me to wait for and hasten your coming in ways that please you.

...now that you have come to know God, or rather to be known by God...
Galatians 4:9

What matters supremely in the last analysis is not the fact that I know God, but the larger fact that he knows me. I am graven on the palms of his hands. I am never out of his mind. All my knowledge of him depends on his sustained initiative in knowing me. I know him because he first knew me. He knows me as friend, one who loves me; and there is no moment when his eye is off me, or his attention distracted from me, and no moment, therefore, when his care falters.

This is momentous knowledge. There is unspeakable comfort—the sort of comfort that energizes rather than enervates—in knowing that God is constantly taking knowledge of me in love, and watching over me for my good. There is tremendous relief in knowing that his love toward me is utterly realistic, based at every point on prior knowledge of the worst about me, so that no discovery now can disillusion him about me in the way I am so often disillusioned about myself, and quench his determination to bless me.

There is, certainly, great cause for humility in the thought that he sees all the twisted things about me that my fellowmen do not see (and I am glad!), and that he sees more corruption in me than I see in myself (which, in all conscience, is enough). There is, however, equally great incentive to worship and love God because, for some unfathomable reason, he wants me as his friend and desires to be my friend and has given his Son to die for me in order to realize this purpose.

Meditate on the comforting, challenging thought: "God knows me through and through."
Turn your thoughts into confession or thanksgiving or both.

*He who has my commandments and keeps them, he it is who loves me; and he who
loves me will be loved by my Father, and I will love him and manifest myself to him.
John 14:21*

There is much prejudice against any attempt to re-emphasize the experiential side of Christianity. Why? Because of the words that Christians use when trying to express their experiences of God. The paradoxical truth is that some of the language they have used, concerning their awareness of and response to God, has been the language of love between the sexes. That is in fact the fittest language for the purpose, since the love of man and woman really is the closest analogy in creation to the relationship with God that the heavenly love intended for us.

Human love was, indeed, always meant to draw lovers closer to this heavenly relationship. In love experiences, both human and divine, one is intensely self-aware. But the height of self-awareness in sexual love is to see yourself as having become part of the other person to the point where the two of you are a single entity.

Christians past and present who have attempted to share in words their sense of being loved by and loving God have sometimes been accused of tuning into the Hindu wavelength. That, however, is nonsense. In Hinduism there is no personal God, no personal distinction between God and myself, and no love fellowship to enjoy with the divine; separate self-hood is thought of as an illusion to be dispelled. But the Christian saint contemplates the Father and the Son, who, though eternally distinct from him (a mere creature), are nonetheless bound to him by redeeming love. It is the heightened self-awareness of receiving love and responding to love that his language of identity with God expresses. He is as far from the Hindu sense of things as he could possibly be.

Grasp firmly (perhaps after more reading) the differences between Hindu and Christian ideas of and goals in communion with God.
Thank God for all the ways in which he has made you aware of his love for you.

So faith, hope, love abide, these three; but the greatest of these is love.
1 Corinthians 13:13

The Greek word *agape* (love) seems to have been virtually a Christian invention—a new word for a new thing (apart from about twenty occurrences in the Greek version of the Old Testament, it is almost non-existent before the New Testament). *Agape* draws its meaning directly from the revelation of God in Christ. It is not a form of natural affection, however intense, but a supernatural fruit of the Spirit (Gal. 5:22). It is a matter of will rather than feeling (for Christians must love even those they dislike—Matt. 5:44–48). It is the basic element in Christlikeness.

Read 1 Corinthians 13 and note what these verses have to say about the primacy (vv. 1–3) and permanence (vv. 8–13) of love; note too the profile of love (vv. 4–7) which they give.

Tongues, prophetic gifts, theological expertise, and miracle-working faith preoccupied the Corinthians; giving everything away and accepting martyrdom may be required of Christians at any time. Yet love matters so much more than these things that without it they all become worthless, and the loveless Christian, however gifted and active, gains nothing and is nothing.

The middle verses make up a portrait of Jesus and correct the bumptious, contentious, suspicious, presumptuous, arrogant, self-assertive, critical, irresponsible spirit of the Corinthians that made Paul have to call them carnal and spiritually babyish.

The greater importance of love appears from the fact that it will last through the life to come when all occasion for tongues, prophecy, and theological instruction will have ceased.

Do I have any experience at all in loving people I dislike?
Lord, show me where I need to receive from you and show to others true agape.

You are the body of Christ.
1 Corinthians 12:27

Union with Christ implies union with all others who are Christ's. In Christ my fellow believer is my brother, for we both belong to the same family. More than that, he is in a real sense part of me. Because we are both vitally linked to our common Savior, we have a vital link with each other (Eph. 4:25).

The New Testament teaching about God's covenant people, the church, rests on this foundation. Writing to the Ephesians, Paul portrays this double union—with Christ and in Christ with each other—by no less than four organic metaphors for the church: the body of Christ, the bride of Christ, the new man in Christ, and the temple. Three of these images point directly to the church's subjection to Christ. He is the body's head, the bride's husband, and the cornerstone of the temple (Eph. 1:22-23; 5:23-24; 2:20-22). Three of the images point to the church's destiny in Christ: the body, the new man, and the temple *grow* toward a predestined perfection (Eph. 4:12-16; 2:21). And three of the images point to the new relationship of mutual involvement and dependence which binds the regenerate together in Christ. In the body, all are members of one another; in the new man racial distinctions (and sexual and social distinctions too—Gal. 3:28) are transcended (Eph. 2:15-22); in the temple the stones are "joined together" for firm integration (Eph. 2:21).

From these passages we learn that in and under Christ, Christians are called to fit in with each other, to feel for one another, and to stand together in love, loyalty, and care.

Individually and in our local church, how seriously do we take this teaching about our unity with all other Christians in Christ?
Lord, help me to make this day's activities, as much as possible, a conscious response to the needs of others (whether those needs are for company, privacy, or practical help).

March 12

*There is neither Jew nor Greek, there is neither slave nor free, there is neither male
nor female; for you are all one in Christ Jesus.*

Galatians 3:28

Body life is a term for the network of mutual relationships which Christ
both calls and causes the limbs of his body to build. Scripture spells out the
ethics of body life in terms of valuation and service.

The racial, social, economic, cultural, and sexual distinctions which operate as restraints on our acceptance and appreciation of each other cannot
be abolished. However, the limits they impose must be transcended. In
Christ's body all must welcome and value each other as "members one of
another" (Eph. 4:25). You might not think it from watching what goes on in
our churches, but God wants life in his new society to be a perfect riot of
affection, goodwill, openheartedness, and friendship. So what on earth are
we all playing at? You tell me!

Service is love in action. Christ's body "upbuilds itself in love" (Eph.
4:16). This love is more than sweet talk or sweet smiles; its measure is the
evil that you avoid inflicting and the good you go out of your way to do.
How is the church upbuilt or edified in love? By "each part...working
properly" in fellowship: sharing what by God's gift we have and are. This
sharing is the service or ministry to which every Christian is called. Either
we all advance toward Christlike maturity together through mutual ministry (lay people to lay people and also to clergy and vice versa), or we all
stagnate separately.

Do I go out of my way to do good and to avoid inflicting evil?
*Lord, deal with us until we learn to value and serve one another as you want us to
for the sake of your church and your world.*

Walk in love.
Ephesians 5:2

A football referee takes pains to familiarize himself with the rules of the game and the proper way of interpreting them. He also takes care always to be in the best position to make a decision. This requires close observation and anticipation, born of experience, as to how each situation may develop. Where necessary, he will consult his linesmen who are better placed to observe some things than he is—though he will not pay attention to the crowd, which is partisan and not well placed. When appropriate, he will invoke the difficult "advantage" rule, which allows him to keep the game going even though an infringement has occurred, if continuance is to the advantage of the wronged side.

Love to God and our neighbor requires us to behave like that referee. First, it directs us to gain thorough knowledge of the whole range of obligations that Scripture requires us to meet. Second, love directs us in each situation to get into the best position for decision-making by securing as much relevant information as we can about actual causes and possible consequences.

Third, love directs us when we are not well placed for decision-making, either from lack of specialist knowledge or through personal involvement biasing our judgment, to turn to others who are better qualified to suggest what should be done; at the same time, it declines to be swayed by loud noises from persons who are passionate but not well informed. Fourth, love directs us on occasions to apply the equivalent of the advantage rule by not jeopardizing a greater good through needless inquiry into doubtful details. So Paul counsels Christians to use their God-given liberty by waiving the idolatry issue and thus in effect playing their advantage rule in the situation (1 Cor. 10:25-29).

Apply love as the referee in the four ways suggested above in a difficult situation in which you are involved.
Lord show me how to see this situation/this person...

If a man is overtaken in any trespass, you who are spiritual should restore him in a spirit of gentleness. Look to yourself, lest you too be tempted.

Galatians 6:1

When Jesus said, "Judge not, that you not be judged," he did not mean that we were not to be concerned about our own and other people's faults. What he was against was a censorious, fault-finding spirit which gets malicious pleasure from pointing out other people's failings and is vociferous about those weaknesses in others which are part of their personality (and which they seem not to have faced up to realistically and honestly).

This is very different from what Paul calls for here: gently and humbly drawing a fellow Christian's attention to something that needs to be put right in his life and actually helping him to do that, aware all the time of our own weaknesses. What we must never do is breeze up to a person beaming and assuring him of our love, point out bluntly all his wrongdoings, and then walk away thinking we have done our bit. We should only rebuke if we are ready to make an effort to restore.

We have to be creative in our relationships. That will mean creating situations in which we are most likely to be heard by the other person and in which he is most likely to feel that we really care about him. We have to put time and prayer into structuring things so that the other person will receive what we have to say and sense our loving commitment to him.

Jesus was marvelously creative in his relationships. He never said more at any stage than the other person was able to hear; sometimes he gave enigmatic answers to their first questions so that they could think their way into what he was saying and then be able to ask better questions and thus take matters further. Love gave him fantastic empathy with others. We need love like that.

Love and self-giving characterize creative relationships. Do they characterize your relationship with. . .? (Review your relationships at home, in your church, and with those you think of as your friends.)

Father, loving self-giving makes me very vulnerable. But if you took that risk, I oughtn't to hold back.

Through death to life

We are. . . always carrying in the body the death of Jesus, so that the life of Jesus may also be manifested in our bodies.
2 Corinthians 4:8,10

Christian baptism, whether administered by immersion, pouring, or sprinkling, is passing under water (signifying death), and then coming out from under (signifying resurrection). The death and resurrection signified are both physical (future) and spiritual (present). And the spiritual death and resurrection that is in view is not just the once-for-all event of becoming a Christian, but the continuing experience of "always carrying in the body the death of Jesus, so that the life of Jesus may also be manifested in our bodies."

For this is the pattern of the Christian's life. Through the self-negations of love and obedience and the tribulations of pain and loss for Jesus' sake, we enter into a thousand little deaths day by day and, through the ministry of the Spirit, we rise out of those little deaths into constantly recurring experiences of risen life with Christ.

It is a life of constant, conscious, expectant faith. The Spirit stirs us to look to Christ for the moral strength we need—gentleness, compassion, willingness to share and forgive; patience, tenacity, consistency, courage, fair-mindedness, forbearance, kindness, and so forth. And as we pray and seek to practice these virtues, we find that we are enabled to do so.

Am I experiencing this pattern?
Lord, don't let the image of joyless martyrs grimly bearing their crosses deflect me from entering into the authentic, enriching, "death into life" experiences you want to take me through.

*We ourselves, who have the first fruits of the Spirit, groan inwardly as we wait for
adoption as sons, the redemption of our bodies.*

Romans 8:23

What do Christians groan inwardly about? They groan about the fact that
their bodies (meaning their total personal selves) are still the seat of indwelling sin; the old anti-God instincts and urges are still *resident*, although not
dominant. As fallen beings, all our physical and mental desires are naturally
inclined to be inordinate, disorderly, and uncontrolled. Gluttony is one
form of inordinate desire which is a problem for some. Others may selfishly
exploit their fellows out of an inordinate longing for advancement and suc-
cess. Desires become inordinate in all sorts of ways because of the kinds of
persons that we are in these unredeemed bodies of ours. Inordinate desires
are constantly seeking to lead us astray and so there is constant tension in
the Christian life.

The believer, who from his heart delights in the law of God, also finds
another principle operating in himself: a law warring against the law of his
mind and inclining him to all sorts of disobedience and self-indulgence
(Rom. 7:22–23). He starts each day saying, "Lord, let it all be right today,"
and ends it admitting, "Lord, it hasn't all been right today." As long as he is
in the body indwelling sin is still with him, much as he wishes it wasn't.

Our physical dispositions and states give us all sorts of difficulties to contend with. Some are saddled with depressive temperaments, or fiery tem-
pers, or butterfly minds, or extreme shyness; menopausal tensions are acute
for some, and all of us have to cope with coming apart at the seams in old
age. These factors constantly occasion sin and obstruct righteousness. They,
too, merit our groans.

Faced with the reality of indwelling sin and the burden of our as yet unredeemed
physical bodies—no wonder we groan (and not always inwardly either!). But
what *else* can we do?
*Lord, keep me open to, aware of, and grateful for, the foretastes which you give me in
my spirit and in my body of what it will be like in heaven.*

*The secret things belong to the LORD our God; but the things that are revealed belong
to us and to our children for ever, that we may do all the words of this law.
Deuteronomy 29:29*

The principle illustrated in this verse is that God has disclosed his mind and
will so far as we need to know it for practical purposes, and we are to take
what he has disclosed as a complete and adequate rule for our faith and life.
But there still remain "secret things" which he has not made known and
which, in this life at least, he does not intend us to discover. And the reason
behind God's providential dealings sometimes falls into this category.

Job's case illustrates this. Job was never told at any stage about the challenge which God met by allowing Satan to plague his servant in the manner
which the book describes. All Job knew was that the omnipotent God was
morally perfect and that it would be blasphemously false to deny his goodness under any circumstances. He refused therefore to curse God even when
his livelihood, his children, and his health had been taken from him (Job
2:9-10).

Did the bewildering series of catastrophes that overtook Job mean that
God had abdicated his throne or abandoned his servant? Not at all—as Job
in due course proved by experience. But the reason why God had for a time
plunged him into darkness was never explained to him. And may not God,
for wise purposes of his own, treat others of his best followers as he treated
Job?

"You have heard of the steadfastness of Job," writes James, "and you have
seen the purpose of the Lord, how the Lord is compassionate and merciful"
(James 5:11).

If my "why's" are unanswered, what am I to conclude, and how should I act?
*Lord, even though you seem to be withholding the answers, don't withdraw your
presence.*

His (Joseph's) feet were hurt with fetters, his neck was put in a collar of iron; until
what he had said came to pass the word of the LORD tested him.

                                                            Psalm 105:18–19

The heart-breaking perplexity of God-given hopes apparently wrecked by God-ordained circumstances is a reality for many Christians today and will be the experience of more tomorrow—just as it was for Joseph.

Youngest in the family, he is given dreams of being head of the clan. His furious brothers sell him into slavery to make sure it never happens. Joseph is doing well in Egypt as right-hand man of a leading soldier-politician. The lady of the house, perhaps feeling neglected by her husband, as wives of soldiers and politicians sometimes do, wants to take Joseph to bed with her. Joseph says no, and this put-down from a mere slave turns the lady's lust to hate (never a hard transition) so that she lies about him and suddenly he finds himself languishing in prison, discredited and forgotten.

There he stays for some years, a model convict we are told, but with no prospects and nothing to think about save the dreams of greatness that God once gave him. Until what God had said was fulfilled, the word of the Lord tested him—and how! Can we doubt that Joseph constantly had to fight the feeling that the God who gave him hopes was now hard at work destroying them? Can we suppose that he found it easy to stay calm and trusting?

Do you have the feeling that God is playing games with you and your life? *Lord, I need to tell you how I honestly feel . . .*

*We are afflicted in every way, but not crushed; perplexed, but not driven to despair;
persecuted, but not forsaken; struck down, but not destroyed.*
2 Corinthians 4:8–9

Some Christians today live with epilepsy, homosexual cravings, ulcers, and
cyclical depressions. Indeed, Philip Hughes is surely correct when he writes:
"Is there a single servant of Christ who cannot point to some thorn in the
flesh, visible or private, physical or psychological, from which he has
prayed to be released, but which has been given him by God to keep him
humble and therefore fruitful? . . . Paul's thorn in the flesh is, by its very lack
of definition, a type of every Christian's thorn in the flesh."

The fact is that, now as then, God uses chronic pain and weakness,
along with other sorts of affliction, as his chisel for sculpting our souls.
Weakness deepens dependence on Christ for strength each day. The weaker
we feel, the harder we lean. And the harder we lean, the stronger we grow
spiritually, even while our bodies waste away.

Living with your complaint uncomplainingly and remaining kind, patient, and free in heart to love and help others, even though every day you
feel less than good, is true sanctification. It is true healing for the spirit. It is
a supreme victory of grace in your life.

Am I/Is my church expecting too much or too little from God as far as present
physical healing is concerned? What can be done about it?
*Lord, show those who lead and teach us what aspect of your truth we need to be
assimilating now—whether it's "You do not have because you do not ask," or "My
grace is sufficient for you" (James 4:2; 2 Cor. 12:9).*

When I am weak, then I am strong.
2 Corinthians 12:10

Grace is God drawing sinners closer and closer to him. How does God in grace prosecute this purpose? Not by shielding us from assault by the work, the flesh, and the devil, nor by protecting us from burdensome and frustrating circumstances, nor yet by shielding us from troubles created by our own temperament and psychology, but rather by exposing us to all these things, so as to overwhelm us with a sense of our own inadequacy, and to drive us to cling to him more closely.

This is the ultimate reason, from our standpoint, why God fills our lives with troubles and perplexities of one sort and another—it is to ensure that we shall learn to hold him fast. The reason why the Bible spends so much of its time reiterating that God is a strong rock, a firm defense, and a sure refuge and help for the weak is that God spends so much of his time showing us that we are weak, both mentally and morally, and dare not trust ourselves to find or follow the right road. When we walk along a clear road feeling fine, and someone takes our arm to help us, likely we would impatiently shake him off; but when we are caught in rough country in the dark, with a storm brewing and our strength spent, and someone takes our arm to help us, we would thankfully lean on him. And God wants us to feel that our way through life is rough and perplexing, so that we may learn to lean on him thankfully. Therefore he takes steps to drive us out of self-confidence to trust in himself, to—in the classic scriptural phrase for the secret of the godly man's life—"wait on the Lord."

What are your strengths and weaknesses? Is there a danger that your strengths are keeping you from being in the position before God that he wants you to be? *Lord, these are my strengths and weaknesses... and this is the situation that I face... May everything serve to draw me closer to you.*

I can will what is right but I cannot do it. For I do not do the good I want, but the evil I do not want is what I do.
Romans 7:18-19

In Romans 7:14–25 Paul speaks in the present tense, having previously spoken in the past. "I was" (v. 9) gives place to "I am" and "I do" (vv. 14, 16). So what he is telling his readers here is that the principle of which he spoke in verses 7–13—that God's law defines, detects, and damns sin in us, showing us how far sin dominates us—still applies now that he's a Christian.

Many commentators feel that in verses 14–25 Paul is simply saying again in present tense what he said in past tense in the preceding seven verses. I don't agree. Anyone who regards Paul as a good communicator must see his shift to present tense as a sign that, having spoken of the past, he is now moving on to speak about his present experience as a Christian. Any rejection of this, the most obvious explanation, accuses Paul of not knowing how to say clearly what he meant. Besides, a person who is not a Christian would never be able to claim truthfully that he delights in the law of God in his inmost self (v. 22) because "the mind that is set on the flesh is hostile to God" (8:7).

Nor do I believe, as some claim, that Paul is here speaking as a Christian in poor spiritual health. Don't ask me to accept that when Paul dictated any part of Romans he was in a low spiritual state! In reality, it is a mark of spiritual health passionately to desire to be perfect for the glory of God and then to be deeply distressed when one finds that sin, though dethroned and no longer dominant, remains within, marauding and trying to regain control, so that one cannot fully achieve righteousness. This healthy distress at the way in which, morally speaking, what one aims for always exceeds what one actually grasps is what Romans 7:24–25 portrays.

Can you recognize in your own life Paul's spiritual conflict? Read the second half of Romans chapter 7 again, using "I" to mean yourself. Does it ring true?
Lord, when we struggle like this it is hard to see how we can at the same time be "more than conquerors" (Rom. 8:37). Help us experience this nonetheless through your Spirit.

. . . called according to his purpose. For those whom he foreknew he also predestined to be conformed to the image of his Son, in order that he might be the first-born among many brethren.

Romans 8:28–29

Paul regularly uses the word "call" to express God's work of causing us to hear, understand, and receive the gospel. In calling us he both invites us to faith in Christ and moves our hearts to respond to that invitation. He evokes the response for which he calls. Paul's readers were Christians who knew they were called in that sense. Such people, Paul says, God foreknew and predestined to glory. Here "foreknew" really means "foreloved." Often in Scripture, knowing includes the idea of affection, as when a husband knows his wife or a friend knows a friend. God, then, foreloved us and predestined us to be conformed to Jesus.

To the question, "What did God want out of this world with its sin, fallenness, and confusion?" one true answer is, "He wanted an extended family." He has one Son, we might say, and wanted more. Of course there are differences between Jesus and the rest of God's sons and daughters. Jesus is the eternal Son of God by nature while we are God's children through Jesus, by adoption and grace. Nevertheless, the glorious truth about redemption is that God wanted to extend his family and have many, many people with him for all eternity bearing the family likeness: "a great multitude which no man could number, from every nation, from all tribes and peoples and tongues" (Rev. 7:9). That was why he sent his Son to die for us and now sends his Spirit to call us to faith, keep us in faith, and renew us in Jesus' image.

Think about the concept of God's extended family and your membership in it.
Father, thank you for wanting a big family, and thank you that I am in it and that you love all your adopted children as much as you love your eternal Son.

You are the salt of the earth. . . You are the light of the world.
Matthew 5:13-14

Salt preserves what would otherwise rot and gives flavor to what would otherwise be flavorless; also, salt creates thirst. So Christians by the quality of their lives and by their actions should restrain evil and keep society from rotting, add savor to community life by, among other things, doing right and treating people with respect, and stir up a thirst for God.

Jesus is really telling his disciples to be what they are: You are salt, he says. Now be it! You're not living by the same scale of values as the rest of men, and people should notice this as they watch you in your homes, in your work, in the wider world. Don't lose your "tang." Be uncompromisingly different. Again, you are the light of the world. Be what you are: a source of illumination, guidance, and hope to all around you.

Make sure that people see your light. "Let your light so shine before men, that they may see your good works and give glory to your Father who is in heaven" (Matt. 5:16). Here Jesus isn't encouraging the "silent servers," those who say, "I can't speak for God so I'll just live a good life and let others do the talking." He is saying that the quality of our lives should back up and make credible the truth of the gospel that we profess and our good works confirm the good words of our testimony to the Savior who transforms sinners into saints. By seeing our lives, people ought to be made to realize that our gospel really works!

What part am I (is my church) playing in restraining evil, doing good, and stirring up a thirst for God in the community?
Father, show me as I wait on you today and in the coming days any ways in which I could and should be exerting a Christian influence.

Do not give dogs what is holy; and do not throw your pearls before swine, lest they trample them underfoot and turn to attack you.

Matthew 7:6

I don't think Jesus means that some people are so rotten that you shouldn't share the gospel with them. What he is warning us against, rather, is failing to understand those to whom we seek to witness and so being insensitive and saying inappropriate things. By such failures we easily provoke fury and so turn our hearers into "dogs" and "swine."

Imagine a person prostrated with pain of bereavement and along comes some pious Pete to deliver a sermon about the precious discipline that God intends through taking away the loved one. The grieving person may have neither the physical nor the verbal resources to throw such a Job's comforter out, but that is what he will want to do. At a time of intense grief, one is simply unable to handle this thought, however true it might be. What one needs at such a time is love, and anything said about God should point the bereaved to God as the supreme source of help in trouble.

Similarly, some people witness to others by buttonholing them and keeping them captive while lecturing them about gospel truth, whether they like it or not. We're not to be insensitive in such ways. Dogs and pigs don't appreciate holy things and pearls. And if we witness in a brutal, loveless way that makes our hearers needlessly angry, they won't appreciate what we're offering them either.

We must learn to empathize with people to whom we want to witness. We must understand them, see where they are "at," what they need, and how much they can, at any given moment, take. Only then should we attempt to share God's precious truths with them.

What is my real motive in speaking to others about God's truth? Guilt? A desire to be well thought of? Love? . . .

Lord, in my contacts with people, help me to focus less on what I want to say and more on what the other person is feeling and needing.

What we preach is not ourselves, but Jesus Christ as Lord.
2 Corinthians 4:5

Basic missionary, evangelistic, and pastoral policy has to do in the first instance not with programs (though these have their place), nor with institutions (though you could not get far without them), but with the message. This is what Paul draws our attention to in 1 Corinthians 2:1-5.

The first maxim for those who engage in missionary work, pastoral care, or evangelism is : Trust your message. Your message is God's own witness to reality. And God can be trusted to honor it.

Paul's words come directly out of his own experience. That makes them much more powerful. Truth in life is always more impressive than truth in formula.

Paul came to Corinth with the aim he had wherever he went: to communicate the gospel with a view to converting his hearers. He unites these two concepts in the single word he often uses to describe his ministry: *persuade.* "We persuade men" (2 Cor. 5:11), Paul says. We persuade men to receive and respond to God's truth.

Communication with a view to conversion ought never to be a matter of dispute among Christians. Beyond all question this is our given task.

Are we all meant to be persuaders for Christ or is that a special calling for some Christians? Are there other means of persuasion, apart from words? What will give the most persuasive force to our words?
Lord, let me not be in any doubt about the truth of the gospel message or the part you want me to play in passing it on.

I did not come proclaiming to you the testimony of God in lofty words or wisdom.
1 Corinthians 2:1

As inheritors of the Greek philosophical culture, the Corinthians appreciated argument, esteemed eloquence, and delighted in debate. But Paul said, "I did not come with eloquence." Nor did he speak with what the Corinthians could recognize as wisdom. Why not?

Paul's thought in answer to this question went something like this: I saw that those expectations of yours were conceited ones, and if I had conformed to them I would have been pandering to your conceit and flattering you.

To catch people's attention and get them listening is one thing. That is good, right, and necessary, and Paul himself would adapt his style of presentation in order to do that. But the further element of cultural and intellectual flattery that so easily enters into communication was not included in his approach. His business as a messenger of God was not to feed God's Word into the arena of debate, but simply to proclaim it with the authority of the Lord himself from whom it comes.

Whether his listeners would hear or turn away, Paul set himself to announce, to explain, and to enforce what God had said. But to be clever? No. And for a very good reason. "You cannot at the same time give the impression that you are a great preacher"—or theologian or debater or whatever—"and that Jesus Christ is a great Savior" (James Denney). If you call attention to yourself and your own competence, you cannot effectively call attention to Jesus and his glorious sufficiency.

Does this mean that God cannot use our eloquence or other "natural" gifts? If not, how can such gifts be used?

Lord, I recognize that my strengths could draw attention to myself, whereas your strength in my weakness would draw attention to you.

*Lift up your eyes, and see how the fields are already white for harvest. . . One sows
and another reaps.*
John 4:35,37

In telling his disciples to lift up their eyes and look on the fields, Jesus is saying something about spiritual priorities. He has already told them: "I have
food to eat of which you do not know," and, "My food is to do the will of
him who sent me, and to accomplish his work" (vv. 32,34). Now in effect
he's saying to them: What you should concentrate on at this moment is not
our picnic, but those people coming across the fields from Sychar led by the
woman to whom I've been speaking.

Whenever opportunity affords, evangelism is to be our first priority. It's
also, or ought to be, a joyful privilege: "He who reaps receives wages, and
gathers fruit for eternal life, so that sower and reaper may rejoice together"
(v. 36). There's nothing more worthwhile than seeking under God to be the
human agent in saving men and women for all eternity.

Evangelism is also a partnership. Jesus said to his disciples, "I sent you to
reap that for which you did not labor" (v. 37). What did he mean? He
meant that he had been witnessing to the Samaritan woman, and she had
been witnessing to her friends and neighbors and now they were coming to
the well. It would be the disciples' privilege to "reap" them: to teach them
more about Jesus and establish them in the kingdom and family of God.

It takes great humility to say, without jealousy or resentment, "I sowed,
now you reap." But that's the pattern. In the winning and nurturing of souls
sometimes we will be the reapers and sometimes we will only be the sow-
ers, preparing the way for others to reap. Yet each role is essential; so we
must be ready to fulfill either.

Am I a willing and contented partner in evangelism?
Lord, make me eager to contribute to sowing or reaping for you.

*To the weak I became weak, that I might win the weak. I have become all things to
all men, that I might by all means save some.*

1 Corinthians 9:22

Paul was a great communicator not because he was eloquent (2 Cor. 10:10;
1 Cor. 2:1–5), but because he knew his own mind and had a great capacity
for identifying with the other person. It is clear that though he had looked
to the Holy Spirit to make his communicating fruitful, he knew that the
Spirit works through appropriate means, and so he was very conscious of
the human factors in persuasion—namely, cogency of statement and empa-
thetic concern—and was always most conscientious in laboring to achieve
them. With that, he set no limit to what he would do, however unconven-
tionally, to ensure that he did not, by personal insensitiveness or cultural inertia, set up barriers and stumbling-blocks in the way of men and women
coming to Christ (1 Cor. 9:19–22).

Paul was a man who could and did share himself unsparingly. From his
letters we know him well, and we can appreciate the trauma that lies behind
the autobiographical passage of Philippians chapter 3 where he tells us how
Christ stripped him of cultural pretensions. "Here was a man who . . . sub-
mitted every part of his historical inheritance to the judgment of the cross.
Nothing could be removed, but everything could be re-interpreted. Those
things which seemed most positive gain could be judged as of no account in
the service of Christ: those things which had seemed to be hindrances and
handicaps might well prove positive assets in the new order of living" (F.W.
Dillistone).

Paul's loving, imaginative adaptability is a shining example to all who engage in communicating the gospel to the world.

What makes a good communicator?
Lord, I submit all my inheritance to you for re-interpreting in your will.

The wisdom of this world is folly with God.
1 Corinthians 3:19

Atheism is a denial of God's existence. Such denial might be expected to create a mood of disillusionment and despair, yet atheism today is often not the gloomy thing we might have expected it to be. Most Western atheists are optimistic humanists, convinced that atheism opens the door to full personhood and true happiness, whereas the real effects of religious belief (which they would call superstition) is to keep people in certain respects sub-human.

The best known version of this thesis is the Marxist contention that Christianity with its two-worldly perspective is "the opiate of the masses," a psychic drug which makes people content when they ought not to be content, a major obstacle in the way of revolution that will bring the classless society where all may attain the dignity of personhood.

But it is not only Marxism that sees belief in God as a barrier to full human development. This valuation of religious belief is found in every type of atheism that Christianity has produced. I say "produced" advisedly because atheism is essentially anti-theism: a reaction against someone else's belief in God. Therefore it is a chameleon, taking its color from the sort of faith in God that it denies. Marxism, with its gospel of a way out of bondage into a hope of glory, is very obviously a Christian harmonic progression transposed into a materialistic key. It could be shown that the other atheisms of history have also been built out of re-angled Christian concepts and secularized Christian ideals.

Try saying to an atheist, "Tell me about the God you don't believe in." If he does, you may be able to assure him that you don't believe in that sort of God either and tell him about the God you *do* believe in!

Help me, Father, to want to understand, care for, and share the gospel with my atheist neighbors.

The serpent said to the woman, "You will not die. For God knows that when you eat of it your eyes will be opened, and you will be like God, knowing good and evil."
Genesis 3:4-5

The ideal which Adam and Eve embraced was to become so mature and wise that they would no longer need God for guidance but would be able to rule themselves. By this choice, they renounced the alternative ideal of living in obedience to God, seeking and doing his will, as contented and worshipping creatures. They refused to accept the fact that they were under probation and were not intended to enjoy the fullest and final maturity until the time of probation was over. They saw the way of godless independence and self-sufficiency as a short cut to the highest happiness. The world has never seen a more tragic error.

All atheism reaffirms this Adamic ideal negatively as well as positively. Its deepest motivation is the longing to be our own God here and now, coupled with the certainty that this is the way to fullest personhood.

Practical atheism, the life of pride and self-will, is as natural to every person as it was to Adam. Theoretical atheism appears as a humanistic reaction and as a denial of the God or gods whom others acknowledge. Love of forbidden things, arrogance of mind, the hurt of disappointment, or disgust at believers may have triggered the reaction, but in every case the deep intention is the same: namely, to clear the stage for man to play God unhindered.

There are many ways of gratifying the impulse to live as God without God, and some of them have been by human standards both virtuous and heroic. Also, atheism is sometimes a lesser evil than that against which it reacts. Yet this does not alter the fact that in all its forms atheism deifies human beings and revolts against any sort of dependence on God.

Read "The Impercipient" by Thomas Hardy to understand the desperate plight of those who want to believe in God but feel that they can't.

Lord, show me whether my atheist neighbor is hung up by pride or by pain.

The wrath of God is revealed from heaven against all ungodliness and wickedness of men who by their wickedness suppress the truth. For what can be known about God is plain to them, because God has shown it to them.
Romans 1:18-19

What is the condition of the professed atheist in the sight of God? Paul tells us the answer to this in the first two chapters of Romans, in the course of his great indictment of a sinful humanity.

Atheists may or may not have known the Jewish law, or for that matter the Christian gospel, but some revelation of God the Creator and his law has reached them, simply through their being alive in God's world and having consciences; this revelation they are suppressing by a process so habitual that they are hardly or rarely aware of it. Atheists are, like the rest of the world, "without excuse" and guilty before the God whom they have ignored (Rom. 1:18-25, 32; 2:1-16).

Human beings in revolt can do no more than make puny gestures of defiance against the God they claim to deny. Meanwhile they reap the reward not of self-fulfillment but of frustration—the frustration of not being able to live life fully because they refuse to live the way they were designed: God's way. Life does not go well when we deny God and make ourselves the center of our world, any more than cars run well when denied oil and filled up with the wrong fuel. The wear and tear of atheism on the human personality may not be apparent on the surface, but it will appear in some form: an inner hardening, an obsessive fixation of pride and prejudice, an atrophying of sensitiveness to spiritual values, a cheapening view of life, a growing temper of cosmic distaste, or an intensifying battle to keep boredom at bay.

How is the wear and tear of being an atheist different (if at all) from that of being a Christian?
Lord, help me to see my atheist neighbor as living in an unreal and hopeless world (Eph. 2:12). Fill me with active, positive compassion.

Let all the house of Israel. . . know assuredly that God has made him both Lord and Christ, this Jesus whom you crucified.

Acts 2:36

Right through the Old Testament the conviction runs that God is managing all human history for the good of his people and that the climax will be the setting up of the kingdom of God under the Messiah, God's anointed King. In the New Testament, Jesus of Nazareth is shown to be that Messiah or Christ. But his role is not only a kingly one, but prophetic and priestly too. Jesus as prophet preached in God's name; as priest, he offered himself in sacrifice for the sins of the people; as king, having risen triumphantly from the dead, he now reigns at God's right hand. "All authority in heaven and on earth has been given to me," he told his disciples (Matt. 28:18). So the early Christians came to see Jesus of Nazareth as the Christ of God, their Teacher, Savior, and living Lord.

Those who believe this have a view of history that differs from the views of those who don't. As Christians we know that Christ is reigning until all things are put under his feet and that we are living in the last days—the period between his first coming, to bring salvation and set up his kingdom, and his second coming, to complete the work of his kingdom in royal triumph and final judgment.

There is increasing chaos and confusion as human history moves to its close, but as Christians we can find stability and hope in Jesus who is the sovereign Lord of history. The Father has promised the Son, "Thy throne, O God, is forever and ever" (Heb. 1:8), and the promise will never fail.

"What do you think of the Christ?" (Matt. 22:42). This is a question to ask ourselves and others: so much depends on the answers we give.

Jesus, I acknowledge you as the focus of human history, God's Messiah, and Lord of all. Be my Lord today—controlling all I do, say, and think.

You are the Christ, the Son of the Living God.
Matthew 16:16

My Lord and my God.
John 20:28

When Thomas called Jesus his Lord and God, he wasn't confusing Jesus with the Father; he was acknowledging that Jesus was God, too. One of the hardest and most mind-blowing things that Christians are called upon to believe is that there are three persons, but one God. It took some centuries for Christian theologians to arrive at a form of words that would safeguard, though not explain, this amazing notion. That formula describes Jesus as being *of one substance with the Father.* In other words, there's nothing in God the Father that isn't also and equally in God the Son, while at the same time the mystery remains: Father, Son, and Spirit are one God and not three.

Another mystery that Christians acknowledge is that Jesus was not only truly and fully divine, but also truly and fully human. He didn't lose his personal deity in becoming flesh. He is as much a human being as any one of us. "He had to be made like his brethren in every respect, so that he might become a merciful and faithful high priest in the service of God, to make expiation for the sins of the people" (Heb. 2:17).

The implications of the fact that Jesus was fully God and fully man are important. God is Jesus-like. If we want to understand the character of God, it's to Jesus we must look. Human nature is also to be understood in terms of Jesus. Man is made to live life for God in the way that Jesus lived his life. For humans to live in any other way is to be less than human. So anyone living without God is less than human—not physically or psychologically, but in the sense that he is not tasting the truly human life for which he was made and which brings the true freedom, fulfillment, and satisfaction.

Am I enjoying the truly human life for which I was made?
Jesus, I want to give more priority-time to my relationship with you.

April 3

The angel Gabriel was sent from God to a city of Galilee named Nazareth, to a virgin betrothed to a man whose name was Joseph, of the house of David; and the virgin's name was Mary.

Luke: 1:26–27

The Bible says that the Son of God entered and left this world by acts of supernatural power. His exit was by resurrection-plus-ascension, and his entry by virgin birth: both fulfilling the Old Testament anticipations (Isa. 7:14; 53:10–12). The entry and exit miracles carry the same message. They confirm that Jesus, though no less than man, was more than man, and they indicate his freedom from sin.

The New Testament gives two complementary accounts of the virgin birth, evidently independent yet strikingly harmonious: Joseph's story (Matt. 1:18–25) and Mary's (Luke 1:26–2:20). Both show every sign of being sober history.

Skepticism about Jesus' virgin birth and his physical resurrection began as part of a quest for a non-miraculous Christianity. Though that quest is now out of fashion, the skepticism still lingers on, clinging to the minds of Christian people as the smell of cigarettes clings to a room after the ashtrays have been cleared. If we acknowledge Jesus as the Word made flesh, these two miracles as elements in the larger miracle of the Son's incarnate life raise no special problem.

Mary was a virgin till after Jesus' birth (Mark 3:31; 6:3). Mariology, which sees her as co-redeemer, rests on the non-biblical teaching that Mary, like Jesus, was born without sin and entered resurrection glory straight after death. But the real Mary, the Mary of Scripture, saw herself simply as a saved sinner. She sets us a marvelous example.

Am I skeptical or gullible about miracles? Is either attitude right? If not, how should I see and respond to miracles?
Lord, help me to be both open and thoughtful like Mary.

Now we see in a mirror dimly, but then face to face. Now I know in part; then I shall understand fully, even as I have been fully understood.
1 Corinthians 13:12

That a man named Jesus was crucified under Pontius Pilate about A.D. 30 is common historical knowledge, but Christian beliefs about Jesus' divine identity and the significance of his dying cannot be deduced from this fact alone. What further sort of knowledge about the cross may Christians enjoy?

The answer is—*faith-knowledge.* By faith we know that God was in Christ reconciling the world to himself. Yes indeed. But what sort of knowledge is faith-knowledge? It is a kind of knowledge of which God is both giver and content. It is a Spirit-given acquaintance with divine realities, given through God's Word. It is a kind of knowledge which makes the knower say in one and the same breath, "Though I was blind, now I see" (John 9:25), and "Now we see in a mirror dimly...Now I know in part."

It is a unique kind of knowledge which, though real, is not full; it is knowledge of what is discernible within a circle of light against the background of a larger darkness; it is knowledge of a mystery, the mystery of the living God at work.

The atonement is one aspect of the total mystery of God; it is a reality which we acknowledge as actual without knowing how it is possible. Charles Wesley expressed it well:

Tis mystery all! The immortal dies!
Who can explore his strange design?
In vain the first-born seraph tries
To sound the depths of love divine!

Meditate on 1 John 4:8–10.
Write and then offer to God in worship a prayer, poem, or song based on your meditation.

God shows his love for us in that while we were yet sinners Christ died for us.
Romans 5:8

As we look at the cross and interpret it, with the help of the Holy Spirit, and in the light of what the Bible says about it, we see many truths that are basic to personal religion:

God condones nothing but judges all sin as it deserves, which Scripture affirms and my conscience confirms to be right.

My sins merit ultimate penal suffering and rejection from God's presence (conscience also confirms this), and nothing I do can blot them out.

The penalty due me for my sins was paid for me by Jesus Christ, the Son of God, in his death on the cross.

Because this is so, through faith in him I am made the righteousness of God (2 Cor. 5:21): i.e., I am justified. Pardon, acceptance, and sonship become mine.

Christ's death for me is my sole ground of hope before God.

My faith in Christ is God's own gift to me, given in virtue of Christ's own death for me: i.e., the cross procured it.

Christ's death for me guarantees my preservation to glory.

Christ's death for me is the measure and pledge of the Father and Son's love for me.

Christ's death for me calls and constrains me to trust, worship, love, and serve.

Express the nine thoughts above in non-theological language so that an unchurched person might understand. Try to find and memorize some of the verses which are the basis for these thoughts (e.g., 2 Cor. 5:19, 21; Gal. 3:13; Rom. 5:8, 18).

Father, thank you for all I can be sure of because Jesus was crucified for me.

For Christ... being put to death in the flesh but made alive in the spirit... went and preached to the spirits in prison, who formerly did not obey, when God's patience waited in the days of Noah.
1 Peter 3:18-20

When Jesus descended into hell, he entered not Gehenna but Hades; in other words, he really died, and it was from a genuine, not a simulated death that he rose (Acts 2:31-32).

1 Peter 3:18-20 tells us briefly what Jesus did in Hades:

First, by his presence he made Hades into Paradise (a place of pleasure) for the penitent thief and, presumably, for all the others who died trusting him during his earthly ministry, just as he does now for the faithful departed (Luke 23:43; Phil. 1:21-23; 2 Cor. 5:6-8).

Second, he perfected the spirits of Old Testament believers (Heb. 12:23; 11:40), bringing them out of the gloom which Sheol (the pit) had hitherto been for them (Ps. 88:3-6, 10-12) into this same Paradise experience. This is the core of truth in the medieval fantasies of the harrowing of hell.

Third, "he went and preached (presumably announcing his kingdom and appointment as the world's judge) to the spirits in prison" who had rebelled in antediluvian times (presumably the fallen angels of 2 Pet. 2:4-10 who are also the sons of God in Gen. 6:1-4). Some have based on this one text a hope that all humans who did not hear the gospel in this life, or who, having heard it, rejected it, will have it savingly preached to them in the life to come. Peter's words provide no warrant for this inference: a first, non-saving announcement to a group of fallen angels does not imply a second saving announcement to the whole host of unsaved human dead. Had Peter believed in the latter, surely he would have said it straightforwardly.

Do Philippians 1:19-26, 2 Corinthians 5:1-10, and 2 Timothy 4:16-18 really express my attitude toward death?
Lord Jesus, thank you that you lead me through no darker rooms than you went through before.

On the third day he rose again

He (David) foresaw and spoke of the resurrection of the Christ... This Jesus God raised up.

Acts 2:31-32

Christians believe that on a precise day—the third day (counting inclusively as they did in those days) after his crucifixion—in Jerusalem, capital of Palestine, Jesus came alive and vacated a rock tomb, and death was conquered for all time.

Can we be sure it happened? The evidence is solid. The tomb was empty and nobody could produce the body. For more than a month afterwards the disciples kept meeting Jesus alive, always unexpectedly, usually in groups (from two to 500). Hallucinations don't happen that way.

The disciples were sure that the risen Christ was not just in their imaginations and tirelessly proclaimed his rising in the face of ridicule, persecution, and even death.

The corporate experience of the Christian church over the centuries chimes in with the belief that Jesus rose; communion with Jesus belongs to the basic Christian awareness of reality.

What is the significance of Jesus' rising from death? It marks Jesus as the Son of God; it vindicates his righteousness; it demonstrates victory over death; it guarantees the believer's forgiveness and justification and his own future resurrection; it brings him into the reality of resurrection life now (John 16:10; Acts 2:24; Rom. 1:4; 4:25; 6:4; 1 Cor. 15:17-18). You could speak of Jesus' rising as the most hopeful (hope-full) thing that has ever happened—and you would be right!

Why is it important to believe in the resurrection as a historical fact?
Because you rose, I/we... (finish the sentence as fully as possible). Thank you, Lord Jesus.

Let us leave the elementary doctrines of Christ and go on to maturity.
Hebrews 6:1

In Hebrews 5:11–14 the writer complains that after years as believers his Jewish Christian readers were neither passing on the truth they knew nor holding it fast themselves, let alone hungering for more as they should have been; instead they had regressed to a sort of spiritual infancy in which even elementary things had ceased to be clear, and they needed to learn the gospel ABC all over again. Blurred vision regularly results from not facing spiritual challenges squarely, and in this case the challenge to patience under persecution was not being faced. In their self-induced infantile state, they could scarcely take the solid food (teaching on Christ's perfect high-priesthood with its implications of finality and exclusiveness) which the writer had for them and gives them in Hebrews chapters 7–10.

What they lacked was *maturity*: the perfection of the fully-developed, clear-sighted, spiritual all-rounder. The sign of immaturity was that they could not see that the ministry of Christ cancels and excludes the typical religion of the Old Testament. Thus, by reverting to Judaism, as they thought of doing, they would gain nothing and lose everything. This blindness showed their lack of discerning good from evil courses—a capacity which requires constant consecrated exercise for its development. Regressing to spiritual babyhood, they had embraced fantasy and lost touch with spiritual realities. To lead them on to the maturity they lacked and needed, the writer resolves to leave the gospel ABC and go on to the more demanding doctrines.

Is it possible to be a mature Christian and an immature person?
Lord, help me to understand what Christian maturity really is and to want it.

*If I have prophetic powers, and understand all mysteries and all knowledge, and if I
have all faith, so as to remove mountains, but have not love, I am nothing.*
                                                                       1 Corinthians 13:2

What the Corinthians had to realize, and what some today may need to relearn, is that, as the Puritan John Owen put it, there can be *gifts* without
graces; that is, we may be capable of performances that benefit others spiritually and yet be strangers ourselves to the Spirit-wrought inner transformation that true knowledge of God brings. The manifestation of the Spirit
in charismatic performance is not the same thing as the fruit of the Spirit in
Christlike character (Gal. 5:22–23), and there may be much of the former
with little or none of the latter. You can have many gifts and few graces;
you can even have genuine gifts and no genuine graces at all, as did Ba-
laam, Saul, and Judas. So no one should treat his gifts as proof that he
pleases God or as guaranteeing his salvation. Spiritual gifts do neither of
these things.

All through the New Testament, when God's work in human lives is spoken of, the ethical has priority over the charismatic. Christlikeness (not in
gifts, but in love, humility, submission to the providence of God, and sensitiveness to the claims of people) is seen as what really matters. This is particularly clear in Paul's prayers for believers (Col. 1:11; Phil. 1:9–11; Eph.
3:14–19).

Any mindset which treats the Spirit's gifts as more important than his
fruit is spiritually wrong-headed and needs correcting. The best corrective
will be a view of the Spirit's work that sets activities and performances in a
framework that displays them as acts of serving and honoring God and
gives them value as such.

Are you/Is your church fellowship overemphasizing or ignoring gifts or graces
from the Spirit?
Pray in the words of Paul's prayers for believers (see above) for yourself and others.

*He chose us in him before the foundation of the world, that we should be holy and
blameless before him.*
Ephesians 1:4

Gospel holiness is quite different from legal holiness: the latter consists
merely of forms, routines, and outward appearances, maintained from self-
regarding motives; the former is simply a consistent living out of our filial
relationship with God, into which the gospel brings us.

Gospel holiness is a matter of the child of God being true to his type, his
Father, his Savior, and himself. It is the expressing of his adoption in his life.
It is a matter of being a good son, as distinct from a prodigal or black sheep
in the royal family. The adoptive relationship provides the motive for this
authentically holy living. Christians know that God "destined us in love to
be his sons through Jesus Christ" (Eph. 1:5) and that they are moving toward a day when this destiny will be fully and finally realized: "We know
that when he appears we shall be like him, for we shall see him as he is"
(1 John 3:2).

What flows from this knowledge? 1 John 3:3 provides the answer: "Everyone who thus hopes in him purifies himself as he is pure." The children
know that holiness is their Father's will for them and that it is a means, condition, and constituent of their happiness, here and hereafter; because they
love their Father, they actively seek the fulfillment of his beneficent purpose.

Paternal discipline, exercised through outward pressures and trials, helps
the process along. In this world, royal children have to undergo extra training and discipline, which other children escape, in order to equip them for
their high destiny. It is the same with the children of the King of Kings.

What pressures and trials face you? Does it help to see them in the light suggested
above?
*Tell God, honestly, how you feel about your pressures and trials, and don't be afraid
to ask him for what you feel you need—respite, encouragement, a way of escape,
someone's help, or whatever.*

Grow in the grace and knowledge of our Lord and Savior Jesus Christ.
2 Peter 3:18

Growth in grace is something that is required of us all. So why is it that some Christians seem content to remain spiritual pygmies? Some, I believe, have never really grasped the fact that we are summoned to grow and mature. Others duck the issue because they're so afraid of change. Again others compare themselves with fellow Christians and decide they're all right by comparison. We all need to take the issue of Christian growth more seriously.

Growth in grace cannot be measured in the way that physical growth can, but it can be and often will be tested. Whether we have been growing or not will be revealed by our response to times of crisis and unexpected pressure. The more we have grown, the steadier we shall stand, and the more resolutely we shall obey.

Growth in grace does not take place at the same speed in every life, nor produce the same experiences, because each of us is different. However, the goal is the same for us all—that we shall bear the full fruit of the Spirit in our lives and become fully like our Master.

We can never be very good judges of whether we have grown in grace because so much of this growth goes on without our being aware of it. But we can realize our progress to some extent by asking questions such as: What does the Lord enable me to do now which once I could not do, and which I could never have done myself apart from his strength? The apostle Peter, had he asked himself that question, could have replied, "The Lord has given me a stability and wisdom which I never had before." So too, John, originally a son of thunder who wanted fire called down from heaven on Jesus' enemies, was turned into the apostle of love: that was how the growth-process showed itself in him.

What has my Lord done for me that I never could have done for myself?
Thank you, Lord, for the evidence of the growth of grace in my heart. I want to go on growing as a Christian; please help me to do so, for Jesus' sake.

I am the least of the apostles.
1 Corinthians 15:9

I am the very least of all the saints.
Ephesians 3:8

I am the foremost of sinners.
1 Timothy 1:15

Humility and a passion for praise are a pair of characteristics which together indicate growth in grace. The Bible is full of self-humbling (man bowing down before God) and doxology (man giving praise to God). The healthy heart is one that bows down in humility and rises in praise and adoration. The Psalms strike both these notes again and again. So too, Paul in his letters both articulates humility and breaks into doxology. Look at his three descriptions of himself quoted above, dating respectively from around A.D. 59, 63, and 64. As the years pass he goes lower; he grows downward! And as his self-esteem sinks, so his rapture of praise and adoration for the God who so wonderfully saved him rises.

Undoubtedly, learning to praise God at all times for all that is good is a mark that we are growing in grace. One of my predecessors in my first parochial appointment died exceedingly painfully of cancer. But between fearful bouts of agony, in which he had to stuff his mouth with bedclothes to avoid biting his tongue, he would say aloud over and over again: "I will bless the Lord at all times; his praise shall continually be in my mouth" (Ps. 34:1). That was a passion for praise asserting itself in the most poignant extremity imaginable.

Cultivate humility and a passion for praise if you want to grow in grace.

Does God mean for us to be both humble and confident? If so, explain this apparent impossibility.

Lord, I'm short on joy. Help me today to bow down before you and then rise to praise you for everything that you are to me and have given or promised to me.

April 13

Growing up in the family
Faith and the surrender of security

By faith Abraham. . . went out, not knowing where he was to go.
Hebrews 11:8

Faith and the surrender of security are two more characteristics that will be found in the life of someone who is growing in grace.

Faith from one standpoint is trust in Christ as Savior; from another, it is "the assurance of things hoped for, the conviction of things not seen" (Heb. 11:1) on the basis of which people are prepared to take risks for God and to accept insecurity for his sake. Years ago a man I chatted with in an electronics shop said, "What you really have faith in is what you're willing to bet your life on." Hebrews chapter 11 is full of people willing to bet their lives on God. Abraham went out not knowing where he was going because he was not sure where the Lord was leading him. Moses left Egypt, not fearing the wrath of the king and "choosing rather to share ill treatment with the people of God than to enjoy the fleeting pleasures of sin" (Heb. 11:24–25). These are just two examples out of very many.

Often we are called upon to show our faith by surrendering our security in one area or another. Perhaps it's financial security that we have to give up or the security of living in a place which we enjoyed until God said to us, "I want you to move somewhere else and start a new work for me." The call comes in different ways, but when it comes, growth in grace can be seen by the way a person expresses faith in taking the risk of responding. It isn't really a risk, though, because the only safe place to be in this world is within the will of God.

Is God asking you to surrender your security in any area?
Lord, if you are calling me to. . . make it clear and make me willing to trust and obey you.

*For his sake I have suffered the loss of all things, and count them as refuse, in order
that I may gain Christ.*
Philippians 3:8

Christ-centeredness and a tender conscience are further characteristics of
lives that are growing in grace. Paul said that he had suffered the loss of everything for Christ's sake and that he counted those things as refuse (dung or
manure) in comparison with what he wanted to gain: Christ (Phil. 3:7–11).
He was willing to let everything go that he might grasp Christ fully. He developed a sensitive conscience about anything which might get in the way
of that objective. And if we are growing in grace, we will be developing
Christ-centeredness and a tender conscience along the same lines.

Then there is love and the instinct for giving. These too are marks of
growth in grace. We see full grown love in Jesus. Even on the cross love tri-
umphed, not only because he was there out of love but because even in the
midst of his pain, his dominating concern was still to bless and be a blessing
to others. To his Father on behalf of those who had crucified him he said,
"Father, forgive them; for they know not what they do" (Luke 23:34); to his
mother: "Woman, behold, your son" (John 19:26); and to the thief on the
cross: "Today you will be with me in Paradise" (Luke 23:43). Like Jesus, our
lives should be increasingly characterized by love and the purpose of bringing good to others.

Is my conscience increasingly sensitive about things and pursuits that take me
away from outward-looking discipleship? Even when things are hard, do I still
long to be a blessing to others?
*Thank you, Lord, for every sign that you are at work in my life and character. I am
aware of my lack of growth in these areas. . .*

*God spoke all these words saying, "I am the LORD your God, who brought you out
of the land of Egypt, out of the house of bondage. You shall have no other gods before me... You shall not covet your neighbor's house... or anything that is your
neighbor's."*

                                                    Exodus 20:1-3,17

It's possible to know the Ten Commandments by heart and still miss much of their meaning as did the Pharisees.

God gave the commandments to Israel in his character as Yahweh, their God and Redeemer. Loyalty to their God and gratitude for his work of grace were to be the motives for their obedience. They were given the Law not to show them how to earn God's favor and acceptance (they had that already), but to guide them in living the life that would please him and bring them the fullness of his blessing.

Though nine of the commandments are negative statements, positive principles are implied: give your God total loyalty; in all your dealings with him, think of him only as he has revealed himself and not in any other terms; always be reverent; use your weekly day of rest to worship your Maker and Redeemer and to help others; respect and love your fellow men and seek their welfare; respect the sanctity of marriage vows and the integrity of the opposite sex; respect property; stay truthful and straight; be content with what God has given you.

Though stated in terms of outward action, the commandments touch the heart, calling for right desires and attitudes.

The commandments were given as God's covenant requirements of Israel, but the principles embodied in them go back to creation. What they are pointing to is the shape of the ideal life, not just for Israelites, but for all human beings.

If the Ten Commandments are meant positively, why do you think they were stated negatively?

Lord, I keep coming back to this message about obedience to you...

You shall worship no other god, for the LORD, whose name is Jealous, is a jealous God.
Exodus 34:14

There are two sorts of jealousy among men, and only one of them is a vice. Vicious jealousy is an expression of the attitude, "I want what you've got, and I hate you because I haven't got it." But there is another sort of jealousy—zeal to protect a love-relationship, or to avenge it when broken, and Scripture consistently views God's jealousy as being an aspect of his covenant love for his own people. The Old Testament regards God's covenant as his marriage with Israel, carrying with it a demand for unqualified love and loyalty. The worship of idols and all compromising relations with non-Israelite idolaters constituted disobedience and unfaithfulness, which God saw as spiritual adultery, provoking him to jealousy and vengeance.

So when God told Moses that his name was Jealous, he meant that he demands from those whom he has loved and redeemed utter and absolute loyalty, and he will vindicate his claim by stern action against them if they betray his love by unfaithfulness.

We must remember, too, that God's jealousy over his people presupposes his covenant love; and this love is no transitory affection, accidental and aimless, but the expression of a sovereign purpose. The goal of the covenant love of God is that he should have a people on earth as long as history lasts, and after that he shall have all his faithful ones of every age with him in glory.

Should we be jealous for God (see 1 Kings 19:10,14)? If so, how?
Father, make me very aware of idols in whatever guise they come—especially when they come in the form of things that are in and of themselves good.

April 17   **Family standards**
                                                        Putting God first

You shall have no other gods before me.
Exodus 20:3

What other gods could we have besides the Lord? Plenty. For Israel there
were the Canaanite Baals, those jolly nature gods whose worship was a
rampage of gluttony, drunkenness, and ritual prostitution. For us there are
still the great gods Sex, Shekels, and Stomach (an unholy trinity constitut-
ing one god: self), and the other enslaving trio, Pleasure, Possessions, and
Position, whose worship is described as "the lust of the flesh and the lust of
the eyes and the pride of life" (1 John 2:16). Football, the Firm, and Family
are also gods for some. Indeed the list of other gods is endless, for anything
that anyone allows to run his life becomes his god and the claimants for this
prerogative are legion. In the matter of life's basic loyalty, temptation is a
many-headed monster.

What will it mean in practice for me to put God first? This much at least.
The 101 things I have to do each day and the 101 demands on me which I
know I must try to meet will all be approached as ventures of loving service
to him, and I shall do the best I can in everything for his sake.

And then I shall find that, through the secret work of the Spirit which is
known by its effects, my very purpose of pleasing God gives me new energy for all these tasks and relationships—energy which otherwise I could
not have had. Self-absorbed resentments dissolve zest for life. Happiness in
doing things and love for others grows great when God comes first.

Does God really come first in my life in practice?
*Lord, I can see that. . . could become/is an idol. I am willing to take action to ensure
that I worship only you. Help me.*

You shall not take the name of the LORD your God in vain.
Exodus 20:7

"In vain" means "for unreality." What is forbidden is any use of God's name that is empty, frivolous, or insincere. This touches at least three things.

The first thing is *irreverence*: speaking or thinking of God in a way that insults him by not taking seriously his wisdom and goodness. Job offered sacrifices on behalf of his children while they were alive for fear that they had "cursed God in their hearts"; and after their deaths when his wife in her bitterness urged him to "curse God and die," he would not do it (Job 1:5; 2:9–10). Whenever sinful self-absorption makes us hate God for what he allows to happen, we break this third commandment.

The second thing is *bad language*: using God's holy name as a swear word to voice unholy feelings. Everyday profanity—for example, "Oh, God," or, "Oh, Christ"—may not be the worst of sins, but it is a nasty breach of the third commandment since it expresses neither faith nor worship.

The third thing, and the one which needs special emphasis because we are so slack here, is *promise-keeping*. If we have invoked God by name in order to give our words credence, it is monstrous irreverence if we then go back on them. And the point goes deeper. When Jesus attacked the Pharisees' idea that we can break without guilt any oath sworn by any sacred object so long as God's name has not been explicitly mentioned, his point was that you cannot keep God out of any transaction. He is everywhere. All promises are made in his presence and involve him whether his name is mentioned or not.

Do I take God's name in vain in any of these ways? How do (should) I react when others do this in my presence?
Lord, I acknowledge that I have taken your name in vain in this way...

The place for sex

You shall not commit adultery.
Exodus 20:14

What is the place and purpose of sex? God intends that the "one flesh" experience should be an expression and a heightening of the partners' sense that, being given to each other, they now belong together, each needing the other for completion and wholeness (Gen. 2:18–24). This is the love that committed couples are to make when they mate. Children are born from their relationship but this is secondary; what is basic is the enriching of their relationship itself through their repeated knowing of each other as persons who belong to each other exclusively and without reserve. So the place for sex is the place of lifelong mutual fidelity, i.e., marriage, where sexual experience grows richer as the couple experiences more and more of each other's loving faithfulness in the total relationship.

It follows that casual sex outside marriage (called adultery if either partner is married, fornication if not) cannot fulfill God's ideal, for it lacks the context of pledged fidelity. In casual sex, a man does not strictly love a woman but uses and so abuses her (however willing she may be). Nor can solitary masturbation fulfill God's ideal; sex is for relationships, not ego trips. And the relationships intended are heterosexual only; God forbids and condemns homosexual practices.

In these days it needs to be said, indeed shouted, that accepting as from God a life without physical sex acts does one no harm nor does it necessarily shrink a person's humanity. Not all who wish for a sexual partner can have one, but what God by circumstances calls us to he will enable us for.

Do we behave as though sexual sins are somehow worse than almost any other and imply that total forgiveness isn't available for them? Is this a biblical/right attitude?
Pray for yourself or anyone else struggling with sexual temptations.

Honor your father and your mother, that your days may be long in the land which the LORD your God gives you.
Exodus 20:12

The way we behave as children and parents is a prime test of both our humanity and our godliness. Love—the caring love of parents who respect their children and want to see them mature, and the grateful love of children who respect their parents and want to see them content—is our great need here.

In these days it is urgent that parents and children together relearn the ways of Christian family life. In the West, yesterday's extended family has shrunk to today's nuclear family; social security and community affluence has reduced the family's importance as an economic unit, and all this has weakened family relationships. Parents are too busy to give time to their children, and young people, identifying with current youth culture, are more prone than ever to write off their parents as clueless old fuddy-duddies. But the fifth commandment recalls us to God's order at this point.

Honoring parents means respecting them for their office and their relationship to us, whatever we may think of their personal limitations or private lives. A school contemporary of mine carved out a brilliant academic career but grew ashamed of his parents (his father was a baker), and would not visit them or let them visit him. But people may not claim to love their neighbor while they shrug off their parents. Some of us have some repenting to do here.

Do I honor my parents? Do we as a church honor the older people among us? Are Christians leading in these matters the way they should?
Lord, thank you for my parents—for their good qualities and actions. . .

You shall not steal.
Exodus 20:15

Love to our neighbor requires us to hold sacred not only his person (sixth commandment) and his marriage (seventh commandment), but also his *property* and his *due*.

Behind the commandment lies the biblical view of property: namely, that ownership is stewardship. By human law, my property is that which I own and may dispose of as I wish, as distinct from that which I am merely allowed to use as borrower or trustee under conditions which the owner imposes. Bible believers, however, know that what human law says I own—my money, goods, legal rights, and titles—I actually hold as God's trustee. In terms of Jesus' parable, (Matt. 25:14-30) these things are *talents*, lent to me by my Lord on a temporary basis to use for him. One day I shall be asked to give account of how I managed those resources of which I was given control.

Temptations to steal property—that is, to deprive another person of what he or she has a right to—arise because fallen man always, instinctively, wants more than he has at present and more than others have. Blind competitiveness, expressing an equally blind jealousy, was the essence of the devil's pride when he rebelled against God, and of Cain's pride when he killed Abel, and of Rebekah's and Jacob's pride when they stole Esau's birthright; it is the essence of the discontented greed condemned in the tenth commandment which is itself the cause of the dishonest grabbing forbidden in the eighth. But it is not God's will for us to have anything that we cannot obtain by honorable means. The only right attitude to others' property is scrupulous concern that ownership be fully respected.

Does Acts 2:43-47 make this commandment obsolete? If not, why not?
Lord, please show me if I am not respecting any of my neighbor's property or what is due him or her (e.g. Have I returned all the books he/she loaned me?)...

Before the mountains were brought forth, or ever thou hadst formed the earth and the world, from everlasting to everlasting thou art God.
Psalm 90:2

Our Bible-reading takes us into what, for us, is quite a new world: namely, the Near Eastern world as it was thousands of years ago—primitive and barbaric, agricultural and unmechanized. It is in that world where the action of the Bible story is played out. In that world we meet Abraham and Moses and David and the rest, and watch God dealing with them. We hear the prophets denouncing idolatry and threatening judgment on sin. We see the Man of Galilee doing miracles, arguing with the Jews, dying for sinners, rising from death, and ascending to heaven. We read letters from Christian teachers directed against strange errors which, so far as we know, do not now exist.

It is all intensely interesting, but it seems very far away. We feel that we are, so to speak, on the outside of the Bible world, looking in. Our unspoken thought is: Yes, God did all that then, and it was wonderful for the people involved, but how does it touch and help us now, living in the space age?

This sense of remoteness from the biblical experience of God springs from seeking the link between our situation and that of the various Bible characters in the wrong place. The link is God himself. For the God with whom they had to deal is the same God with whom we have to deal. We could sharpen the point by saying *exactly* the same God; for God does not change.

Being linked to God is the most mind- and spirit-expanding relationship anyone could ever have; the Bible is just one of the vast treasure-houses that open up to us when we are in Christ and know his Father as ours.

Father, as I read the Bible, make that long-ago, far-away world totally relevant to my life for your glory, by the Holy Spirit, through Jesus.

Let all the earth fear the LORD, *let all the inhabitants of the world stand in awe of him! For he spoke, and it came to be; he commanded, and it stood forth.*
Psalm 33:8

Every quality that confers authority is found in God, and every form of authority finds both its origin and archetype in him. His veracity (Titus 1:2) imparts to all that he says the authority of truth. All authority in human society derives from him.

Human beings, the Bible tells us, were made for authority: made to live under the rule of their Maker. The idea that freedom and happiness can be found by casting off God's authority was and is Satan's lie, but many people believe it. The Western world is suffering from a breakdown of authority in every department of life with disastrous consequences. And the churches which ought to be mediating the authority of God to others are not doing so because they themselves have been infected. The result of a century of liberalism has been the destruction of the authority of Scripture, its teaching, and its God in our churches. It is no accident that where God's Spirit has been powerfully poured out, there the sense of the inspiration and authority of Scripture has been preserved and that there has never been a revival, only barrenness, wherever liberal theology has gone.

The greatest need of our society is for a renewed sense of the authority of God and of his Christ and of his Word. And a revived church, with a renewed experience of the authority of the Word of God, is where it all has to stem from.

For meditation or discussion: The man who is set against God is always set against some of his neighbors too.

Lord, I accept that "what Scripture says, God says." Help me to submit and serve you and others according to your Word.

I have laid up thy word in my heart, that I might not sin against thee.
Psalm 119:11

One morning in the 1620s, in a little village church, a preacher named John
Rogers was preaching on the subject of the Bible in the Christian's life. He
allowed himself some pulpit dramatics. First, he acted the part of God telling the congregation: "Well, I have trusted you so long with my Bible; you
have slighted it; it lies in such and such houses all covered with dust and
cobwebs; you care not to listen to it. Do you use my Bible so? Then you
shall have my Bible no longer." And he took the pulpit Bible away.

Then he knelt down and impersonated the people crying to God: "Lord,
whatever thou dost to us, take not thy Bible from us; kill our children; burn
our houses; destroy our goods but spare us thy Bible."

Then he acted God again: "Say you so? Well, I will try you a while
longer; and here is my Bible for you" (replacing it); "I will see how you will
use it, whether you will love it more, observe it more, practice it more, live
more according to it."

At this the whole congregation dissolved in tears. What had happened?
Rogers, under God, had touched a nerve, reminding them of their need to
pay close attention to the Bible because reverence for God meant reverence
for Scripture and serving God meant obeying Scripture.

Do we need to recapture some of the same attitude today? Surely disre-
garding the Bible is the greatest possible insult to its divine author.

A critic has said, "A book is a mirror: if an ass peers into it, you can't expect an
apostle to look out." Does this hold true if the book in question is the Bible? If not,
why not?
Lord, I pray for those who do not have the privilege of reading a Bible of their own.

My soul is consumed with longing for thy ordinances at all times.
Psalm 119:20

The biggest thing that keeps us from getting the full benefit of Scripture is simply that we do not feel needy enough. Leaders are particularly prone to feel that they are fully competent; they have got it made; they know it all. This sense of self-sufficiency is a satanic temptation. A moment of realistic thought should remind leaders and anyone else that each of us is as needy as another before God.

I find it most helpful to remind myself at the beginning of my devotional time who God is and what I am. I remind myself that God is great, transcendent—that he loves me and wants to speak to me right now. And I recall that I am the original sinner, the perverse and stupid oaf who misses God's way constantly. I have made any number of mistakes in my life up to this point and will make a lot more today if I don't keep in touch with God and stay with Christ, my Lord and Savior, as I should.

There is nothing like a sense of hunger to give me an appetite for a meal, and there is nothing like a sense of spiritual emptiness and need to give me an appetite for the Word of God. Let that be the theme of our first minute or two of prayer as we come to our devotional times, and then we will be tuned in right. The quantity of theological notions in our minds, even correct ones, doesn't say anything about our relationship with God. As a professional theologian I need to keep reminding myself of the difference between knowing notions and knowing God.

"Open your mouth wide, and I will fill it" (Ps. 81:10).
Lord, show me how wide open my mouth is—how hungry and thirsty I am for you. And make me hungrier and thirstier yet.

For whatever was written in former days was written for our instruction, that by steadfastness and by the encouragement of the scriptures we might have hope.
Romans 15:4

How may we get the most from the Bible? First, we must value it properly. Psalmists, prophets, and apostles testify that we need the Word of God as *light* for guidance, *food* for growth, and a *sword* for battle. Out of his awareness of man's natural ignorance and perversity when it comes to knowing and pleasing God, the psalmist cries, "Thy word is a lamp to my feet and a light to my path" (Ps. 119:105). To young and not-so-young Christians, Peter writes: "Like newborn babes, long for the pure spiritual milk, that by it you may grow up to salvation" (1 Pet. 2:2). This milk is the living and enduring Word of God (1 Pet. 1:23–25). "Thy words were found, and I ate them, and thy words became to me a joy and the delight of my heart" (Jer. 15:16). As good food nourishes the body, so biblical truth feeds the soul, and as babies who get no milk waste away, so do Christians who neglect their prescribed diet.

Also, there is a war to be fought. Satan is on the attack; and for that Paul directs: "Take...the sword of the Spirit, which is the word of God" (Eph. 6:17).

Where would any of us be without Bible truth? Lost, starving, and defenseless, according to the divine analysis. We undervalue and neglect it at our peril.

We show how much we value people or things by the amount of time and the intensity of care and thought we lavish on them. So, on that criterion, how much do you value the Bible?

Lord, increase my desire for and my delight in every word that proceeds from the mouth of God.

Give me understanding, that I may keep thy law.
Psalm 119:34

We cannot arrive at a true understanding of God's Word by detaching texts
from their contexts to find personal meaning in them and by feeding them
into the world of our private preoccupations and letting that world impose
new senses on old phrases.

A theological student whom later I knew as a senior friend had committed himself to starting his ministry in the north of England when he received
a very attractive invitation to join a teaching institution in South Wales instead. He did not feel able to withdraw from his commitments, but one day
he read in Isaiah 43:6 (Authorized Version), "I will say to the north, Give
up," and concluded that this was God telling him that he would be provi-
dentially released from his promise and so set free to accept the second invitation. No such thing happened, however, so he went north after all,
wondering what had gone wrong. Then he reread Isaiah 43:6 and noticed
that it continued,". . .and to the south, Do not withhold." At this point it
dawned on him that he had been finding meaning in the text that was never
really there. Instead, the concerns which he brought to his reading of the
text had governed his interpretation of it.

To impose meaning on the text is not the way to learn God's Law. Yet we
constantly do this (don't we?), and it is one chronic obstacle to understanding.

Is there a difference between imposing a personal meaning on some words in the
Bible and experiencing God specifically applying those words to a particular situation in your life?
*Lord, I don't want to impose meaning on your Word nor do I want to rule out any
means by which you might speak to me.*

Give me understanding, that I may know thy testimonies!
Psalm 119:125

Imagine a seminar in which the instructor, himself an authority, comments on someone else's essay so skillfully and profoundly that you, as a member of his class, learn all you need to know about the subject just by listening. This is how God teaches us from the Bible. We are drawn into the middle of God's dealings with Bible characters and his address in and through the biblical books to their original recipients. By observing and overhearing, we learn what God thought of their attitudes, assumptions, ambitions, and activities, and what changes in their mindset and lifestyle he wanted to see, and this shows us what he must think of us and what changes he must want to see in us.

Now imagine yourself being coached at tennis. If the coach knows his stuff, you are likely to experience him as a perfect pest. You make strokes as you have done for years, the natural, comfortable way. He interrupts, "Hey, not like that; that's no good; do it this way instead." In the same way God corrects us, constantly working to change us.

The understanding of which the psalmist speaks is a matter of receiving that *teaching* (first illustration) and *reproof* and *correction* that leads to *training in righteousness* (second illustration) for which Paul said Scripture was *profitable* (2 Tim. 3:16). It means knowing what God's truth requires today in our lives. Such understanding does not come naturally, but is the gift of God.

Is my church receiving teaching and correction and training in righteousness from the Bible, or is the balance not right at the moment?
Lord, please continue to correct me whenever I need it.

Give me understanding that I may live.
Psalm 119:144

God gives understanding of the Bible through the Holy Spirit. That does not cancel out the need for study any more than it invalidates the rules of interpretation. Never oppose the work of the Spirit in giving understanding to your work as a student seeking it; the Spirit works through our diligence, not our laziness. Understanding what God's written Word means for me comes through seeing what it meant when it was first put on paper and applying that to ourselves.

It is in application specifically that we need divine help. Bible commentaries, Bible classes, Bible lectures and courses, plus the church's regular expository ministry can give us fair certainty as to what Scripture meant. We should make full use of them to that end. But only through the Spirit's illumination shall we be able to see how the teaching applies to us in our situation. So we should look not only to the commentators for exegesis but also to the Spirit for the application.

I'd like to suggest three questions which we could ask as we read the Bible. What does this passage tell me about *God:* his character, power, and purpose; his work, will, and ways in creation; providence and grace? What does this passage tell me about *people:* the human situation, man's possibilities, privileges, problems, right and wrong ways of living, man in sin, and man in grace? What is all this showing me and saying to me about *myself* and my own life? Lift your heart to God and ask for the Spirit's help as you work through these three questions in the divine presence, and you will certainly be given understanding.

Am I praying before reading as well as after reading the Bible?
Lord, I can't hope to understand everything here and now, but please give me understanding of all that I need to know in order to live fully.

Give me understanding according to thy word!
Psalm 119:169

God gives understanding of the Bible through the Christian community. Psalm 119 does not say this, but Paul does (Eph. 3:16–19; Col. 3:16). Only as we gratefully share with the others what we know and receive from them what they know will the Word of Christ (the Christian message) dwell in us *richly* (abundantly and enrichingly) in the way that produces *wisdom.*

I don't question the value of private Bible reading and study. Nor do I forget that over and over again people who had no biblical preaching within reach nor any fellowship have been wonderfully taught by God; or that a Christian may not finally surrender his judgment to anyone (1 Thess. 5:21; 1 Cor. 10:15). I am only saying that the New Testament expects that as we sit under the preaching and teaching of the Word and share with each other about it, rather than isolating ourselves in spirit to commune with the Bible as solitary individuals, we shall be given understanding most fully.

It follows that we should take most seriously the preaching under which we sit in our churches, and the value of group Bible study and practicing fellowship with Christians outside our own circle by reading their books.

If we do these things, we will stand a much better chance of being delivered from the tyranny of being tied to our own thoughts, our own time, and our own heritage.

Am I listening to preachers in order to criticize or to learn? How much do I pray for them and prepare myself prayerfully to hear them?
Lord, help me not to be afraid of reading beyond my own tradition and preferences.

Three persons

...in the name of the Father and of the Son and of the Holy Spirit.
Matthew 28:19

Notice that it is "name" (singular), not "names" (plural). The incredible yet inescapable truth that the one God is tri-personal runs through all the New Testament. Jesus called God his Father, claiming to be both his son and his equal, and allowed Thomas to worship him as "my Lord and my God" (John 5:18–23; 10:30; 20:28). Also, he promised to send the Holy Spirit— "another (that is, a second) Counselor"—to replace him and carry on his ministry to the disciples (John 14:26; 15:26; 16:7–15). Thus he made plain that within the unity of the Godhead are three divine persons working together. Other passages show the same thing.

At Jesus' baptism the Holy Spirit descended on him while the Father declared from heaven: "This is my beloved son" (Matt. 3:16–17). To Nicodemus Jesus explained the need to be born of the Spirit and believe in the Son who was given to the world by the Father (John 3:1–16). Paul wishes the Corinthians the blessing of each of these persons (2 Cor. 13:14), through whose joint work, as he elsewhere explains, we are saved (Rom. 8; Eph. 1:3–14; 2:13–22; 2 Thess. 2:14–15; 1 Pet. 1:2).

It is sometimes thought that the Spirit is just the active influence of the Father and the Son, but the New Testament tells us that he speaks, testifies, helps, searches, is lied to, grieved, and resisted—things that could be said only of a person.

The truth of the Trinity is verified in Christian experience. The Spirit dwells *in* us (Rom. 8:9) and the enthroned Lord stands *by* us (2 Tim. 4:17) to strengthen us for the worship and service of our heavenly Father who is *above* us.

Does your experience verify the truth of the Trinity? How?
Pray with a reawakened awareness of the three persons of the Trinity: pray to your heavenly Father in the name of the Son through the Holy Spirit.

The LORD our God is one LORD.
Deuteronomy 6:4

I am the LORD and there is no other, besides me there is no God.
Isaiah 45:5

There is no God but one.
1 Corinthians 8:4

The central issue of belief today is between faith in one God (monotheism) and disbelief in any God (atheism); but in Bible times it was between believing in one God and in many (polytheism). The Bible is hot against polytheism, for one who believes in many gods cannot regard any of them as having absolute power or total claim on his life, nor dare he serve any of them exclusively to the disregard of others. But Scripture insists throughout that there is only one God, the Maker and Lord of all.

So what is this one God like? To the fourth question of the Westminster Shorter Catechism, "What is God?" the following answer is returned: "God is a Spirit, infinite, eternal, and unchangeable in his being, wisdom, power, holiness, justice, goodness, and truth." No better account of God has ever been framed in so few words. Two points stand out:

First, *God's existence is eternal.* He is God "from everlasting to everlasting" (Ps. 90:2), all-powerful, all-knowing, self-sustaining, and needing nothing (Acts 17:25). "Thou art the same, and thy years have no end" (Ps. 102:27).

Second, *God's character is unchanging.* This is how he proclaimed himself to Moses: "The LORD, a God merciful and gracious, slow to anger, and abounding in steadfast love and faithfulness, keeping steadfast love for thousands, forgiving iniquity and transgression and sin, but who will by no means clear the guilty" (Exod. 34:6–7). This is God's character still for "he cannot deny himself" (2 Tim. 2:13).

What is God to you? What names can you give him, and what qualities can you ascribe to him, from your own experience of him?
Turn your answers into thanksgiving and worship.

The head of the family
God the judge

It is God who executes judgment.
Psalm 75:7

Arise, O God, judge the earth.
Psalm 82:8

Why do men shy away from the thought of God as a judge? Why do they feel unworthy of him? The truth is that part of God's moral perfection is his perfection in judgment. Would a God who did not care about the difference between right and wrong be a good and admirable being? Would a God who put no distinction between the beasts of history, the Hitlers and Stalins (if we dare use names), and his own saints be morally praiseworthy and perfect? Moral indifference would be an imperfection in God, not a perfection. And not to judge the world would be to show moral indifference. The final proof that God is a perfect moral being, not indifferent to questions of right and wrong, is the fact that he has committed himself to judge the world.

It is clear that the reality of divine judgment must have a direct effect on our view of life. If we know that retributive judgment faces us at the end of the road, we shall not live as otherwise we would. But it must be emphasized that the doctrine of divine judgment, and particularly of the final judgment, is not to be thought of primarily as a boogieman, with which to frighten men into an outward form of conventional righteousness. It has its frightening implications for godless men, it is true; but its main thrust is as a revelation of the moral character of God, and an imparting of moral significance to human life.

"Shall not the Judge of all earth do right?" (Gen. 18:25). The answer of *faith* and the answer of *sight* (i.e., judgment by appearances) to this question might be very different. Think about this in relation to yourself.
God the Judge, thank you that you are also God my Savior.

I will have mercy on whom I have mercy, and I will have compassion on whom I have compassion.
Romans 9:15

Ancient paganism thought of each god as bound to his worshippers by self-interest because he depended on their service and gifts for his welfare. Modern paganism has at the back of its mind a similar feeling that God is somehow obliged to love and help us, even though we don't deserve it. This was the feeling voiced by the French freethinker who died muttering, "God will forgive—that's his job." But this feeling is not well founded. The God of the Bible does not depend on his human creatures for his well-being (see Ps. 50:8-13; Acts 17:25), nor, now that we have sinned, is he bound to show us favor. We can only claim from his justice—and justice, for us, means certain condemnation.

God does not owe it to anyone to stop justice from taking its course. He is not obliged to pity and pardon; if he does so it is an act done, as we say, "of his own free will," and nobody forces his hand. "It depends not upon man's will or exertion, but upon God's mercy" (Rom. 9:16). Grace is free because it is self-originated and proceeds from the One who was free not to be gracious. Only when one realizes that what decides each man's destiny is whether or not God resolves to save him from his sins, and that this is a decision which God need not make in any single case, can one begin to grasp the biblical view of grace.

If I am not staggered by the grace of God, is it because I've lost sight of it, or never really grasped, where I'd be without it?
Lord, you freely chose, at great cost to yourself, to show mercy and grace to every repentant sinner. Lord Jesus Christ, be merciful to me, a sinner.

The head of the family
God's generous goodness
The Lord is good to all.
Psalm 145:9

God's truthfulness and trustworthiness, his unfailing justice and wisdom, his tenderness, forbearance, and entire adequacy to all who penitently seek his help, his noble kindness in offering people the exalted destiny of fellowship with him in holiness and love—these things together make up God's goodness, the sum total of his revealed excellences. "This God—his way is perfect" (Ps. 18:30).

However, there is more to be said. Within the cluster of God's moral perfections there is one in particular to which the term goodness points. This is the quality of *generosity*. Generosity means a disposition to give to others in a way which has no mercenary motive and is not limited by what the recipients deserve, but consistently goes beyond it. Generosity expresses the simple wish that others should have what they need to make them happy. Generosity is, so to speak, the focal point of God's moral perfection; it is the quality which determines how all God's other excellences are to be displayed.

Many of the psalms extol God's generosity in its different aspects. There is God's generosity in bestowing natural blessings: every meal, every pleasure, every possession, every bit of sun, every night's sleep, every moment of safety, everything else that sustains and enriches life (Ps. 145). But the mercies of God on the natural level, however abundant, are overshadowed by the greater mercies of spiritual redemption: God's mighty acts in saving Israel from Egypt; his willingness to forbear and forgive when his servants fall into sin; his readiness to teach men his way; his mercy in grafting "wild" Gentiles into his olive tree (Ps. 106; 86:5; 119:68; Rom. 11:22).

Read Psalm 18, asking yourself how far your testimony matches up to that of David.
Spend some time giving thanks to the Lord for his generous goodness to you.

To all who received him. . . he gave power to become children of God.
John 1:12

When we cry, "Abba! Father!" it is the Spirit himself bearing witness with our spirit
that we are children of God.
Romans 8:15–16

God's fatherly relationship with Jesus implies four things. First it implies *authority*. The Father commands and disposes; the initiative which he calls his Son to exercise is resolute obedience to his Father's will. Second, it implies *affection*; third, *fellowship*; fourth, *honor:* God wills to exalt his Son.

All this extends to God's adopted children. In, through, and under Jesus Christ their Lord, they are ruled, loved, accompanied, and honored by their heavenly Father.

As Jesus obeyed God, so must they (1 John 5:1,3). As God loved his only-begotten Son, so he loves his adopted sons (John 16:27). As God had fellowship with Jesus, so he does with us (1 John 1:3). As God exalted Jesus, so he exalts Jesus' followers, as brothers and sisters in one family (John 12:32; 17:24).

In these terms the Bible teaches us to understand the shape and substance of the parent-child relationship which binds together the Father of Jesus and the servant of Jesus.

Which aspect of God's fatherly relationship with you are you least aware of or failing to benefit fully from? Let the relevant Bible words soak into your mind and stay with you throughout the day.
Tell your Father how you feel about him and what he means to you.

He cannot deny himself.
2 Timothy 2:13

Does omnipotence mean that God can do literally anything? No, that is not the meaning. There are many things God cannot do. He cannot do what is self-contradictory or nonsensical, like squaring the circle. Nor (and this is vital) can he act out of character. God has a perfect moral character, and it is not in him to deny it. He cannot be capricious, unloving, random, unjust, or inconsistent. Just as he cannot pardon sin without atonement because that would not be right, so he cannot fail to be faithful and just in forgiving sins that are confessed in faith and in keeping all the other promises he has made. Moral instability, vacillation, and unreliability are marks of weakness, not of strength: but God's omnipotence is supreme strength, making it impossible that he should lapse into imperfection of this sort.

The positive way to say this is: though there are things which a holy, rational God is incapable of intending, all that he intends to do he actually does. "Whatever the LORD pleases he does" (Ps. 135:6). As when he planned to make the world, "he spoke, and it came to be" (Ps. 33:9), so it is with everything that he wills. With people "there's many a slip twixt cup and lip," but not with him.

What else can't God do (because for him to do it would be a denial of himself)? *Lord, I thank you that you do as you please because I know that you are perfect and so all your intentions and actions are perfect too.*

As they were looking on, he was lifted up, and a cloud took him out of their sight.
Acts 1:9

The Father withdrew Jesus from the disciples' gaze by taking him up—not sideways or down, but *up*. What does it mean when we say that someone has gone up in the world? It means that they have been promoted. And the fact that Jesus went up into heaven was a sign to the disciples that he had been advanced to God's throne. Jesus had been king from the beginning of his ministry, but the ascension was the public sign of his monarchy, corresponding to the coronation of a human monarch—an event which can take place later than actual entry upon royal dominion. Having ascended, so we are told, Jesus sat down at the right hand of God—the prime minister's seat in any first-century palace, the place of executive power and authority. What does this mean for us?

First, we need to realize that though Jesus was withdrawn physically from the world, his ministry still continues. Before his ascension Jesus had told Mary not to hang on to him (John 20:17) because he wanted her to realize that she must get used to not being able to stretch out her hand and touch him physically; but he would still be real and close to her and to all his disciples. The Acts of the Apostles, which could equally well be called the Acts of the Ascended Lord, show us just how real and close Jesus still was as he continued his ministry on earth. The Christ who was absent in body was powerfully present by the Spirit, and the world was turned upside down as a result.

Second, the ascension meant that Jesus would no longer be localized in Palestine; he would be present anywhere and everywhere so that all who seek his presence can find it and all who call on him can receive his undivided attention, wherever in the world they may be.

Third, we have the wonderful prospect of one day being with Jesus where he is. The Lord who is *sitting* at God's right hand (Acts 2:34–35) will *stand* to welcome us into his home at the end of our time on earth (Acts 7:56)!

I know Jesus will come again, but what would my honest reaction be if I knew he would be coming again today?
Jesus, help me to find the balance between gazing up at you and doing your work right here.

Christ Jesus...died...was raised from the dead...is at the right hand of God...intercedes for us.

Romans 8:34

Following the resurrection came the *ascension*—the withdrawal of Jesus from human sight to reign till his return. This event was presented to the eyes of the disciples as a movement up into misty cloud, a sign that Jesus had gone "into heaven"—God's immediate presence—to occupy the place of power as the reigning Lord (Acts 1:9-11).

Jesus is the "one mediator between God and men" (1 Tim. 2:5), and in heaven his *mediatorial work* goes on—not in the form of continued offering of himself as a ransom for sins (that work is finished now), but in the form of *intercession* (Rom. 8:34; Heb. 7:25).

Jesus' intercession is his effective intervention in our interest, as our guardian and champion, when we are in trouble; it ensures that the benefits of Calvary are actually received and that when we approach "the throne of grace" we find without fail "grace to help in time of need" (Heb. 4:16).

But Jesus is not only "in heaven" but also "in us," through the Holy Spirit. The New Testament tells us that born-again believers are here and now united with Christ in a vital relationship whereby they die with him (finishing their former life) and rise with him (beginning an endless new life of fellowship with their Lord—Rom. 6:1-11; Col. 2:9-15; 3:1-4).

Lord, even if I cannot understand the paradox of your being in heaven and in me at the same time, help me to *experience* you as my heavenly intercessor and king and my everyday friend and companion.
Because Jesus is alive, earth is "slight momentary affliction" and heaven is "glory beyond all comparison" (2 Cor. 4:17). True for you? If it is, thank God now.

You he made alive, when you were dead through. . .trespasses and sins.
Ephesians 2:1

Paul speaks clearly in Ephesians 2:1-10 and elsewhere of the new birth as
the act of God by which those who were spiritually dead are made alive in
Christ.

When he describes people as being spiritually dead, he means that they
are unresponsive to God (corpses don't answer when you address them);
they are separated from God's fellowship and exposed to God's wrath. Such
people follow a course of life dictated by the world, the devil, and the
flesh—a life of disobedience to God.

Concerning God's quickening of the spiritually dead, Paul points out:

It springs from *love, mercy, grace,* and *kindness* so completely that it is
largely beyond our thought.

It takes place *in Christ.* Jesus Christ is the mediator of all God's gifts to us,
including newness of life.

It catches us up into God's act of *raising Christ from the dead.* The church
is the extension of the resurrection. Those raised with Christ sit in the
heavenlies: they enjoy a hidden life which puts them always "on top" since
he who is ruling the world makes all things work for their good.

A course of *God-planned obedience* is its goal.

How does Ephesians 2:1-10 apply to people who have been Christians for as long
as they can remember—you, perhaps?
*Father, I don't feel very "on top" today. Give me a truer perspective on this situation
as I talk to you about it. . .*

On the evening of . . . the first day of the week, the doors being shut where the disciples were, for fear of the Jews, Jesus came and stood among them, and said to them, "Peace be with you."

John 20:19

"Grace . . . came through Jesus Christ," John wrote at the beginning of his gospel (1:17); ultimately grace is Jesus himself, coming into a situation of human need to speak a word of love, coming in person to save people who are in need and distress.

The disciples had disastrously failed in their discipleship. They had said they would stand by Jesus but as soon as the troops came to arrest him, they had run away, and Simon Peter had passionately denied that he knew the Master. Now they were scared, for the Jews had disposed of Jesus and would no doubt be after them now. So there they were, guilty and panicky, huddled behind locked doors for fear of the Jews.

I believe many people today are running scared with bad consciences. I know there's a lot of talk about Christless people being happy as they are, and certainly many of them claim to be, but I don't think their feelings necessarily match their words. Deep down, many of them feel that they are failures and are missing out on what life's all about and are afraid of the future. Christians who have slipped feel the same. The disciples represent a great section of the human race.

Jesus came through the locked doors, stood in the midst of his troubled people, and spoke to them of the peace, the program, and the power that he had come to give them (20:19–23). He still breaks through the barriers which we wittingly or unwittingly set up and presents himself to us in our frightened, guilty, helpless state as the loving friend who brings us new hope and new life. And that's the essence of grace.

Lord, I would love to see you in person as the disciples did, but please help me to be content for now to know the blessing of "those who have not seen and yet believe" (John 20:29).
Whom do I know who's running scared with a bad conscience for whom I could pray and to whom I could show something of Jesus' grace?

While they were talking and discussing together, Jesus himself drew near and went with them.
Luke 24:15

Read the story of the walk to Emmaus (Luke 24:13–35) and see Jesus the great physician and counselor at work. Here were two people in a very distressed state, unable to think straight.

First of all Jesus *asked questions:* he got them to talk, established a relationship, and so made them receptive to what he had to say. His opening gambit drew from Cleopas only rudeness (people who are hurt often react in this way) but he persisted and they shared their trouble. In this way healing was able to begin.

Second, he *explained Scripture,* showing them that what had been puzzling them—the death of the one whom they thought would redeem them by ending the Roman occupation—had actually been prophesied centuries before as God's way of redeeming, in the sense of ending the burden and bondage of sin.

Finally, he *revealed his presence.* "Stay with us" they had said to him on reaching Emmaus. In the deepest sense he did, even after they ceased to see him. What a blessing for them that they were given to hospitality! What they would have missed had they not been!

Jesus is still the great physician and counselor today. We shall receive his healing as we tell him our trouble, let him minister to us from Scripture, and ask him to assure us that as we go through what may feel like fire and flood, he goes with us and will stay with us till the road ends.

Do you believe Hebrews 4:15? Then put Hebrews 4:16 into practice.
Lord, with confidence I come to you for mercy and grace in this situation...

He (Abraham) was called the friend of God.
James 2:23

God wants us as friends. In the Old Testament, Abraham and Moses are called friends of God (2 Chron. 20:7; Exod. 33:11), and in the New Testament, Jesus tells his disciples: "No longer do I call you servants...but I have called you friends" (John 15:15).

For some reason, we don't assure one another of this as often as we should. We often say that God wants us as his children or as his beloved bride. But if there isn't real friendship between parent and child and husband and wife, something vital is missing in that family or that marriage. Friendship, both ways, should be basic in both relationships. And God calls us to be his friends. Doesn't this blow your mind? It should.

Who is this God? He's a plurality; he's Father, Son, and Holy Spirit, three persons who in some unimaginable way constitute the one and only Creator. Jesus came into the world, identified himself as the Son, and prayed to his Father—that makes two persons; also, he promised to send the Spirit whose ministry, he said, would be a continuation and carbon copy of his own, and that makes three. From all eternity Father, Son, and Spirit were together in a fellowship of love and friendship; their communion and communication was perfect. But the nature of love is that it wants to share, so a plan was formed to make creatures like us who could share that loving relationship. To put it colloquially, Father, Son, and Holy Spirit now say to us in chorus, "Join the club! Come and share our life of love." And Jesus has died for us so that this, God's original plan for us, might be fulfilled. Being friends with our heavenly Father and our divine Savior is what life in and through Jesus is about, both here and hereafter. What amazing grace!

What are the characteristics of a good, rich friendship? Is my friendship with God showing any of these characteristics?

Father, Son, and Holy Spirit, it is staggering that you want my friendship. Thank you.

If any one serves me, he must follow me; and where I am, there shall my servant be also; if any one serves me, the Father will honor him.
John 12:26

As I get older, I find that I appreciate God and people and good and lovely and noble things more and more intensely; so it is pure delight to think that this enjoyment will continue and increase in some form (what form, God knows, and I am content to wait and see), literally forever. In fact Christians inherit the destiny which fairy tales envisaged in fancy: *we* (yes, you and I, the silly saved sinners) *live* and live *happily,* and by God's endless mercy will live happily *ever after.*

We cannot visualize heaven's life and the wise man will not try to do so. Instead he will dwell on the doctrine of heaven, where the redeemed will find all their heart's desire: joy with their Lord, joy with his people, and joy in the ending of all frustration and distress and in the supply of all wants. What was said to the child—"If you want sweets and hamsters in heaven, they'll be there"—was not an evasion but a witness to the truth that in heaven no felt needs or longings go unsatisfied. What our wants will actually be, however, we hardly know, except the first and foremost: we shall want to be "always...with the Lord" (1 Thess. 4:17).

What shall we do in heaven? Not lounge around but worship, work, think, and communicate, enjoying activity, beauty, people, and God. First and foremost, however, we shall see and love Jesus, our Savior, Master, and Friend.

Do I personally expect and look forward to heaven?
Lord, let me tell you why this present life can never fully satisfy me...

*I am Jesus. . .I have appeared to you. . .to appoint you to serve and bear witness to
the things in which you have seen me and to those in which I will appear to you,
delivering you from the people and the Gentiles—to whom I send you to open their
eyes, that they may turn from darkness to light and from the power of Satan to God,
that they may receive forgiveness of sins and a place among those who are sanctified
by faith in me.*

Acts 26:15–18

Evangelism is first of all *a work of God*. God the creator is both God the
redeemer and God the evangelist. He made us; he loves us; he ransoms us;
he reclaims us.

Evangelism is also a work of man or rather *a work of God through man*.
God sends Christian men and women to be heralds, ambassadors, and
teachers in his name and on his behalf. The task which God gives to his
messengers is primarily and essentially one of proclamation but this proclamation is not to be made on a casual take-it-or-leave-it basis; the end in
view is to persuade, convert, or turn the sinner.

Evangelism, again, is *a work of God through men proclaiming Jesus
Christ and the new community in him*. Christian communication is not
evangelism unless the full truth about Christ is preached. And the new
community belongs to this central message, for the call to become a disciple
is also a call to become a partner with all other disciples.

Is my concept of evangelism too man-centered?
Lord, help us to think rightly about evangelism and to get on with it.

What is the evangelistic message?

God was in Christ reconciling the world to himself.
2 Corinthians 5:19

It's sometimes not stressed enough that the gospel is a message about God. He is our maker, in whom we exist and move each moment, and in whose hands, for good or ill, we always are; and we, his creatures, were made to worship and serve him and live for his glory. These are the foundation truths of theism and upon them the gospel is built.

The gospel is also a message about sin. It defines sin as failure to meet the holy Creator's total claim and it diagnoses sin in us, telling us that we are helpless slaves of our own rebelliousness, showing us to be under the righteous judgment of God and assuring us that nothing we can do for ourselves can put us right.

The gospel is a message about the person and work of Christ—an interpreted story of the earthly life, death, resurrection, and reign of God's Son.

Again, the gospel is a message about new birth, telling us that our plight in sin is so great that nothing less than a supernatural renewing of us can save us.

And the gospel summons us to faith, repentance, and discipleship. Faith is credence and conviction regarding the gospel message, as well as a casting and resting of ourselves on Christ and his promises. Repentance is a changed attitude of heart and mind leading to a new life of denying self and serving the Savior as king. And discipleship is a matter of relating to the living, exalted Christ and to the rest of Christ's disciples.

Are all these points taken into account in my church's evangelism—including the preparation of outreach and follow-up leaflets?
Praise God and pray for the people who brought you the evangelistic message, perhaps at different times and in different ways.

We beseech you on behalf of Christ, be reconciled to God.
2 Corinthians 5:20

Christians are sent to convert, and they should not allow themselves to aim at anything less. Evangelizing therefore is not simply a matter of teaching, instructing, and imparting information to the mind. It includes the endeavor to elicit a response to the truth taught. It is communication with a view to conversion. It is a matter not merely of informing but of inviting. It is an attempt to gain or win or catch our fellow human beings for Christ. Jesus depicted it as fisherman's work.

Paul knew himself to be sent by Christ not only to open people's minds by teaching them the gospel, but also to turn them to God by exhorting and applying the truth to their lives. So his avowed aim was not just to spread information but to save sinners: "that I might by all means save some" (1 Cor. 9:22). Thus there was in his evangelistic preaching both instruction—"God was in Christ reconciling the world to himself"—and entreaty—"we beseech you on behalf of Christ, be reconciled to God" (2 Cor. 5:19–20). His responsibility extended not only toward the gospel which he was charged to preach and preserve but also toward the needy people to whom he was sent to impart it and who were perishing without it. As an apostle of Christ, he was more than a teacher of truth; he was a shepherd of souls, sent into the world not to lecture sinners but to love them.

What difference does it make when we see evangelism as a particular way of fulfilling the law of love to our neighbors?

Pray for any evangelists you know who seem to concentrate on lecturing sinners rather than reaching out in compassion to them, and ask that they may be given the attitude expressed in 1 Thessalonians 2:7–8.

If I speak in the tongues of men and of angels, but have not love, I am a noisy gong or a clanging cymbal.
1 Corinthians 13:1

Evangelism should be an enterprise that springs from a genuine interest in those whom we seek to win and a genuine care for their well-being and should express itself in a genuine respect for them and a genuine friendliness toward them.

A famous old evangelist once said: *"Whenever I am justified in choosing my subject of conversation with another,* the theme of themes (Christ) shall have prominence between us so that I may learn of his need and if possible meet it."* The words in italics remind us of the need for courtesy and indicate that personal evangelism normally needs to be founded on friendship.

We are not usually justified in choosing the subject of conversation with someone else until we have already begun to give ourselves to that person in friendship and established a relationship in which he feels that we are respecting him, interested in him, and treating him as a human being and not as some kind of "case." With some people we may establish such a relationship in five minutes; with others it may take months.

The right to talk intimately to another person about the Lord Jesus Christ has to be earned and we earn it by convincing people that we are their friends and really care about them. Therefore the indiscriminate button-holing, the intrusive barging into the privacy of other people's souls, the thick-skinned insistence on expounding the Word of God to reluctant strangers who are longing to get away—these modes of behavior should be written off as a travesty of personal evangelism. Rudeness of this sort dishonors God, creates resentment, and prejudices people against the Christ whose professed followers act so objectionably.

Allow 1 Corinthians 13:1 to change, if necessary, your day's agenda.
Lord, I would be a noisy gong if I were to do/say this. . .with my present attitude. Please change me in the following way. . .

The Lord gives the command; great is the host of those who bore the tidings.
Psalm 68:11

We have a responsibility for making the gospel known. "Go. . .and make disciples" (Matt. 28:19) is Christ's command to the whole church. We are all under orders to devote ourselves to spreading the good news and to use all our ingenuity and enterprise to bring it to the notice of the whole world. The Christian must therefore be constantly searching his conscience, asking himself if he is doing all that he might be doing in this field.

But we must also keep the thought of divine sovereignty very much in mind. We must never forget that while it is our responsibility to proclaim salvation, it is God who saves. It is he who brings men and women under the sound of the gospel to faith in Christ. Our evangelistic work is the instrument that he uses for this purpose, but the power that saves is not the instrument: it is in the hand of the one who uses the instrument. We must not at any stage forget that. For if we forget that it is God's prerogative to give results when the gospel is preached, we shall start to think that it is our responsibility to secure them. And if we forget that only God can give faith, we shall start to think that the making of converts depends, in the last analysis, not on God but on us. And this line of thought consistently followed will lead us far astray.

What are the dangers of forgetting the sovereignty of God in evangelism?
Lord, "I know that thou canst do all things, and that no purpose of thine can be thwarted" (Job 42:2); help me to believe this in relation to my present situation, in which. . .

Necessity is laid upon me. Woe to me if I do not preach the gospel!
1 Corinthians 9:16

A classic instance of overemphasis on the sovereignty of God in evangelism (so the story goes) was provided in the eighteenth century by the chairman of the ministers' fraternal at which William Carey discussed the founding of a missionary society.

"Sit down, young man," said the old warrior. "When God is pleased to convert the heathen, he will do it without your aid or mine!"

This man had learned to take the sovereignty of God perfectly seriously but he was forgetting to take the church's evangelistic responsibility equally seriously. He was forgetting that God's way of saving people is to send out his servants to tell them the gospel and that the church has been charged to go out into the world for that very purpose.

Christ's command means that each of us should be devoting all our resources of ingenuity and enterprise to the task of making the gospel known in every possible way to every possible person. Unconcern and inaction with regard to evangelism are always inexcusable.

In Jesus' parable of the talents, the good and faithful servants were those who furthered their master's interests by making the most enterprising lawful use that they could of what was entrusted to them. The servant who buried his talent and did nothing with it beyond keeping it intact no doubt imagined that he was being extremely good and faithful, but his master judged him to be wicked, slothful, and unprofitable. For what Christ has given us to use, we must put to use. We may apply this to our stewardship of the gospel. The truth about salvation has been made known to us not simply for us to preserve (though we must certainly do that), but also and primarily for us to spread: "You are the light of the world" (Matt. 5:14).

What are the dangers of forgetting human responsibility in evangelism?
Lord, you have given me... Am I really putting these gifts to good use for you?

It pleased God through the folly of what we preach to save those who believe.
1 Corinthians 1:21

Paul saw himself as Christ's herald. When he describes himself as an appointed preacher of the gospel (2 Tim. 1:11), the noun he uses means a herald, a person who makes public announcements on another's behalf. When he declares "we preach Christ crucified," the verb he uses denotes the herald's appointed activity of blazoning abroad what he has been told to make known. When Paul speaks of "my preaching" and "our preaching" and lays it down that after the world's wisdom had rendered the world ignorant of God "it pleased God through the folly of what we preach to save those who believe," the noun he uses doesn't mean the activity of announcing, but the thing announced, the proclamation itself, the message declared.

Paul, in his own estimation, was not a philosopher, not a moralist, not one of the world's wise men, but simply Christ's herald. His royal master had given him a message to proclaim; his whole business was to deliver that message with exact and studious faithfulness, adding nothing, altering nothing, and omitting nothing. And he was to deliver it not as another of people's bright ideas, needing to be beautified with the cosmetics and high heels of fashionable learning in order to make people look at it, but as a word from God spoken in Christ's name, carrying Christ's authority and authenticated in the hearers by the convincing power of Christ's Spirit (1 Cor. 2:1-5).

What are the characteristics of a good herald? How might this be applied to our thinking about and training of evangelists?

Lord, sometimes when I am speaking to others about you I sense that my words sound like folly to them; at times, they even sound like folly to me. Help me to be prepared to look and sound foolish for you. Reassure me with your reality.

Spiritual assurance

*You did not receive the spirit of slavery to fall back into fear, but you have received
the spirit of sonship.*
Romans 8:15

One of the things which a Christian may be tempted to fear is that his fellowship with God will be broken because of his weak and wobbly, up-and-
down sort of Christian life. But Paul answers that fear by pointing out that
we have been adopted for all eternity into God's family and that God's
Spirit within us is constantly assuring us that we are God's children. This
assurance takes the form not so much of an arresting feeling as of a filial instinct and a sustained confidence. "When we cry, 'Abba! Father!' it is the
Spirit himself bearing witness with our spirit that we are children of God,
and if children, then heirs, heirs of God and fellow heirs with Christ" (Rom.
8:15–17).

It is the Spirit's work to keep the Christian aware that as a forgiven sinner
he has become God's child, that his life must be lived out of that adoptive
relationship, and that his hope of glory is precisely the prospect of inheriting his father's riches. God has made us joint heirs with Christ, destined to
share all the glory and joy that is his, and he will not go back on that; so we
need not fear that the uneven quality of our Christian lives will rob us of
our present standing in God's favor. It is heaven on earth to find oneself unable to doubt that this is so—and that is the essence of the God-given spirit
of sonship.

Though we cannot be robbed of our present position in God's family, we can certainly abuse it. How? To what forms of presumption and unworthy conduct are
you most prone?
*Father, thank you with all my heart that I'm in your family forever. Show me if I'm
abusing my position in any way or failing to take full advantage of all that you have
given me for my own and other people's blessing.*

The anointing which you received from him abides in you, and you have no need
that any one should teach you; as his anointing teaches you about everything, and is
true, and is no lie, just as it has taught you, abide in him.

1 John 2:27

My conviction is that the key to understanding the experiential aspects of life in the Spirit is to be found in his work of making Jesus Christ, our crucified, risen, reigning Savior, real and glorious to us moment by moment (John 16:14). And I claim that John is referring to this ministry of the Spirit when he declares that "his anointing teaches you about everything" (everything, he means, concerning Jesus and his glory), and leads us to "abide in him" (to maintain not just a true confession about him, but a disciple relationship to him as living Lord).

I contend that when John calls the Spirit "the witness" (1 John 5:7-8), he has in view the Spirit's ministry of making us sure that the apostles' Christ is real and is ours. I believe that the breathtaking certainty of mind, confidence of manner, and evident rapture of heart with which Augustine, Bernard, Luther, Calvin, Owen, Whitefield, Spurgeon, and many more have celebrated and commended the Lord Jesus is a direct fruit of this ministry. I believe that all those in whom the Spirit fulfills this ministry will speak of Christ the same way. And I maintain that apart from this God-given certainty concerning the Christ of the New Testament and this God-taught habit of abiding in him by faith and love and obedience and adoration, there is no authentic Christian living and no genuine sanctification—for indeed, where these things are lacking, there is in reality no new birth.

Study the Bible verses above in their context with the help of commentaries, and decide in your own mind what you think they mean. Writing down or speaking aloud the meaning, as if to an inquiring friend, can be helpful.

Lord, may your anointing Spirit abide in me and teach me, as I abide in him.

If by the Spirit you put to death the deeds of the body you will live.
Romans 8:13

This is a very liberating verse, for it shows us that when particular forms of sin trouble us it is actually possible for us to put them to death through the Spirit's power. It is easy to despair of ever making headway against moral weaknesses that have ensnared us again and again. But by praying for the Spirit's help to watch against them, especially in times of temptation, and by letting the Spirit lead us to love Christ more so that we love sin less, we may drain the life and energy out of these ugly habits.

There's an old story about a missionary and an ex-cannibal who had become a Christian. His grandfather had been a cannibal of distinction and a wild man in other ways, and the missionary told him to think of his own continuing impulses to sin as grandfather in his bones. After some years of furlough, the missionary returned and asked him, "How is grandfather in your bones these days?"

"He's still alive," came the reply, "but he don't get around like he used to!"

Every Christian's experience ought to be like that. Sin is still in us and the war is not yet over, but we may win victories over it constantly and weaken its power and allure as we follow the Spirit's prompting to look to the Lord and say no to the temptation. As when, trusting the Lord, we resist the devil we find that he flees (as James 4:7 says he will), so when, still trusting the Lord, we resist each temptation we find that it retreats, and attacks less strongly as time goes by. Have you not found this already? It is your privilege to prove it, starting today. The crucial question is: are you willing to see your beloved sins die in this way?

What "deeds of the body" (sinful behavior patterns) are you least willing to put to death? We all have favorite, besetting sins.
Lord, I'm dwelling too much on . . . and not enough on . . . in my personal battle for holiness. Help me to get my moral priorities right.

Concerning spiritual gifts, brethren, I do not want you to be uninformed.
1 Corinthians 12:1

A spiritual gift is an ability to express and communicate in some way one's knowledge of Christ and his grace. It is not a mere natural endowment, though usually it is given through the sanctifying of a natural endowment. Spiritual gifts have a spiritual content: they display the riches of Christ by manifesting something we receive from him. All forms of service which do this involve an exercise of spiritual gifts for profit (1 Cor. 12:7) and edifying (Eph. 4:2,16).

There are many gifts, and there is no reason to treat even 1 Corinthians 12:28–30 as an exhaustive list; indeed, it is doubtful in principle whether such a list could be compiled. Gifts vary in value according to whether they give more or less help to others; thus speaking the word of God in intelligible terms is better than speaking in a tongue. What are the higher gifts (1 Cor. 12:31)? Those that communicate Christ best to others, showing them his reality either by word or by deed. Nor should gifts of service be rated below gifts of speech: each gift is equally important in its place (1 Cor. 12:14–21).

Paul's charge to his readers to use their gifts (Rom. 12:6–21) starts with the ministry of the Word but soon broadens into a general plea for mutual service in the exercise of Christian graces towards others. No doubt gifts and graces are distinct in idea, but in practice much using of our gifts is a matter of exercising our graces informally and spontaneously in giving what help we can according to people's needs.

All can serve others in some way and all are called to do so; such service, whatever its form, falls under the definition of an exercise of gifts. And the purpose of all gifts is edification—building up Christians and leading them forward toward their ultimate perfection.

Assess your local church in the light of Romans 12, 1 Corinthians 12, and Ephesians 4.

Lord, what do you want me to do about these new insights I have gained?

Since you are eager for manifestations of the Spirit, strive to excel in building up the church.
1 Corinthians 14:12

Fellowship, which means the give-and-take of sharing the things of God, is carried on through the reality of spiritual gifts. So what is a spiritual gift? It is in essence a God-given capacity to express or minister Christ so that those to whom the service is rendered will see Christ and grow in Christ, to his glory. It may be a gift of speech, behavior, conduct, or service in any form. It may be the practical gift of relieving needs, Samaritan-style, or the teacher's gift of explaining things from God's Word. It may be a natural talent sanctified or an ability newly bestowed. But whatever form it takes, it is a God-given ability to make Christ known.

When gifts are exercised in the power of the Spirit by whom they are bestowed, the reality of the situation is this: Christ himself, on his throne but through his Spirit in us, is ministering still as he ministered to people in the days of his flesh. We become his mouth, his hands, his feet, to fulfill his ministry to others by exercising the spiritual gifts we have been given. Christ now ministers to his people through his people, and through them to other people too.

Usually others see our gifts better than we see them ourselves. Usually others can tell us more exactly what we can and cannot do for the Lord than we are able to discern by self-review and introspection. Realizing then that the finding and use of gifts is fellowship business, we should ask others to watch us and tell us what our gifts are, and so be guided by them as we seek to serve.

If you haven't already done so, try to discover, in the fellowship of the Christians who know you best, what your own spiritual gifts are, and go on from there.
Lord, if what I do for others seems to be drawing attention to myself rather than to you, show me what to do about this.

Pray... in the Spirit.
Ephesians 6:18

"Pray in the Holy Spirit" (Jude 20). What does this mean?

It means that we're not to pray in our own strength or with our own insight, but with the strength and insight that God supplies through his Spirit in our hearts. There are at least three thoughts implicit in this idea.

To pray in the Spirit is to pray as a child of God (Gal. 4:4–6). It's the Spirit who prompts the attitude which treats, approaches, and cries to God as our Father in heaven.

To pray in the Spirit also means to pray with our eyes on God. The Spirit has been given to open our eyes to see the good things that God has for us. "What no eye has seen, nor ear heard, nor the heart of man conceived, what God has prepared for those who love him, God has revealed to us through the Spirit" (1 Cor. 2:9–10). The Spirit is the teacher of God's people: he opens the eyes of our understanding and keeps us looking to God, focusing on him and his resources of grace and power so that we are able to pray with confidence.

To pray in the Spirit means, too, relying on the Spirit's support. "Likewise the Spirit helps us in our weakness; for we do not know how to pray as we ought, but the Spirit himself intercedes for us with sighs too deep for words" (Rom. 8:26). Sometimes we want to pray for something, but we find that we can't put our thoughts and desires into words: we end up tongue-tied before the Lord. At such times, the Spirit in us is praying for us, and God "who searches the hearts of men knows what is the mind of the Spirit, because the Spirit intercedes for the saints according to the will of God" (Rom. 8:27). "If we ask anything according to his will he hears us" (1 John 5:14). But when we don't know what specifically to ask for, and can only bring a name or need before God in general terms, he hears us too. This also is prayer in the Spirit. That's a tremendously encouraging truth.

Above are three insights into what praying in the Spirit means. Can you add others from the Bible?
Lord, here is this need...I wish I knew how to pray about it but I don't yet... Thank you that you know my heart and hear the Spirit interceding for me.

Restore us again, O God of our salvation, and put away thy indignation toward us!
Psalm 85:4

Renewal is a general experiential deepening of the life in the Spirit which is the foretaste and first installment of heaven itself. Assurance of both the shameful guiltiness and the total pardon of our sins; humble but exalted joy in the awareness of God's love for us; knowledge of the closeness of the Father and the Son in both communion and affection; a never-ending passion to praise God; an abiding urge to love, serve, and honor the Father, the Son, the Spirit, and the saints, and the inward freedom to express that urge creatively and spontaneously—these things will be the essence of the life of heaven. They are already the leading marks of spiritually renewed individuals and communities in this world.

It is in renewal that love for Jesus and fellowship with him become most clear-sighted and deep. The most obvious evidence of this is the hymnology of renewal movements.

Through renewal, believers are drawn deeper into their baptismal life of dying with Christ in repentance and self-denial and rising with him into the new righteousness of combating sin and living in obedience to God.

Renewal takes place through the action of the Holy Spirit doing his New Covenant work of glorifying the glorified Christ before the eyes of the understanding of his disciples.

In renewal God's people experience the termination of the impotence, frustration, and barrenness which have been the tokens of divine displeasure at unfaithfulness. Joy replaces the distress which they felt at God's displeasure, and God's kingdom is extended through the impact of their revitalized lives (Ps. 85:4–6; Zech. 8:23).

Do I focus on notions and dreams of renewal that do not follow the principles/ guidelines above?
Lord, help me not to be afraid of any genuine *spiritual experience.*

The Spirit of the family
Hindrances to spiritual renewal

This people honors me with their lips, but their heart is far from me.
Matthew 15:8

God is sovereign and takes action to answer prayer at his own speed and in his own good time. Yet we can bring spiritual quickening or renewal nearer by breaking with things that are in their own nature Spirit-quenching.

For instance, surely *clericalism* as a leadership style is Spirit-quenching. Some leaders embrace this because it gives them power; others embrace it because they fear that people ministering with them will overshadow them, or because they feel incapable of handling an every-member-ministry situation. But every-member-ministry in the body of Christ is the New Testament pattern, and anything which obstructs or restricts it is an obstacle to a renewing visitation from God.

Again, surely *formalism* as a worship style is Spirit-quenching. But many churches seem to view worship in a way that can only be called formalistic, for their interest is limited to performing set routines with suitable correctness, and there is no apparent desire on anyone's part actually to meet God.

Yet again, surely personal attitudes of *complacency* are Spirit-quenching. To what extent do you see in your own church fellowship the reality of worship, faith, repentance, knowledge, holiness? Do the members resolutely, energetically, and passionately love the Lord? Do they love each other? How do they pray and give? How much support do they get from each other in times of personal need? How much do they share their faith? Those led often become like their leaders. If you are a leader, does the thought of those led by you becoming like you appall you or please you? Why?

Examine your own church fellowship in light of the above.
Lord, how can I bring renewal closer today?

Wilt thou not revive us again, that thy people may rejoice in thee?
Psalm 85:6

Revival is a visitation of God which brings to life Christians who have been sleeping and restores a deep sense of God's near presence and holiness. Thence springs a vivid sense of sin and a profound exercise of heart in repentance, praise, and love, with an evangelistic outflow.

Each revival movement has its own distinctive features, but the pattern is the same every time.

First *God comes.* On New Year's Eve 1739, John Wesley, George Whitefield, and some of their friends held a "love feast" which became a watchnight of prayer to see the New Year in. At about 3 a.m., Wesley wrote, "the power of God came mightily upon us, insomuch that many cried for exceeding joy, and many fell to the ground." Revival always begins with a restoration of the sense of the closeness of the Holy One.

Second, *the gospel is loved* as never before. The sense of God's nearness creates an overwhelming awareness of one's own sins and sinfulness, and so the power of the cleansing blood of Christ is greatly appreciated.

Then *repentance deepens.* In the Ulster revival in the 1920s shipyard workers brought back so many stolen tools that new sheds had to be built to house the recovered property! Repentance results in restitution.

Finally, *the Spirit works fast:* godliness multiplies, Christians mature, converts appear. Paul was at Thessalonica for less than three weeks, but God worked quickly and Paul left a virile church behind him.

Is our church fellowship longing and praying for revival?
Lord, send revival and let it begin with me. Quicken my heart.

You are not lacking in any spiritual gift.
1 Corinthians 1:7

Strive to excel in building up the church. . .Let all things be done for edification. . .
All things should be done decently and in order.
1 Corinthians 14:12,26,40

---

1 Corinthians chapters 12–14 make extremely painful reading for thoughtful, evangelical believers. Why? Is it because Corinthian public worship was such a chaotic uproar? Is it because of the apparent unseemliness of services in which many people were talking at once, some in ecstatic gibberish, and in which some women were screeching to be heard above the general noise? No. These chapters make painful reading because, whatever evils they confront us with, they do at least show us a local church in which the Holy Spirit was working in power. So one is made painfully aware of the impoverishment, inertia, dryness, and deadness of so many churches today.

If our only reaction to these chapters is to preen ourselves and feel glad because our churches are free from Corinthian disorders, we are fools indeed and ought to think again. I fear that many of our churches today are orderly simply because they are asleep. And in many cases, I fear it is the sleep of death. It is no great thing to have perfect order in a cemetery!

These Corinthian disorders were due to an uncontrolled overflow of Holy Spirit life. There was real carnality and immaturity in these Corinthians. It was deplorable enough, and Paul censures it strongly. But this must not blind us to the fact that they were nevertheless enjoying the ministry of the Holy Spirit in a way which most today are not.

The Corinthians came to worship—eager, excited, and expectant. How does that compare with your attitude to worship?
Talk to God about your attitude to worship and about any blocks which you or others in your church family may have with regard to it.

A directory of prayer

Pray at all times in the Spirit, with all prayer and supplication. To that end keep alert with all perseverance, making supplication for all the saints, and also for me, that utterance may be given me in opening my mouth boldly to proclaim the mystery of the gospel.
Ephesians 6:18–19

Here we have a little directory of prayer. Though there are only two verses, they are marvelously comprehensive. Notice the four "all"s: "at all times," "with all prayer," "with all perseverance," and "for all the saints."

These verses have something to say about the nature, the time, the enabler, the discipline, the matter, and the range of prayer. All these deserve study but I want to focus now on the range of prayer suggested.

We're not to pray just for ourselves but for all the saints, all the family of God—or at least for all the family members known to us and involved with us in some way. We need to ask God which of his saints and which of their activities in particular he wants us to be praying for on a regular basis. Let the Lord lead here. He leads Christians differently in these matters.

Some feel they should pray intensively for a small range of people and concerns; others less intensively for a wider range. However, the general formula, for whichever way he leads you in detail, is that we are to make supplication for all the saints as they and their needs are known to us. Christian prayer must be family-oriented, not just individual-oriented. There's to be a network of mutual service not only at the level of face-to-face contact and personal helpfulness, but also at the level of intercession for one another at God's throne of grace. Christian fellowship must include this discipline of praying for one another.

Am I praying for all the saints or even any of them regularly?
Lord show me which of your saints and which Christian causes you want me to pray for generally and specifically.

They lifted their voices together to God and said, "Sovereign Lord. . ." . . . And when they had prayed, the place in which they were gathered together was shaken; and they were all filled with the Holy Spirit and spoke the word of God with boldness.
Acts 4:24,31

Free prayer meetings are a basic form of Christian fellowship and this is the first one to be described for us (Acts 4:23–31). Talking together to God should be as natural and spontaneous as talking together with one another. Prayer together for each other's needs should always be part of the pattern which the church fulfills of mutual support and help.

This particular prayer meeting and the things for which the Christians prayed were a reaction to threats from officialdom. As always in biblical praying, they built on the reality of God's dominion, as Maker and Lord of all, and on the Spirit-given revelation which he has embodied in the Scriptures (in this case the revelation that the rulers of this world regularly oppose the king whom God has anointed). They prayed, not in hope of getting this situation changed, but in order to gain strength to live and serve God in it. Strikingly, therefore, they asked not for an abating of the threats or a leave of absence from Jerusalem, but for boldness to proclaim the Word in the face of opposition and for further confirmation of their witness to Jesus' lordship of the kind given when the lame man was healed. They were thinking not of their own safety but of the cause of God.

It was the right prayer and it was wonderfully answered. Pentecost almost came again! They felt the place shaken—vast divine energy was let loose. And with the Spirit's power strong in them they witnessed boldly just as they had asked that they might. Prayer for boldness in witness will always be answered positively, if we dare to make it. But do we?

What could we learn from this prayer model?
Lord, teach us to lift our voices together in the same way and spirit.

After he had dismissed the crowds, he went up into the hills by himself to pray.
Matthew 14:23

Each Christian's prayer life, like every good marriage, has in it common factors about which one can generalize and also uniquenesses which no other Christian's prayer life will quite match. You are you, and I am I, and we must each find our own way to God; and there is no recipe for prayer that can work for us like a handyman's do-it-yourself manual or a cookery book, where the claim is that if you follow the instructions you can't go wrong.

Praying is not like carpentry or cookery; it is the active exercise of a personal relationship: a kind of friendship with the living God and his Son Jesus Christ, and the way it goes is more under divine control than under ours. Books on praying, like marriage manuals, are not to be treated with slavish superstition, as if the perfection of technique is the answer to all difficulties; their purpose, rather, is to suggest things to try. But as in other close relationships, in prayer you have to find out by trial and error what is right for you, and you learn to pray by praying.

Some of us talk more, others less; some are constantly vocal, others cultivate silence before God as their way of adoration; some slip into glossolalia, others make a point of not slipping into it; yet we may all be praying as God means us to do. The only rule is: Stay within the biblical guidelines, and within those guidelines, as John Chapman put it, "Pray as you can, and don't try to pray as you can't."

Do I need to stop worrying about how other people pray and spend more time simply praying by myself?
Spirit of Jesus, pray with me and for me.

Turn thou to me, and be gracious to me; for I am lonely and afflicted.
Psalm 25:16

The wonderful thing about God is that he returns again and again to his needy people. He's never exhausted and his interest in us never lapses. The pattern of Christian life is awareness of need followed by God coming to meet that need. This is what the covenant relationship is all about. God turns and returns to those who seek him in their need.

No one reading this will be completely carefree. Each of us has some trouble, problem, burden, difficulty, thorn in the flesh to contend with. And there's nothing godly about not turning to the Lord with these, but saying instead, "I'm a Christian so I must expect troubles," and then feeling that you're really rather heroic to be bearing so much. Self-sufficient stoicism is in truth a kind of Spirit-quenching arrogance that Christians should be careful to avoid.

The Christian, like the psalmist, makes no bones about crying out to God: "Turn thou to me, and be gracious to me; for I am lonely and afflicted." He looks to God with confidence, expecting help and deliverance as soon as God sees fit to send them—and why not now? He asks with boldness for healing and strength now. Maybe God will give him all that he seeks today. Maybe God will reserve some of it for tomorrow or next week or next year. The Christian is prepared to settle for whatever God decides is best in the heavenly timetable. But his plea is that God will help him now, according to his needs now, and he knows that one way or another his present needs are going to be met.

Am I in danger of feeling rather heroic about the amount of work I can do, the pressures I can work under, or the number of people who depend on me in one way or another? Beware! As someone wrote: "I was given weakness that I might feel the need of God."
Turn thou to me, and be gracious to me; for I am... (fill in your own problem here).

Blessed be the LORD, for he has wondrously shown his steadfast love to me when I was beset as in a beseiged city.
Psalm 31:21

As we read the Psalms, we learn how to behave in the prayer relationship. The psalmists waited on God. They didn't lose hope and confidence altogether, supposing that God had forgotten them. Instead they waited patiently, sustaining their faith by meditating on and reminding themselves of all that God is; of all God's resources; of all that he'd done for them in the past; of all that he'd promised to do for them in the future. Often they told God to remember what he had done for them, and in doing so they recalled these things themselves and took confidence from their memories of what had happened. As someone has said, "Faith must make use of experiences and read them over to God out of the register of a sanctified memory."

Remember how David reacted when Saul told him that he was only a boy and couldn't hope to beat the giant Goliath. He reminded himself and told Saul of how a lion and bear had come to attack his flock and God had delivered him from them both; this same unchanging God could deliver him again, he said.

When we are downhearted, we need to call to mind what we know of God and have experienced of God, in order to give ourselves new energy and hope. It's important to treasure up our memories of God's gracious dealings with us in the past, and then use them to sustain our faith and hope as we wait patiently for his deliverance and help in the present.

Do I need to start keeping a spiritual journal—writing down what God says to me and does for me—so that I can sustain my faith (or another's) in time of trouble? *Lord, I remember with gratitude . . .*

We have not ceased to pray for you, asking that you may be filled with the knowledge of his will in all spiritual wisdom and understanding, to lead a life worthy of the Lord, fully pleasing to him, bearing fruit in every good work and increasing in the knowledge of God.

Colossians 1:9–10

Praying for fellow Christians is a basic Christian responsibility. Colossians 1:3–14 helps us to see how to discharge it. In this passage Paul asks God to give the Colossian Christians four things:

Christian knowledge: He prays that they will know both God's will (his plans, ways, and commands) and God himself. The Greek word for knowledge implies full, thorough knowledge, as does the verb "filled." "Understanding" relates to principles of truth, "wisdom" to application of those principles in life (v. 9). Worthy living depends on this knowledge; he who does not know God's will cannot do it. Knowledge of God increases as we live up to it (v. 10).

Christian practice: He prays that they will lead a life worthy of Christ the king to whom they owe their salvation, and a life pleasing to God at every point by every activity (vv. 10,13–14).

Christian patience: He prays for their cheerful endurance in dealing with trying people and situations with actual rejoicing as tribulation grinds on (v. 11). Paul specifies that all God's strength, power, and might are needed to produce such a reaction!

Christian thankfulness: He prays that they will be grateful for grace, the major motive of Christian living. According to the truth of the gospel (v. 5), Christian doctrine is grace throughout and Christian ethics are gratitude all the way.

How much time do I spend praying for fellow Christians and how does the content of my prayers for them compare with the above?
Pray for other Christians in general or a few by name along the lines of Paul's prayers for the Colossian Christians.

*Let the words of my mouth and the meditation of my heart be acceptable in thy
sight, O LORD, my rock and my redeemer.
Psalm 19:14*

Meditation—thinking about God in God's presence—is a helpful preparation for speaking to God directly and one which we seem to need regularly.
In this world, interviews with persons of some standing are handled with
ceremony, both out of respect for the persons themselves and also in order
to gain most benefit from the interview.

To rush to God randomly babbling about what is on our mind at the moment, with no pause to realize his greatness and grace and our own sinfulness and smallness, is at once to dishonor him and to make shallow our
own fellowship with him. I, for one, want to do better than that. Like others, I find it good to preface my prayers about needs by reading Scripture
and thinking through what my reading shows me of God and turning that
vision into praise before I go further.

A little reverent thought about God before opening our mouths to address him makes a lot of difference in the quality of fellowship with him
that follows. Remembering, and reviewing who God is, is never time
wasted; it is, rather, a vital means of *knowing* God, just as prayer itself is.

Use the whole psalm for an aid to your meditation before prayer.
*Lord, I only see and know you dimly, yet I am aware of something of your glory
and greatness as I bring my petitions to you. . .*

Unless your righteousness exceeds that of the scribes and Pharisees, you will never enter the kingdom of heaven.

                                                                    Matthew 5:20

The scribes and Pharisees venerated, studied, and expounded the Law of God—or so they thought. The rabbis in Jesus' day had agreed that in the Old Testament there were 248 commands and 365 prohibitions. These numbers give us an indication of what their error was. They supposed that the Law had only to do with behavior patterns, being thus like traffic regulations or an industrial rule book, and that keeping it meant no more than conforming to these outward patterns and rules.

But Jesus challenges the narrow Pharisaic understanding of the law's requirements. He overthrows the external rule—the righteousness which the Jewish religious leaders practiced—and replaces it with a righteousness which is of the Spirit as well as the letter and starts in the heart before it finds expression in the life.

This righteousness will only be found in those who have been born again. Jesus doesn't explicitly state this here, but it becomes obvious as you read through the Sermon on the Mount that no one by nature can fulfill the standards he sets out. The righteousness he requires reflects God's heart and character, and such behavior cannot issue from our own heart and character till we are born of and animated by the Holy Spirit. So in the Sermon on the Mount (especially in Matthew 5:21–48) Jesus isn't just saying, "Don't do this, or that," but "Be this kind of person:" a new person, made new by God's saving grace.

Read Matthew chapter 5 slowly and let the verses, through the Spirit, search your heart and life.

Lord, thank you that I am a new creature in Christ, renewed in my heart for righteousness in my life. Help me to be what I am.

*You have heard that it was said to the men of old, "You shall not kill; and whoever
kills shall be liable to judgment." But I say to you...*
Matthew 5:21-22

The supposition of the Pharisees was that the sixth commandment was
only about murder as an act. Jesus tells his disciples (Matt. 5:21-26) that it
goes much further than that, prohibiting also malice, ill-will, contempt,
hostility. The principle here is that the law of God covers not only acts (actually killing someone), but attitudes (wishing to see someone dead).

Jesus illustrates this from relationships within the fellowship of his disciples. If you are angry with your Christian brother, or insult him, or call him
a fool, he says, you're in danger of final spiritual ruin, for your heart is
wrong. So if you come to worship and remember that your brother has
something against you because you've shown him ill-will or contempt,
show repentance toward God and love toward him by putting things right
at once, before you worship God, or you will re-enact the sin of Cain. Similarly, if someone accuses you, make friends at once and settle matters out of
court; don't let hostility hang on. Paul's advice is relevant: "Be angry but do
not sin; do not let the sun go down on your anger, and give no opportunity
to the devil" (Eph. 4:26-27). Anger is a given ingredient in human nature,
so what is in question is not whether we're going to be angry (we are!), but
what we shall do when we're angry. Says Paul: Don't cherish the anger you
expressed; make peace at once; ask God's and your brother's forgiveness for
venting anger as you did, otherwise you'll be giving the devil a foothold in
your life.

Jesus wants to make it very clear that the sixth commandment, like the
rest of the Law, covers attitudes as well as actions: in this case, anger as well
as murder. We must control our desires as well as our actual doings.

Should we wait till our motives are perfect before doing right actions?
Lord, make me aware of my wrong attitudes...

You have heard that it was said, "You shall not commit adultery." But I say to you...
Matthew 5:27-28

The Pharisees supposed that the seventh commandment was just a prohibition against loose sex. But Jesus adds that everyone who indulges in lustful fantasies about others has already committed adultery in his or her heart (Matt. 5:28).

This is the example Jesus gives to illustrate a very important principle for interpreting the Law: namely, that the Law covers desires and dreams as well as deeds. We mustn't suppose that because we haven't done something, God won't mind that we would have liked to do it. "The LORD looks on the heart" (1 Sam. 16:7) and sees the lustful thoughts and the indecent fantasy, just as he notes the lustful action and indecent behavior.

So Jesus goes on to say (Matt. 5:29-30), be tough with yourself: "If your right eye causes you to sin, pluck it out and throw it away." He says the same in relation to the right hand. "But I can't do without my right eye or right hand," someone says. If they're causing you to stumble, get rid of them at all costs, replies Jesus. Better that than ending up in hell! C.S. Lewis's picture of lust on the sinner's shoulder begging not to be killed is a wonderful commentary on this.

There are some things we have to cut out of our lives (not only in relation to sexual matters) if we want a clean heart. God's standards in this area as in others are very high and his instructions are very clear: lust as well as adultery is prohibited, and we may well need to be ruthless with ourselves if we are not to ruin our souls.

Is there anything in my life that is constantly causing me to sin? What should I do? *Thank you, Lord, that your death on the cross covers all sins—open sins and secret ones too. I confess this secret sin to you now...*

*It was also said, "Whoever divorces his wife, let him give her a certificate of divorce."
But I say to you. . .*
Matthew 5:31–32

It was the general Jewish view that divorce was all right if one adhered to
Old Testament procedure (Deut. 24:1–4). Elsewhere (Matt. 19:3–9) Jesus
makes it clear that God does not like divorce and that his intention from the
beginning was lifelong monogamous marriage. Here however he makes one
point only, saying in effect: Have you considered that the man who divorces his wife, when she has not already committed sexual sin, thereby
causes her and the man whom she marries afterwards to commit sexual sin?
In first century A.D. Palestine there was no social security, no public welfare
for a divorced woman, and no possibility for her to follow a career as
would be possible today. So the only thing she could do was to find another
man who would look after her. Whether she formally married the man or
not, she would enter with him into a relationship of marriage type. Thus,
by frivolously divorcing his wife, a man would set going a train of far from
ideal consequences and virtually ensure that she would become an adulter-
ess and her partner an adulterer.

The underlying principle here is that just as we must seek to keep ourselves from sin, so we must seek to keep others from sin. We have a responsibility not to lead nor push other people into sins precipitated by our
actions. If we are true disciples of Jesus we must consider the effect on others of what we do in this matter of divorce as in every area of our lives.

The buck of guilt stops at our table, if we put others under strong constraint to sin.
*Show me, Lord, if I'm doing or planning anything that would make it hard for some-
one else to resist a wrong course of action.*

*Again you have heard that it was said to the men of old, "You shall not swear falsely,
but shall perform to the Lord what you have sworn." But I say to you...*
                                                               Matthew 5:33–34

The Pharisees had developed some rules about oaths, one of which was
that it did not matter if you broke minor oaths which didn't involve the
name of God directly. But Jesus' point is that the law about oaths is really
about truthfulness, the keeping of one's word. His directive is that we
should say a calm "yes" or a calm "no" and stick to our word every time (vv.
35–37): no extra verbiage; no "cross-my-heart-and-hope-to-die" type of ad-
ditions; no oaths at all. Remember Simon Peter's oaths when he was trying
to convince the people at the high priest's house during Jesus' trial! People
often add oaths to persuade others to believe that what they are saying is
the truth, even when it is not.

Keep clear of all that, says Jesus. Don't deceive people with weasel words
and verbal sleight of hand. Let your "yes" be yes and your "no" be no; "anything more than this comes from evil."

The principle underlying this discussion of swearing is that the specifics
of the Law must be interpreted in terms of its spirit. Here the spirit of the
law is that in all we say we should value and hold sacred the truth and keep
our word, as God keeps his. Any rules not in line with that two-fold principle are not part of the Law of God.

Is what I say and how I say it really under the lordship of Jesus?
*Lord, write your law on my heart so that I will be able to keep both the letter of your
law and its spirit more and more each day.*

You have heard that it was said, "An eye for an eye and a tooth for a tooth." But I say to you...
Matthew 5:38,39

The rightness of retaliation is widely accepted, as it was in Jesus' day. But Jesus tells his disciples that "tit for tat" must not be the principle by which they live. Instead, startlingly he tells them: "Do not resist one who is evil" (Matt. 5:39). He then gives them four examples of how this revolutionary principle could be applied.

First: if anyone hits you on the right cheek, turn your left cheek to him too. Second: if anyone sues you for your coat, let him have your cloak too. Third: if a Roman soldier conscripts you to carry his bag, shield, or anything else for a mile, carry it for two miles. Fourth: give and lend freely. Don't be held back by the thought that the other person may not repay you. Learn the kind of generosity that doesn't ask, "What am I going to get back out of this?" but is only concerned for the other's well-being.

But Jesus goes even further. His disciples must do more than simply refrain from resisting evil. They must love their *enemies* and pray for their *persecutors* if they want to be sons of their Father who is generous in all kinds of ways not only to those who love and appreciate him, but also to those who set themselves against him (Matt. 5:44–48).

Think of how Jesus exemplified this principle. As they were nailing him to the cross he was praying, "Father, forgive them; for they know not what they do" (Luke 23:34). There lies our hope, for in our own strength and with our own resources we couldn't possibly live out this principle of loving self-denial in our response to and treatment of others. But Jesus, who did it himself, can enable us to do it.

"Do not resist one who is evil" (Matt. 5:39). "Resist the devil" (James 4:7). Is there a contradiction here or not?
Lord, in my responses to others, am I living at a sub-Christian level, i.e., by the law of retaliation?

When you fast, do not look dismal.
Matthew 6:16

Jesus assumes that his disciples will fast and tells them how those who are "pure in heart" will fast; their motivation and manner will be distinctively different from those of people not in the family relationship with him and his Father (Matt. 6:16–18).

In Scripture we see several purposes for fasting. It's part of the discipline of self-control; it's a way of sharing that we depend on God alone and draw all our strength and resources from him; it's a way of focusing totally on him when seeking his guidance and help, and of showing that you really are in earnest in your quest; it's also, at times, an expression of sorrow and deep repentance, something that a person or community will do in order to acknowledge failure before God and seek his mercy.

We tend to think of fasting as going without food. But we can fast from anything. If we love music and decide to miss a concert in order to spend time with God, that is fasting. It is helpful to think of the parallel of human friendship. When friends need to be together, they will cancel all other activities in order to make that possible. There's nothing magical about fasting. It's just one way of telling God that your priority at that moment is to be alone with him, sorting out whatever is necessary, and you have cancelled the meal, party, concert, or whatever else you had planned to do in order to fulfill that priority.

If you have fasted—has your motive been to make time for undivided, uninterrupted time with God? Or has some thought of merit or magic crept into your thinking? If you haven't ever fasted yet, don't rule out this expression of deep friendship for and deep commitment to your God.

Lord, there are times when I long for you with my whole heart. May these times be more and more frequent as I live in your family moment by moment.

All scripture is inspired by God and profitable for teaching, for reproof, for correction, and for training in righteousness, that the man of God may be complete, equipped for every good work.
2 Timothy, 3:16–17

The word translated "inspired by God" really means *"breathed out* by God," the product of his creative Spirit, as the world itself was (Gen. 1:2; Ps. 33:6). The Bible analysis of inspiration is that "men moved (carried along) by the Holy Spirit spoke from God" (2 Pet. 1:21), and the documents resulting from inspiration are both man's witness to God and God's witness to himself. What is said of the Lord Jesus must also be said of the biblical books: he was and they are both fully human and fully divine. This is how our Lord and the apostles could quote the Old Testament both as what Moses, David, and Isaiah said, for example (Mark 7:6,10; 10:3–6; Acts 2:25,34; 3:22), and also as what God or the Holy Spirit said (Matt. 19:5; Acts 28:25; Heb. 1:5–13; 3:7; 10:15).

It appears that sometimes the processes of inspiration were conscious and sometimes not. Certainly the inspired writers were not psychologically passive, writing at dictation; their individuality comes out clearly in all that they wrote. But this does not put question marks against their inspiration, any more than the genuineness of our Lord's manhood throws doubt on the truth of his deity.

Being God's own teaching, the Bible may properly be called a revelation. First and foremost, however, we should think of it as the inspired record and interpretation of the revelation which God gave in history by visions and verbal messages, by mighty acts of mercy and judgment, and supremely by the life, death, and resurrection of the Lord Jesus Christ.

As you read the Bible in the coming days try to keep in mind that it is God telling us what he has done and what he now calls us to do.
Lord, thank you for what you have done/call me to do in this matter...

Beginning with Moses and all the prophets, he interpreted to them in all the scriptures the things concerning himself.

Luke 24:27

Because the Bible is a human book and God chose to convey his teaching to us in the form of the inspired instruction of his human penmen, the way into his mind is necessarily via their minds. So the basic discipline in biblical interpretation must always be the attempt to determine as exactly as possible just what the writer meant by the words he wrote and how he would explain the sense of his statements could we cross-question him about them.

Because the Bible is a divine book, its sixty-six separate documents being products of a single divine mind proclaiming a single message, we must seek to integrate the fruit of our study of the individual books and writers into a single coherent whole. We know that the human author's thoughts are God's own thoughts too. As we seek to synthesize all the different thoughts, we become aware that at point after point God's thoughts go further and embrace more than those of any human writer did or could. The full significance of each passage only appears when it is set in the context of all the rest of Scripture—which its own human author, of course, was never able to do.

The Bible appears like a symphony orchestra with the Holy Spirit as its Toscanini; each instrumentalist has been brought willingly, spontaneously, creatively, to play his notes just as the great conductor desired, in full harmony with each other, though none of them could ever hear the music as a whole. We, however, are privileged to do precisely that.

Am I both breaking down Bible passages and/or books for detailed study and reading them whole?
Lord, may my life be more and more like a symphony orchestrated by the Holy Spirit.

O Timothy, guard what has been entrusted to you.
1 Timothy 6:20

The church no more gave us the New Testament canon than Sir Isaac Newton gave us the force of gravity. God gave us gravity by his work of creation; similarly he gave us the New Testament canon by inspiring the
individual books that make it up. Newton did not create gravity but rather
recognized it by considering (so it is said) the fall of an apple; similarly the
various churches of Christendom, through a gradual, uncoordinated, seemingly haphazard and erratic process covering several centuries, came to recognize the extent and limits of the God-given canon by checking and
cross-checking the pedigree and contents of the many books that bore apostolic names or were alleged to proceed from the apostolic circle, to find out
which of them could make good their claim to be genuine apostolic products, embodying the revealed truth of which the apostles were trustees.

Had someone suggested to Christians of the second, third, or fourth century that by this means the church was creating a canon for itself, choosing
some good-quality Christian literature to authorize as a standard of faith
for the future, they would have shaken their heads and marveled that anyone could dream up an idea so perverse and far from the truth. The belief
that apostolic writings as such were inspired and therefore intrinsically authoritative was the presupposition of their whole inquiry. All the churches
were trying to do was to see which of the books claiming to be in some sufficient sense apostolic really were so—a question primarily of historical
fact, though one in which character and content were also held to bear both
positively and negatively.

Why is it important to say that the church collected rather than composed the
Bible?
Lord, you have entrusted your Word to me; help me to guard and share it.

Do you think that I cannot appeal to my Father, and he will at once send me more than twelve legions of angels? But how then should the scriptures be fulfilled, that it must be so?

Matthew 26:53–54

There is really no disputing that Jesus and his apostles held and taught that the Jewish Scriptures (our Old Testament) were God's witness to himself in the form of man's witness to him. There is no disputing that Jesus, God's incarnate Son, viewed these Scriptures as his Father's Word; or that he quoted Scripture to repel Satan; or that he claimed to be fulfilling both the Law and the prophets; or that he ministered as a rabbi (Bible teacher), explaining the meaning of texts of which the divine truth and authority were not in doubt; or that he went to Jerusalem to be killed and, as he believed, to be raised to life again because this was the way Scripture said God's Messiah must go. Nor is there really any disputing that God raised him from the dead thereby vindicating all he had said and done as right—including the way he had understood, taught, and obeyed the Scriptures.

So too it is clear that the apostles saw the Scriptures as the God-given verbal embodiment of teaching from the Holy Spirit. They claimed not merely that particular predictions were fulfilled in Christ but that all the Jewish Scriptures were written for Christians, and that they took over the Old Testament for use in the churches alongside their own teaching. The apostles saw their own teaching and writings as inspired in just the same sense as the Old Testament was inspired (i.e., God speaking and teaching in and through what men say in his name).

Are we being led by the Bible as given or by the Bible as we privately edit and reduce it?

Lord, I take my lead from you and your apostles on the divine authority of the Bible...

This is my beloved Son; listen to him.
Mark 9:7

What does it mean to hear God's written Word? According to Hebrews it means, quite concretely, receiving and responding to God's propositional word (that is, his message) which he has spoken to us from heaven through the lips of his personal Word (that is, his Son), and also through the utterances of prophets and apostles, concerning the great salvation which the Son of God won for us by the shedding of his blood for our sins. God's personal Word appears as the central subject of his propositional word both when spoken and written. What Jesus said of the Scripture of the Old Testament—"It is they that bear witness to me" (John 5:39)—can be said of both Testaments with equal truth.

To hear God's written Word, therefore, means, in the last analysis, doing as God commanded at the transfiguration when he said, "This is my beloved Son; listen to him"; which in turn means not just accepting Jesus' moral teaching but receiving him as our living Savior, relying on his shed blood for the pardon for our sins, and living henceforth as his bondslave—one of those who "follow the Lamb wherever he goes" (Rev. 14:4).

Do I hear God's Word (written, spoken and personal) in the biblical sense of attending to it, assenting to it, and applying it? What kind of follow-up of the sermons is there in our church? Do we attempt to work out their implications and check whether we are obeying what we are being taught and being changed by it? *Father, clear away all the clutter in our lives so that we may truly come with open hearts and ears to your Word.*

He will judge the world with righteousness, and the peoples with his truth.
Psalm 96:13

We have to choose whether we will accept the biblical doctrine of Scripture as it stands or permit ourselves to refashion it according to our fancy. We have to choose whether to embrace the delusion that human creatures are competent to judge and find fault with the words of their Creator or whether to recognize this idea for the blasphemy that it is and drop it. We have to decide whether to carry through our repentance on the intellectual level or whether we shall still cherish our sinful craving for a thought-life free from the rule of God. We have to decide whether to say that we believe the Bible and mean it or to look for ways whereby we can say it without having to accept all the consequences.

If the human mind is set up as the measure and test of truth, it will quickly substitute for man's incomprehensible Creator a comprehensible idol fashioned in man's own image; man wants a god he can manage and feel comfortable with and will inevitably invent one if allowed. He will forget (because he cannot understand) the infinite gulf that separates the Creator from his creatures and will picture to himself a god wholly involved in this world and wholly comprehensible (in principle, at any rate) by the speculative intellect. It was no accident but a natural development that made the liberal theology of the nineteenth century so strongly pantheistic. Once people reverse the proper relationship between Scripture and their own thinking and start judging biblical statements about God by their private ideas about God, instead of vice versa, their knowledge of the Creator is in imminent danger of perishing and with it the whole idea of supernatural redemption.

Can you see that it's right to say that we should make *the* truth *our* truth but wrong to say that *our* truth is *the* truth?
Lord, may your truth become more and more my truth by which I live and move and have my being.

There are some things in them hard to understand, which the ignorant and unstable twist to their own destruction, as they do the other scriptures.
2 Peter 3:16

Many of us would agree with Peter when he says that parts of Paul's letters are hard to understand! And there are difficulties and apparent discrepancies in other parts of the Bible too. On this matter of discrepancies, I remember reading something written by an old seventeenth-century Puritan named William Bridge. He said that harping on discrepancies shows a very bad heart, adding: "For a godly man, it should be as it was with Moses. When a godly man sees the Bible and secular data apparently at odds, well, he does as Moses did when he saw an Egyptian fighting an Israelite: he kills the Egyptian. He discounts the secular testimony, knowing God's Word to be true. But when he sees an apparent inconsistency between two passages of Scripture, he does as Moses did when he found two Israelites quarreling: he tries to reconcile them. He says, Aha, these are brethren, I must make peace between them.' And that's what the godly man does."

Another point about discrepancies: each generation seems to have a different set of them. One generation's problems seemed to be solved in the next generation which in turn throws up a fresh set of problems for the following generation to solve, and so on.

The fact is, there are seeming discrepancies of detail, and it seems to be part of the discipline of the life of faith to live with them, acknowledging that because the Bible is the Word of God, these things must be optical illusions. If we can't understand something we can still trust God about it, and perhaps our children, as knowledge increases, will understand it, just as we today understand some of the things which perplexed our parents.

The alternative, to abandon the doctrine of the Bible as inerrant and authoritative, makes the Bible into wax which can be bent any way by anyone.

What is my attitude to difficulties and discrepancies in Scripture?
Lord, in this difficulty . . . help me to trust harder and dig deeper.

June 22   **Family standards**
God's law

I the LORD love justice, I hate robbery and wrong.
Isaiah 61:8

God loves some types of action and hates others (Zech. 8:16–17; Jer. 44:6; Amos 5:21; Rev. 2:6). In the Ten Commandments God forbids various types of actions which he hates: disrespect and distrust towards himself in a number of forms; disrespect for parents, and by parity of reasoning, with other bearers of God-given authority too; disrespect for human life, for the marriage bond, and for property; and disrespect for truth, especially truth about other people. Most of the Bible's ethical teaching is elaboration and enforcement of these principles.

In the New Testament Jesus focused positively on the two proper overall purposes of actions (Matt. 22:36–40) which the Ten Commandments illustrated negatively. The Ten Commandments said in effect: Do nothing which in any way dishonors your God or your human neighbor who bears his image. Jesus' formula effectively said: Do everything that expresses the purpose of pleasing and exalting your God and benefitting your neighbor.

In both Testaments God's Law is not a minutely detailed code of all our actions every moment, but a set of broad guiding principles with sample applications to get us going.

Examine your life in light of what God hates and loves. (See the references above and find others with the help of a concordance.)

Father, help me to keep your standards always before me—standards which may be different even from those of the so-called "decent majority" or "decent minority."

You shall be holy; for I the LORD your God am holy.
Leviticus 19:2

A nineteenth-century pastor, Robert Murray McCheyne of Dundee, Scotland, once said, "My people's greatest need is..." How would you have expected him to finish that sentence? Many pastors would say, perhaps, "My people's greatest need is that I should have counseling, expository, or other ministerial skills." McCheyne said, "My people's greatest need is *my personal holiness.*" Do we think in those terms? Is that our vision? I fear not.

We are preoccupied with controversy, scholarship, liberty in ethical matters, and we are disillusioned, I think, with the holiness teaching on which we were brought up. And perhaps that is not too wrong a reaction. There has been a type of holiness teaching which has been sterile and inadequate. Yet I was a little bothered, as well as amused, by what an inner-city pastor once said to me. When I asked, "What do you think of the victorious Christian life?" he replied, "It's all right if you've got the time and the money for it." You can see why I was amused. But can you see why I was bothered? Should Christians be able simply to shrug off the quest for holiness, as if it were a matter of secondary importance? According to the New Testament, at the very heart of our Christian living should be a passion in all things to obey God, imitate our Savior, resist sin, and please our gracious Father. Nothing can alter that priority.

What are the differences between biblical holiness and what the word "holiness" conveys to the man in the street?
Lord, thank you that as I focus on Jesus and obey you each day, you are producing in my life and character the fruit of holiness which the world needs to see in each of us, your people. But Lord, give me more of it!

If you love me, you will keep my commandments.
John 14:15

Keeping the Law out of love is the true path of holiness. This is something biblical Christians have not always managed to grasp well. On the one hand there have always been those who have claimed that if the Spirit indwells you and the motive of love is strong within you, you do not need to study God's Law in Scripture in order to learn his will, for you will always be made immediately aware in every situation what it is that he wants. On the other hand there have always been those whose zeal for law-keeping has so dried up their love that they ended up more like Pharisees than Christians. Augustinian, Wesleyan, and Keswick teaching, though differing in many points, would all agree that the way to show that you love God and man is to keep God's Law.

Perhaps, however, none of these three traditions has laid enough stress on the fact that Jesus Christ himself is, so to speak, the Law incarnate and is also the Christian's lawgiver through the teaching he began on earth and completed from his throne via the apostles. Yet it is so, and a fundamental part of the Holy Spirit's work is to lead Christians to acknowledge and honor Jesus in both capacities as they obey his teaching and follow his example. I believe that the Spirit is calling us all to explore more diligently the theme of the imitation of Christ inasmuch as Jesus-likeness of character and attitudes is the truest holiness for us all.

"Love God and do what you like." In what sense is this right/wrong?

Lord, you know my tendency to scoff at rules and respond spontaneously to situations and people (or to be law-abiding but lacking in love): teach me by your example and change me by your indwelling Spirit, so that I may learn to get the balance right, for your glory.

Whatever you wish that men would do to you, do so to them; for this is the law and the prophets.
Matthew 7:12

Jesus told his disciples to treat others as they would have others treat them. This he said summed up the teaching of Scripture so far as our dealings with others is concerned. He gives us this short, simple guideline, sometimes called the golden rule, to help us judge whether the way we behave toward others, or the way we are planning to treat others, is right or not. What a different place the world would be if we kept this rule!

And within the Christian family, if we all adhered to this command of Jesus, things would be very different too. Many of us, perhaps particularly Christian workers, can begin to think that we're among the elite so we needn't bother with menial tasks or ordinary courtesies and acts of thoughtful kindness. "Let someone else clean out the toilets. I'm a Christian minister: I shouldn't have to do that sort of thing!" But we must not give ourselves airs like this. If we do, we are not coming up to the standards for the true disciple that were set out and lived out by Jesus. We must treat others in the kind, thoughtful, sympathetic, interested, supportive way in which we would want them to treat us, setting no limits to what we do for them when they are in need.

The golden rule is easy to say but takes a lifetime of putting into practice. And if my experience is anything to go by, it's especially easy for those in positions of leadership and responsibility to ignore it, and to assume that they would be treated as top people who cannot be expected to care for others in the way that others care for them, just because they're about the Lord's business in a special way. Not so, says Jesus! The golden rule is for leaders no less than followers.

Have I fallen into the error of thinking that I'm too important to be bothered about treating others thoughtfully, courteously, and kindly?
Lord Jesus, your example in this matter leaves me ashamed and inspired. . .

June 26 Family standards

How can you say to your brother, "Let me take the speck out of your eye," when there is a log in your own eye?

Matthew 7:4

Read Matthew 7:1–5. What do these verses mean for us? In Jesus telling us not to evaluate and assess others at all? No. It's human nature to form judgments; we might not share our private evaluation of people and events, but we can't avoid using our evaluative faculties.

Jesus is not telling us to deny our humanity and stop using our minds in this way. But he is warning us against a particular pitfall by pointing out that we should judge ourselves by the standards which we bring to the judgment of others.

We must expect God to judge us as we judge others; so, if we want him to judge us compassionately, we had better judge others compassionately. Also, we need to make sure that our judgment of others is preceded by honest judgment of ourselves before the Lord on those matters for which we criticize others. So often we compensate for our own uneasiness in some area by coming down heavily on someone else for failing in that same area. It's a compensation mechanism which counselors know all about—and so does Jesus. That is why he warns his disciples against being the sort of hypocrites who try to straighten other people out as an alternative to recognizing and dealing with their own failures and omissions.

Are you about to correct the faults of another? Ask God to show you whether you have this same fault and need to attend to that first.

Lord, I see this situation/this person as wrong. . . Search my heart, and then, if I do need to take action, keep me remembering the purpose and the spirit which I need to have (Gal. 6:1).

If any one would sue you and take your coat, let him have your cloak as well; and if any one forces you to go one mile, go with him two miles.
Matthew 5:40–41

Here is a sample application of God's Law, couched in typical Eastern hyperbole. It shows that the purpose of the applications was not so much to give models for mechanical imitation as to give cartoons highlighting required attitudes. These cartoons convey the idea by simplifying and exaggerating, but most of the detailed applying of the principles is left to us to manage as creatively as we can. Four aids are given to us in Scripture for this task.

First we have the calculus embodied in Jesus' so-called golden rule (Matt. 7:12). If, for instance, I find myself longing to be listened to more and understood better, there may well be self-pity in my attitude, but that is not relevant here; what matters is that the rule makes me realize (from my own feelings) how much more, in the way of attentive patience and imaginative identification, love to my neighbor requires of me than I had at first realized.

Second, there is the scriptural teaching on man's nature and destiny; such teaching gives us a strong lead on many issues, from human rights and business management to family ideals and the priority of evangelism.

Third, there is the summons to imitate God and Jesus Christ (John 13:15; 15:12–14; 2 Cor. 8:9; Eph. 5:25–33; Phil. 2:1–8; Heb. 12:1–4; 1 Pet. 1:16; 2:21; 1 John 3:16).

Fourth, there is the principle expressed in Paul's prayer for the Philippians (Phil. 1:9–11), that they would choose what was best.

Try to grasp the four tests of or aids to determining right conduct and then apply them to real or imagined situations.
Lord, help me to be aware of my own and other people's dignity and potential and to have my and their highest good in mind in all my decisions and actions.

For our boast is this, the testimony of our conscience that we have behaved in the world, and still more toward you, with holiness and godly sincerity, not by earthly wisdom but by the grace of God.

2 Corinthians 1:12

One aspect of God's image in us is our conscience, classically defined by Thomas Aquinas as man's mind making moral judgments. It functions in the style of a voice within actually addressing us to command or forbid, approve or disapprove, justify or condemn. Conscience does not feel like the spontaneous working of my mind which it actually is; it feels, and is divinely intended to feel, like a monitor from above. The description of conscience as a voice from God highlights the unique character of this particular mental operation. We must not, however, suppose that divine finality attaches to all deliverances of conscience, because it is deficient and needs educating by Scripture and experience. So it might be truer to say that conscience is the capacity for hearing God's voice rather than an actual hearing of it in each verdict that conscience passes.

Attempts have been made to analyze conscience in emotional terms only, as nothing but feelings of liking and disliking. This has been labeled the "Boo–hurrah" theory (coconut? murder? *boo!* curry? promise-keeping? *hurrah!*). If this analysis were true, moral reasoning would be comparable to, "Try this, you'll like it!" and, "Don't eat that, it's horrid," and no universal moral standards could ever be agreed upon, any more than it could ever be agreed that henceforth everyone shall like curry and dislike coconut. But conscience itself tells us that morality is essentially a matter not of taste but of truth; not of feeling, in the first instance, but of judgment, based on principles which are in themselves universally valid and claim everyone's assent.

Do you feel guilty about something? If so, should you?
Lord, do you or does anything in your Word condemn me in this matter. . . or not?

By rejecting conscience, certain persons have made shipwreck of their faith.
1 Timothy 1:19

Freud gives the name of conscience to the various neurotic and psychotic phenomena of obsessive restriction, compulsion, and guilt. His model of man pictures the psyche as a troubled home, where the *ego* on the ground floor (the self-conscious self with doors and windows open to the world) comes under pressure both from the *id* (aggressive energy rushing up from the cellars of the unconscious) and from the *super-ego* (an unnerving voice of command from upstairs, whereby repressed prohibitions and menaces from parents and society are introjected into conscious life in portentous disguise and with disruptive effect). The super-ego, each man's tyrannical, psychic policeman, is the culprit to which neuroses and psychoses are due; and the goal of psycho-analysis is to strengthen one's ego to unmask the super-ego and see it for the hodgepodge of forgotten traumas which it really is, thus winning freedom to discount it.

Since Freud's view equates the super-ego with conscence, it might seem to us, as it certainly did to him, directly to undermine any concept of conscience as God's voice; but in fact what Freud talks about is what Christian pastors have learned to recognize as the "false conscience"—a more or less irrational scrupulosity which shows the mind to be not so much godly as sick.

But what Freud calls conscience is precisely not conscience in the Christian view. For the Christian, conscience is practical, moral reason consciously exercised, growing in insight and sureness of guidance through instruction and use, and bringing inner integration, health, and peace to those who obey it. Freud doesn't deal with this at all.

What are the differences between false conscience and true conscience?
Lord, I need your help to reject false conscience and hear only, more and more clearly, your voice in my inner being.

Our charge is love that issues from a pure heart and a good conscience and sincere faith.

1 Timothy 1:5

Traditionally, and surely correctly, conscience has been believed to involve two faculties by which we are enabled to see general moral truths and then to apply them to particular cases. It was unquestioned among both Protestants and Roman Catholics till this century that the working of conscience takes the form of a *practical syllogism*, e.g., "Stealing is wrong; taking the umbrella would be stealing; therefore taking the umbrella would be wrong," or, "Bank robbers deserve punishment; I robbed a bank; therefore I deserve punishment."

As we can see from these examples, conscience judges particular actions and cases on the basis of general principles. If a person's conscience condemns him where no general principle is involved, we can assume that what he feels is guilt or obsessions masquerading as conscience and that this needs to be relieved or dispelled.

Being God's voice in and to us, our conscience binds us and must always be conscientiously followed; but when through ignorance or confusion its dictates are not God's voice, our conscientiousness will not lead to our pleasing God. So a Christian with an uninstructed conscience is stuck: he cannot please God by either obeying or disobeying his conscience. How vital it is that Christians should study biblical morals and doctrines and experience God's daily forgiveness!

What does the Bible teach about conscience and how it can be reshaped?
Lord, go on reshaping my conscience to make it healthier and more sensitive.

The words of the Preacher, the son of David, king in Jerusalem. Vanity of vanities,
says the Preacher, vanity of vanities! All is vanity.
Ecclesiastes 1:1-2

Try to find time to read the whole book of Ecclesiastes in the next few days.
Read it both from the vantage point of our New Testament faith and hope
(1 John 3:1-3; Phil. 4:4-7) and as a human being for whom experiences of
disillusionment and apathy, disappointment and hopelessness, despair and
a sense of meaninglessness are still realities even though we belong to
Christ. It's the only book in the Bible that is written out of the awareness of
these somber moods and seeks to minister directly to people experiencing
them.

I believe that the author is not Solomon himself but someone playing the
role of Solomon-turned-preacher, presenting a message neither of facile op-
timism nor of bitter pessimism but of sober realism. He's a wisdom writer,
concerned as all such writers are to teach his readers the way to go, starting
from where they are. He wants to help them find joy, purpose, and meaning where at present they see only vanity, pointlessness, and meaninglessness. His ministry in this matter is very rich indeed.

At the end of the book the writer comments directly on the Solomon role
in which he has written. "Besides being wise, the Preacher also taught the
people knowledge, weighing and studying and arranging proverbs with
great care. The Preacher sought to find pleasing words, and uprightly he
wrote words of truth" (Eccles. 12:9-10). The sayings of the wise, he continues, will spur the reader on and will stick in his mind and memory "like
nails firmly fixed"—helping him to walk with God more faithfully than before (Eccles. 12:11-14).

Can you remember times in your life when you felt that everything was pointless
and meaningless? Stay with those feelings for awhile. Try to remember their effect
on you and their context.
Lord, I pray for. . .who seems to see everything in the same somber light. . .

*It is an unhappy business that God has given to the sons of men to be busy with. . .
He who increases knowledge increases sorrow.*

Ecclesiastes 1:13,18

What produces the feeling of world-weariness and pointlessness which is so vividly conveyed in Ecclesiastes? Life's hurts are largely responsible. Everyone who has ever lived in this world experiences in one way or another that life hurts and it's no good pretending that it doesn't.

I heard of a funeral at which the daughters of the bereaved lady wore white dresses for "mummy's marriage to Jesus." The person who told me the story seemed to think this was marvelous but I didn't agree with him at all. It seemed to me to smack of the attitude that as Christians we are not to feel pain and grief but to exude joy and peace and euphoria all the time. But we can't—not if we're being honest. There are times when we hurt dreadfully and God's ways seem totally incomprehensible.

I know a Christian man whose younger brother is in a mental institution; his sister died of rheumatic fever; his father died of a heart attack in his early forties after being housebound for years; his mother died of cancer; his wife gave him five children and then died of cancer too. When we hear of things like this, we want to exclaim with Saint Theresa of Avila, "Lord, if this is how you treat your friends, no wonder you have so few." Think of what Paul had to endure—and he was a top apostle who needed to have a clear mind, a calm soul, and a body in really good shape to do the responsible hard work to which God had called him (2 Cor. 11:23–29). Yet God appointed for him strain from physical hardships, pain from human hostilities, and a constant thorn in the flesh.

God is inscrutable. "What on earth is he doing?" we ask. What sense do these miseries make? God however does not tell us, so we have to be content not to know.

What encouragement or help can you find—for yourself or someone else—in 2 Corinthians 1:3–5; 4:7–11; Romans 5:3–5; Hebrews 12:9–11,14; James 1:2–3? Lord, you don't owe me any explanations but give me some light in my gloom.

The purposes of life reviewed

What has a man from all the toil and strain with which he toils beneath the sun? For all his days are full of pain, and his work is a vexation; even in the night his mind does not rest. This also is vanity.
Ecclesiastes 2:22–23

In Ecclesiastes 2:11–23 the writer reviews the purposes of life.

One such purpose is to gain wisdom. He tells us that he tried that, and "saw that wisdom exceeds folly as light exceeds darkness." Yet acquiring wisdom seems ultimately pointless; the wise man and the fool both meet the same fate: they die and are forgotten. "So I hated life, because what is done under the sun was grievous to me; for all is vanity and a striving after wind" (vv. 12–17).

A second purpose of life is to build something that will last, but the writer's attempt to do this led to the same sort of feeling. "I hated all my toil in which I toiled under the sun, seeing I must leave it to the man who will come after me; and who knows whether he will be a wise man or a fool?" (vv. 18–23).

Then comes the recurring refrain of the book, the word of light and hope that appears several times. "There is nothing better for a man than that he should eat and drink, and find enjoyment in his toil" (v. 24). So there *is* such a thing as enjoyment, satisfaction, happiness. It is a divine gift. "This also, I saw, is from the hand of God; for apart from him, who can eat or who can have enjoyment? For to the man who pleases him God gives wisdom and knowledge and joy" (vv. 24–26).

Work that has God in it is the secret. God made us to work. Work that is done not just for our own contentment but for the glory of God and the good of others has meaning and brings its own happiness.

What is my attitude to my work? Am I giving it not enough or the wrong sort of significance?
Lord, I take my work as from your hands and know that this will make a difference to how I do it, how I feel about it, and what it achieves.

July 4

For everything there is a season, and a time for every matter under heaven. . . I know
that whatever God does endures for ever. . . The fate of the sons of men and the fate
of beasts is the same.

Ecclesiastes 3:1,14,19

Ecclesiastes chapter 3 sets before us three fixed facts in the midst of life's
changing scenes:

One—there are right times and seasons for everything (vv. 1–8). As we
read these haunting verses we should ask ourselves, "Do I look for, and can
I discern, God's timing in all these areas of my life?" Sometimes we aren't
looking; at other times, we try to find God's timing but get it wrong and so
frustration sets in. Many of life's frustrations occur through our failing to
discern the right time for action. Here the writer says there is a right time
for doing and experiencing everything. We need to keep on trying to fit in
with God's wise timing for us.

Two—there is a divine lordship over everything (vv. 9–15). God "has
made everything beautiful in its time." We can agree with that. If we look
for beauty on a day-to-day basis, we shall find it everywhere: beautiful people, places, experiences. We should thank God for that. At the same time
"he has given us the desire to know the future, but never gives us the satisfaction of fully understanding what he does" (v. 10, *GOOD NEWS BIBLE*). He
is the hidden Lord and we are not intended to comprehend all his ways in
this world.

Three—death is a certainty for everyone (vv. 16–22). The writer's question is: How can I find meaning in life when I don't know what happens
after death? His answer is a good one, though only a partial one for us who
have the New Testament before us. He says: The best thing we can do, as
God allows, is enjoy our work, irrespective of what we see of its short and
long-term consequences. There's much sense in that. Not having enough to
do leads to discontent. Worthwhile labor always brings joy.

How do these immovable truths affect my life and thinking today?
Lord, help me to live within your timetable, redeeming the time (Eph. 5:16;
Col. 4:5).

I turned my mind to know and to search out and to seek wisdom and the sum of things, and to know the wickedness of folly and the foolishness which is madness.
Ecclesiastes 7:25

The whole thrust of Ecclesiastes chapters 6–8 is that it is better to seek and practice wisdom than to pursue pleasure. Earlier in the book (Eccles. 2) the writer showed what a barren activity the pursuit of pleasure is. Christians, like others, know very well from experience that if you seek pleasure it eludes you, while if you pursue something worthwhile you find pleasure en route; or, as George Bernard Shaw (I think) expressed it, "Happiness is something that you find when you're looking for something else."

The "something else" suggested here is wisdom, which means in essence knowing the way to go in life. Wisdom sees what is best in each situation; it accepts and adjusts to the fact that we can't always understand God's ways and teaches us how to live under the enigma of God's rule, practicing humility and restraint at all times.

The opposite of wisdom is folly, meaning the short-term self-indulgence which marks out the person who doesn't think about long-term priorities and goals but lives on a day-to-day basis, asking, "What is the most fun thing to do now?" There's another paradox here, similar to the one already mentioned. If you're only trying to amuse yourself, you will soon find that you fail to do even that; if you're trying to do something worthwhile, you will find that a great deal of what you're doing will prove to be fun.

Have you experienced the truth of these words? Think of other people (whom you know or know of) whose lives illustrate what has been said above.
Lord, I turn my mind to know and search out and seek the way to go in this situation. . .

*As you do not know how the spirit comes to the bones in the womb of a woman
with child, so you do not know the work of God who makes everything.*
Ecclesiastes 11:5

Among the seven deadly sins of medieval lore was sloth (*accidie*) — a state of
joyless apathy of spirit. There is a lot of it around today in Christian circles;
the symptoms are personal spiritual inertia combined with critical cynicism
about the churches and supercilious resentment of other Christians' initiative and enterprise. Behind this morbid and deadening condition often lies
the wounded pride of one who thought he knew all about the ways of God
in providence and then was made to learn by bitter and bewildering experience that he didn't. This is what happens when we do not heed the message of Ecclesiastes. For the truth is that God in his wisdom, to make and
keep us humble and to teach us to walk by faith, has hidden from us almost
everything that we should like to know about the providential purposes
which he is working out in the churches and in our own lives.

What the preacher in Ecclesiastes wanted to show his young disciple —
who, like many since, was inclined to equate wisdom with wide knowledge
acquired through diligent bookwork (Eccles. 12:12) — was that the basis of
true wisdom is a frank acknowledgment that this world's course is enigmatic, that much of what happens is quite inexplicable to us, and that most
occurrences "under the sun" bear no outward sign of a rational, moral God
ordering them at all.

Am I spending time and energy trying to understand and explain God's actions to
myself or someone else? Is this productive?
*Lord, these are some questions to which you have not so far given me any answers
. . . Am I to live with them? How, Lord? Help me.*

Fear God, and keep his commandments.
Ecclesiastes 12:13

What is true wisdom? Does the preacher in Ecclesiastes give us any guidance about this? Indeed he does, in outline at any rate.

Trust and obey God, reverence him, worship him, be humble before him, and never say more than you mean when you pray to him (Eccles. 12:13; 5:1–7); do good (3:12); remember that God will someday take account of you (11:9; 12:14), so avoid, even in secret, things of which you will be ashamed when they come to light during God's final judgment (12:14). Live in the present and enjoy it thoroughly (7:14; 9:7–10; 11:9–10)—present pleasures are God's good gifts.

Though the writer of Ecclesiastes condemns flippancy (7:4–6), he clearly has no time for the super-spirituality which is too proud or pious ever to laugh and have fun. Seek grace to work hard at whatever life calls you to do (9:10), and enjoy your work as you do it (2:24). Leave to God the issues of life; let him measure its ultimate worth. Your part is to use all the good sense and enterprise at your command in exploiting the opportunities that lie before you (11:1–6).

This is the way of wisdom. Clearly it is just one facet of the life of faith. For what underlies and sustains it is the conviction that the inscrutable God of providence is the wise and gracious God of creation and redemption. We can be sure that the God who made this marvelously complex world-order, and who compassed the great redemption from Egypt, and who later compassed the even greater redemption from sin and Satan, knows what he is doing and "has done all things well" (Mark 7:37).

True wisdom is claimed to be not a sharing in all God's knowledge, but a disposition to confess that he is wise and to cleave to him and live for him in the light of his Word through thick and thin. Do you agree?
Turn your thoughts into prayer.

I searched with my mind how to cheer my body with wine... and how to lay hold on folly, till I might see what was good for the sons of men to do under heaven during the few days of their life.

Ecclesiastes 2:3

The basic question in Ecclesiastes is: Is there any meaning or joy in life? Up to chapter 6 the acuteness of the problem has been pointed out by two facts: things won't satisfy, and God won't be domesticated. In C.S. Lewis's Narnia books, Aslan is not a tame lion! Wild things happen in God's world. Alongside his delineations of disappointment, doubt, and despair, the writer gives us clues as to how it is possible to experience life as constantly frustrating and yet find joy and meaning in it.

He gives us hints as to where joy and meaning are to be found in Ecclesiastes 2:24–26; 3:22; 5:18–20; 8:15; 9:9. In these verses he tells us two things: that there is simple, basic satisfaction to be found in work and food and married love, and that all joy is God's gift.

In the second passage, he lists the three things which he has seen to be "good for the sons of men to do under the heaven during the few days of their life." Enjoy your work, he says; accept your lot; and live in the present. Elsewhere he pinpoints mistakes to avoid: don't expect joy from your achievements as such; don't expect life to be a bed of roses now that you belong to God; don't resent the way things are; don't be jealous; don't be lazy; don't live on illusions.

All this is low key advice but very sensible and necessary.

Do I tend to despise people with practical, commonsense attitudes and solutions as not being "spiritual"? Should I?
Lord, thank you for those saints who haven't the temperament for hours of contemplation but who get on and do the things that need to be done.

Go, eat your bread with enjoyment, and drink your wine with a merry heart; for God has already approved what you do.
Ecclesiastes 9:7

Joy isn't strictly a feeling. It's a state of mind in which you're content with what you've got and you wouldn't exchange it for the world. This state of mind presupposes acceptance of the limits that God lays upon us. What limits? First, our inability to control events and our ignorance of God's plans; second, the inescapability of strain and pain; third, the certainty that nonetheless everything counts, so that one day, when God brings everything to judgment, we will all discover that what we chose to be and do in this world has determined our destiny for us.

We don't like these limits. We are fallen beings and our natural reaction is to say, "I'd rather not be living under these constraints. I'd rather have everything go the way I wished it to. I resent a world in which wishing doesn't make things so, and happy endings are not guaranteed. It's scandalous that God's up in heaven and I'm on earth and he doesn't tell me the meaning of the things he does so that I'm left in the dark (Eccles. 11:5–6). How can I believe in a God of love when he's set me in a world full of evil and trouble that I can't control?"

Joy depends first on recognizing that Christ's death for us on Calvary is the all-time guarantee to us of our heavenly Father's love, and second, on accepting the limits imposed by our relative powerlessness and ignorance. John in C.S. Lewis's *Pilgrim's Regress* runs away from all that he was taught in his youth but later he returns or regresses to humble Christian faith under the guidance of a wisdom he didn't have when he fled from it. Chastened, he stops rejecting and rebelling, and quiet joy breaks in.

Do I need to regress to acceptance of certain things I hoped to transcend or tried to run away from?

Lord, I am not wise enough to understand everything; I can't foresee and avoid trouble; I don't understand what you're doing much of the time. As I accept these limits set by you, fill me with your joy.

Family attitudes and lifestyle
Enjoying the present

If a man lives many years, let him rejoice in them all.
Ecclesiastes 11:8

Another habit that is essential if we are to know joy is the habit of living in the present (Eccles. 9:7-9). The preacher tells us in effect to enjoy every pleasure each day as God gives it. That's one expression of the childlikeness to which we pilgrims are called. In one sense we should be living in the future, remembering all that God has prepared for those who love him, but not to the extent that it robs us of delight in the present. A wise rabbi in the second century said that when we appear before God, he'll not only ask why we did the bad things we shouldn't have done, but also why we didn't enjoy to the full all the good things he gave us.

For this reason, the preacher directs the young man to rejoice in his youth and let his heart cheer him in the days of his youth (Eccles. 11:9). Youth is a gift from God; we should enjoy it. "Walk in the ways of your heart and the sight of your eyes," he says. In other words, "Do all the things that you'd like to do while you're young enough to do them." He's assuming, of course, that the things we'll choose will be right in themselves. He isn't telling us to kick over the rules and go crazy—hence the last part of the verse: "But know that for all these things God will bring you into judgment."

There's no extra value attached to youth; the point is that we should be taking and tasting to the full every worthwhile thing that God gives us or makes available to us in every present, passing moment.

Do I make the most of life's simple joys? If not, why not?
Lord, deliver me from the "when this or that has happened, I'll really start living" type of attitude. Help me to receive each present moment from you.

Thou dost show me the path of life; in thy presence there is fullness of joy, in thy right hand are pleasures for evermore.
Psalm 16:11

Modern Christians tend to make satisfaction their religion. We show much more concern for self-fulfillment than for pleasing God. Typical of Christianity today (at any rate in the English speaking world) is its massive rash of how-to books for believers, directing us to more successful relationships, more joy in sex, becoming more of a person, realizing our possibilities, getting more excitement each day, reducing our weight, improving our diet, managing our money, licking our families into happier shape, and so on.

For people whose prime passion is to glorify God, these are doubtless legitimate concerns, but the how-to books regularly explore them in a self-absorbed way that treats our enjoyment of life rather than the glory of God as the center of interest. Granted, they spread a thin layer of Bible teaching over the mixture of popular psychology and common sense which they offer, but their overall approach clearly reflects narcissism—(self-ism or me-ism as it is sometimes called)—the way of the world in the modern West.

Now self-absorption, however religious in its cast of mind, is the opposite of holiness. Holiness means godliness and godliness is rooted in God-centeredness. Those who think God exists for their benefit rather than themselves existing for his praise do not qualify as holy men and women. It is an ungodly sort of godliness that has self at its center. And, not surprisingly perhaps, it is a godliness lacking the joy that God gives to those who seek him.

Do I pay myself too much or too little attention? Can I see why both attitudes are unhelpful?
Lord, I want you to become more and more my quiet, inner center.

*These things I have spoken to you, that my joy may be in you, and that your joy
may be full.*

                                                                    John 15:11

Joy is not the same as "having fun." Many people go through life having fun
but have no joy—hence their frenzied search for pleasures. In fact, it is possible to have a great deal of joy and very few pleasures—as the world mea-
sures pleasures.

Joy is not the same thing as a cheerful temperament either. In my youth I
remember hearing a speaker say that Christians should have "teapot" faces
(round and smiling), not "coffee pot" ones (long and serious-looking).
When I thought about that, I realized that he was talking about bone structure, which none of us can do much about at present! We're stuck with the
present shape of our faces until we get our new bodies. Of course I knew his
point was that we should radiate cheerfulness rather than gloom. Fair
enough; so we should. But being naturally cheerful is not the same as being
joyful, and it is perfectly possible to be joyful even though God may not
have given you a naturally cheerful temperament. Don't suppose that if you
are by nature phlegmatic or melancholic, then you are debarred from
Christian joy.

On the night of his betrayal, Jesus shared secrets with his disciples so
that, as he said, "my joy may be in you, and...your joy may be full." He
knew well enough what was coming—Gethsemane was only about an
hour away and after that there was the appalling experience of the cross to
face. So he was far from cheerful or carefree. But even while anticipating all
that, his joy remained in him. And we too can know joy even when in painful situations. A Christian's soul is larger than that of others; there is room
in it for grief (at losses, crosses, and messes) and joy (in and from the Lord)
at the same time.

What things had Jesus said to his disciples so that they would be joyful
(John 13-17)?
*Thank God for each of these things and remind yourself of them if ever you feel
"down" today.*

*The kingdom of God does not mean food and drink but righteousness and peace
and joy in the Holy Spirit.*
Romans 14:17

To know that you are loved—that is one source of joy. No one has joy who
does not know that there is someone who values him, cares for him, accepts him. To feel that nobody cares for me, treats me as a person, or both-
ers with me, and that I matter to nobody is a great joy-killer. Now the
Christian knows love in a way that nobody else does, for he knows that
God so loved the world that he gave his only Son to die in shame for us on
the cross, that we who believe in him might have eternal life (John 3:16;
Rom. 5:8; Gal. 2:20). The measure of God's love to us is how much he gave
for us. To know that Christ "loved me and gave himself for me" is to realize
divine love in a way that brings endless joy. God cares for me! He redeemed
me!

Discontent is another great joy-killer, whereas to accept our situation is a
source of joy. Now Christians can always do that because they know that
all their circumstances are planned out for them by a loving heavenly Father (Rom. 8:28). Speaking from prison with the death sentence hanging
over him, Paul wrote: "I have learned, in whatever state I am, to be content"
(Phil. 4:11).

Joy comes too from an awareness that we have something worth having.
People say, "My spouse, children, home, books, hobbies, and so on are a
joy to me." But Paul speaks of "the surpassing worth of knowing Christ Jesus my Lord" (Phil. 3:8). With Paul, the Christian says: "I have Jesus, the
pearl of great price. I will let anything go in order to hold on to him and
enjoy him fully."

Meditate on these sources of joy, looking up the references.
Father, I have good cause for joy . . .

Rejoice in the Lord always; again I will say, Rejoice.

Philippians 4:4

Another source of joy is the knowledge that you are giving something worth giving; a belief that you have significance for others because of what you have to impart to them. Giving is a supreme source of joy. If you have something that is supremely worth giving, you will find joy in trying to share it even when you feel sorrow that the gift is not being accepted. Paul knew that joy, for Paul gave himself, his whole life, to bring light into people's sin-darkened lives by sharing with them the blessings of the gospel. Like him, we will find joy in passing on God's best gift.

Once we know the sources of spiritual joy, we need to choose it. That is what the command to rejoice in the Lord requires of us. How do we choose joy? By practicing the art of Christian thinking. By choosing to dwell, over and over again, on our sources of joy, saying to ourselves and perhaps to others also: Yes, he loves and accepts me. Yes, my circumstances are sent by God for my good. Yes, I have something supremely worth having: the knowledge of my Savior. Yes, I am doing something supremely worth doing in seeking every opportunity to share Jesus Christ with others. As we think over these things, joy wells up spontaneously. You choose joy, you see, by directing your thoughts to that which triggers it.

Jesus wants our joy to be full and has made abundant provision for its fullness. Once we learn the art of Christian thinking, streams of joy will flow out into our hearts every day of our lives. This is one aspect of the victory that overcomes the world, even our faith, from which comes the joy which no man can quench and which gives us strength for service we never knew we had.

Meditate again on our sources of joy and think about the people who show the joy of the Lord in their lives. How does this quality show? Does it put off or encourage others? Why?

Lord, thank you for wanting your disciples to be full of joy (John 15:11). Make me so.

Extol the LORD our God; worship at his footstool! Holy is he!
Psalm 99:5

To worship God is to recognize his worth or worthiness; to look God-ward, and to acknowledge in all appropriate ways the value of what we see. The Bible calls this activity "glorifying God" or "giving glory to God," and views it as the ultimate end, and from one point of view, the whole duty of man (Ps. 29:2; 96:6; 1 Cor. 10:31).

Scripture views the glorifying of God as a sixfold activity: praising God for all that he is and all his achievements; thanking him for his gifts and his goodness to us; asking him to meet our own and others' needs; offering him our gifts, our service, and ourselves; learning of him from his Word, read and preached, and obeying his voice; telling others of his worth, both by public confession and testimony to what he has done for us. Thus we might say that the basic formulas of worship are these: "Lord, you are wonderful"; "Thank you, Lord"; "Please, Lord"; "Take this, Lord"; "Yes, Lord"; "Listen everybody!"

This then is worship in its largest sense: petition as well as praise, preaching as well as prayer, hearing as well as speaking, actions as well as words, obeying as well as offering, loving people as well as loving God. However, the primary acts of worship are those which focus on God directly—and we must not imagine that work for God in the world is a substitute for direct fellowship with him in praise and prayer and devotion.

Which facets of worship have to do with the first commandment and which have to do with the second? Have I got my priorities right here, remembering that the first must be given priority but should lead to the second?
Lord, show me/us in what ways my/our worship is deficient and whether there are any steps I/we can take about this.

July 16 **The family at prayer**
Thinking big about God

*Blessed be the name of God for ever and ever, to whom belong wisdom and might.
He changes times and seasons; he removes kings and sets up kings; he gives wisdom
to the wise and knowledge to those who have understanding.*

Daniel 2:20-21

The central truth which Daniel taught Nebuchadnezzar (Dan. 2,4) and reminded Belshazzar (5:18-23); which Nebuchadnezzar acknowledged (4:34-37); which was the basis of Daniel's prayers and his confidence in defying authority; which formed the staple substance of all the disclosures God made to Daniel, is the truth that "the most High rules the kingdom of men" (4:25). He knows and foreknows all things, and his foreknowledge is foreordination. He, therefore, will have the last word, both in world history and in the destiny of every person. His kingdom and righteousness will triumph in the end, for neither human beings nor angels shall be able to thwart him.

These were the thoughts of God which filled Daniel's mind, as his prayers witness—always the best evidence for a man's view of God (2:20-23; 9:4-19). Is this how we think of God? Is this the view of God which our own prayer expresses? Does this tremendous sense of his holy majesty, his moral perfection, and his gracious faithfulness keep us humble and dependent, awed and obedient, as it did Daniel? In all honesty, how much or how little do we know God?

Worship God aloud using Daniel's words (2:20-23) or your own version of that song of praise celebrating God's greatness.
Have I lost sight of the greatness of God? How about setting time aside for studying this theme in the Bible as a corrective to my thinking?

My eyes are ever toward the LORD, for he will pluck my feet out of the net.
Psalm 25:15

There won't be any prayer where there's no consciousness of need. The writer of Psalm 25 is very conscious of need. He feels that a net has enveloped and imprisoned him. What is this net? It seems to have outer and inner meshes. The outer meshes symbolize his enemies—"Consider how many are my foes, and with what violent hatred they hate me" (v. 19)—and the difficulties caused by being up against these people—"I am lonely and afflicted. Relieve the troubles of my heart, and bring me out of my distresses" (vv. 16–17).

The inner meshes symbolize what he feels when he remembers his sins: "Remember not the sins of my youth, or my transgressions"; "Pardon my guilt, for it is great" (vv. 7,11). The memories bring fear that he might finally go under and end up as a total failure: "Let me not be put to shame" (vv. 2,20).

Aren't we all aware of a similar net around us? Aren't we too facing opposition, adverse circumstances, difficulty after difficulty, the memory of our sins, fear of failure? We need to do what the psalmist did: take all these matters to the Lord spontaneously, repeatedly and uninhibitedly, by the help of the Holy Spirit, and ask him to pluck us out of the meshes of the net with which the devil, patron of all distress and discouragement, seeks to entrap us.

What is your net: the things, people, and circumstances which are threatening to get you down?
Bring each aspect of your difficulties or fears to God and remind yourself of what he's like and what he's promised.

If you ask anything of the Father, he will give it to you in my name. . . Ask, and you will receive, that your joy may be full.

John 16:23–24

If we ask anything according to his will he hears us.
1 John 5:14

These verses come from two passages which seek to lead us deeper into prayer than most of us have ever gone (John 16:23–27; 1 John 5:13–17).

The aim of prayer is not to force God's hand or make him do our will against his own, but to deepen our knowledge of him and our fellowship with him through contemplating his glory, confessing our dependence and need, and consciously embracing his goals. Our asking therefore must be *according to God's will* and *in Jesus' name*.

The context of such asking is assured faith. In that day when Jesus teaches them, by the Spirit, plainly of the Father, there will be no question of enlisting Jesus' support in prayer, as if he were more merciful than the Father or could influence him in a way that they could not; in that day they will know inwardly that as believers they are the Father's beloved.

To ask in Jesus' name is not to use a verbal spell but to base our asking on Christ's saving relationship to us through the cross; this will involve making petitions which Christ can endorse and put his name to. When God answers in Jesus' name, he gives *through* Jesus as our mediator and *to* Jesus as the one who will be glorified through what is given.

Central to the life of prayer is letting ourselves be taught by Christ through his Word and Spirit what we should pray for. To the extent that we *know*, through the Spirit's inner witness, that we are making a request which the Lord has specifically given us to make, to that extent we *know* that we have the answer even before we see it.

Am I willing to be shaped by God through his Word and Spirit? Have I ever sought to pray that way?
Lord, I need a more assured faith. Please help me. . .

The prayer of a righteous man has great power in its effects.
James 5:16

In James 5:13–18 James says that we should pray for ourselves and for other Christians. In prayer, we look up from our distresses to gaze on God, the merciful ruler who will in due course deliver his suffering servants. Prayer brings stability and strength; seeing temporal problems in eternal perspective cuts them down to size.

People who are sick may ask their pastors to pray over them; elders must be ready to do this on request. This is not a magic formula for a cure: while Jesus' miracles show that there is indeed bodily healing for us in the atonement, his attitude to Paul's thorn in the flesh indicates that it is not his will for every Christian always to enjoy perfect health in this body—though when we get our new bodies it will be different! But we must be clear that the benefits of the atonement are one thing, God's time and manner for conveying them is another. Solemn prayer over the whole range of the sick person's needs is what James counsels, on the principle that illness is always God's summons to consider our ways.

Such a prayer may well result in healing, and prayer for one another's spiritual well-being should not be limited to those who are physically sick. The efficacy of the prayer depends on uprightness of life and motive, wholehearted and sustained earnestness in the person praying, and how far it conforms to God's revealed purposes and ways. The story of Elijah illustrates these three principles either explicitly or by implication.

Study and put into practice, preferably in small groups, the Bible teaching about right-thinking and effective prayer. (For starters, try Deut. 11:13–17; 1 Kings 17; Ps. 73; Mark 2:3–12; Rom. 8:18; 2 Cor. 4:7–18; James 1:6–8; 2:14–26; 4:3.)
Lord, help us as a church to pray with, over, and for people as much and as effectively as possible.

I will pray with the spirit and I will pray with the mind also.
1 Corinthians 14:15

We should seek from God the requests to make in each situation and recognize that it is the Holy Spirit's task, in addition to the rest of his ministry in our prayers, to guide us here as we lay the facts before the Lord. Often we enjoy no special leading and are only enabled to pray for needs in general terms, but sometimes the Spirit prompts very specific requests and leads us to make them with unusual confidence.

Once the theological institution of which I was principal was going to be closed by episcopal order. The community fixed a day of prayer about it. Two hours into the day, I found I knew exactly what to ask God for: a merger with another institution on specific terms so controversial that they seemed unrealistic. I could share this with no one at the time, but I held to the vision as best I could, and within a year all I had been led to pray for happened. Glory to God!

Again, a friend was in the hospital for an exploratory operation; cancer symptoms were present. Many prayed. Laying the situation before God, I found myself drawn (for the only time in my life so far) to pray specifically and confidently for a miracle of healing. Walking home from church on Sunday morning and praying thus, I felt I was being told that the prayer was heard and I need not continue to press it. On Monday the operation revealed no trace of cancer. Once more, glory to God!

We must always be consciously open to being led by God in the things we pray for.

If my prayers seem to be getting nowhere in a particular situation, do I need to stop and wait on God to discover what I should be praying for?
Lord, show me what to pray for in this situation. . .

Make me to know thy ways, O LORD... Who is the man that fears the LORD? Him will he instruct in the way that he should choose.
Psalm 25:4,12

God wants us to understand the principles on which he deals with us so that we will understand what he is doing. So we have the psalmist speaking of how God "instructs sinners in the way" (v. 8) and "teaches the humble his way" (v. 9). He also wants to teach us the way that we should go.

How do we learn God's way of dealing with us and his way for us to travel? We learn it from the Bible through the Holy Spirit. From the Scriptures we learn the way of God with his people and the way we should go in obedience to him.

God teaches these things to his people in the prayer relationship. We wait on God, we meditate in God's presence, and we feed both prayers and meditations from the Scriptures in the presence of God.

To whom will God teach his way? To the person who *"fears the LORD"* (v. 12) (the word "fears" signifies not panic but reverent devotion). Such a person will have discovered from God's Word that he is a sinner, and that God "instructs sinners in the way" (v. 8). He will have heard God proclaiming his greatness and man's smallness and will therefore have a humble and quiet spirit before God, and that God "teaches the humble his way" (v. 9). Also, he will have learned from God about the covenant of grace and how to keep it, and that "all the paths of the LORD are steadfast love and faithfulness, for those who keep his covenant" (v. 10).

Is God teaching me his way? If not, am I too casual, conceited, self-willed, or double-minded in my prayers for God's teaching to come through?
Lord, I want to express my feelings to you... Show me if this is the attitude of reverent devotion which you require in those to whom you want to teach your way of working.

Ever since the creation of the world his invisible nature, namely, his eternal power and deity, has been clearly perceived in the things that have been made.

Romans 1:20

Calvin spoke of a "general revelation" of God to people through nature (the created order with which all of us are in contact every day of our lives). In our own nature, too, there is revelation, a communication from God. It reaches us in the same way that our awareness of light reaches us. It is immediate, inescapable, undeniable. But fallen human beings deny it nevertheless and turn the light that is in them to darkness.

Calvin speaks very strongly about this. He says that God has so revealed himself "in the whole workmanship of this world" that "men cannot open their eyes without being compelled to see him... This skillful ordering of the universe is for us a sort of mirror in which we may contemplate God, who is otherwise invisible... The universe... was founded as a spectacle of God's glory... The Lord represents himself and his everlasting kingdom in the mirror of his works."

The awareness of the Creator comes through in all our commerce with his creatures, in all our knowledge and awareness of ourselves, in our identity, the workings of our conscience, and the thoughts of our own hearts. But people deny this awareness and turn it into darkness and superstition. So the world, for all its wisdom, does not know God even though this general communication of God through nature is a reality for every person.

Am I aware enough of God's general communication to me and to others?
Lord, everything you have made must communicate something about you. Help me to look more closely if a superficial judging by appearances doesn't seem to tally with this. Help me to convey this truth to others.

No one knows the Son except the Father, and no one knows the Father except the Son and any one to whom the Son chooses to reveal him.
Matthew 11:27

God has added to the general communication of himself in the natural order a special communication of himself in grace, in which there are three stages.

Stage one is *redemption in history.* By words and works God makes himself known on the stage of history in saving action. The words are basic, for first God tells people what he is going to do. Then he acts, fulfilling his word. That is how he proceeded at the Exodus when he saved Israel out of captivity in Egypt. That is what he did when in the fullness of time he sent his Son born of a woman to redeem those who were under the Law. He sent Christ to sinners like us so that we might receive the adoption of sons and so become children in his family.

Stage two is *revelation in writing,* which is the work of God inspiring the Scriptures. God caused interpretive records to be written of what he had said and done, so that all people in all generations might know him, and through this knowledge might come into the enjoyment of the redemptive revelation that he had made. The written record is our Bible, from which all our knowledge about God as redeemer derives.

The third stage in the communicative process is *reception by individuals* of the realities of redemption declared in the Scriptures. This reception becomes a reality through the work of the Holy Spirit who opens our hearts to give the Word entrance and renews our hearts so that we might turn around again to face God. Then communication is complete, and we know God through Christ in a personal relationship.

Meditate on the implications for you personally of Matthew 11:27; 16:17; 2 Corinthians 4:6; Galatians 1:15–16.
Praise God for the wonder of what you have just learned about his personal communication to you.

I am an ambassador in chains.
Ephesians 6:20

Paul considered himself Christ's ambassador. What is an ambassador? He is the authorized representative of a sovereign. He speaks not in his own name but on behalf of the ruler whose deputy he is, and his whole duty and responsibility is to interpret that ruler's mind faithfully to those to whom he is sent.

Paul used this "ambassador" image twice—both in connection with his evangelistic work. Pray for me, he wrote from prison, "that utterance may be given me in opening my mouth boldly to proclaim the mystery of the gospel, for which I am an ambassador in chains; that I may declare it boldly, as I ought to speak" (Eph. 6:18–20). He wrote also that God "gave us the ministry of reconciliation. . .So we are ambassadors for Christ, God making his appeal through us. We beseech you on behalf of Christ, be reconciled to God" (2 Cor. 5:18–20).

Paul called himself an ambassador because he knew that when he proclaimed the gospel facts and promises and urged sinners to receive the reconciliation effected at Calvary, he was declaring Christ's message to the world. The figure of ambassadorship highlights the authority Paul had, as representing his Lord, as long as he remained faithful to the terms of his commission and said neither less nor more than he had been given to say.

Meditate on the images suggested in Philippians 2:14–18. Are today's evangelists to see themselves as Paul saw himself?
Lord, how can I shine as a light in your world today?

*Though I am free from all men, I have made myself a slave to all, that I might win
the more. To the Jews I became as a Jew, in order to win Jews; to those under the law
I became as one under the law. . . that I might win those under the law. To those outside the law I became as one outside the law. . . that I might win those outside the
law.*
1 Corinthians 9:19-21

Communicating the Christian gospel is not easy; in fact, there's nothing
necessarily wrong with what we're doing if in a particular situation at a particular time the task proves cruelly hard. Jesus was a prince and paragon
among communicators, yet even he failed constantly to anchor his message
in his hearers' hearts.

However, in communicating Christianity there are guidelines which cannot be ignored. If we do not stay with the biblical story and the scriptural
text and most of all with the person of the Savior; if, while observing the
distinction between milk and meat, foundation and superstructure, we do
not labor to make known the whole revealed counsel of God; if we do not
seek, as part of our communicative strategy, to show the gospel shaping relationships in home and family, in imaginative gestures of neighbor-love,
and to ring the changes on *both* the Christianizing of existing culture *and*
the forming of an alternative culture as true and necessary modes of Christian expression; if, finally, we decline to show any respect for cultures, however pagan, other than our own; then there is no reason to expect
communication to proceed well in any context, whether in our local church
down the road or on the other side of the world.

Is my church leavening in any way the society around it and showing it an alternative lifestyle?
Lord, shake us up if we have become complacent and tunnel-visioned.

Jesus said to her, "Everyone who drinks of this water will thirst again, but whoever drinks of the water that I shall give him will never thirst."

                                                                    John 4:13–14

The story of Jesus and the woman at the well (John 4:1–42) is a marvelous example of how personal evangelism ought to be done. See how ingeniously Jesus approaches the person who is there (the woman) by talking about the provision that is there—the water.

Jesus asks the woman for a drink. Her reply is (v. 9), "How is it that you, a Jew, ask a drink of me, a woman of Samaria?" Jesus answers (v. 10), "If you knew the gift of God, and who it is that is saying to you, 'Give me a drink,' you would have asked him, and he would have given you living water."

The woman is confused and a little defensive. She asks: Can you really offer anything better than this well given to us by our father Jacob? Jesus will not be drawn into an argument about his relationship to Jacob; he goes on talking about water. Everyone who drinks of this well-water will thirst again, but those who drink the water I can give will never thirst again, he tells her.

The woman still doesn't understand but her interest is held by the thought of never feeling thirsty or having to trudge to the well again, so she says (v. 15), "Sir, give me this water." Before Jesus can do that, however, he has to take her a little further into the discovery of her own need, so that her heart might thirst for a new life. No one comes to adult faith without this thirst of heart.

Think of other incidents in the life of Jesus or the lives of his disciples in which he or they opened the conversation or message by appealing to something relevant and interesting to the hearers.

Lord, please help me to take the time and trouble to identify with the thoughts and feelings of those with whom I want to share your truth.

Jesus said to her, "Go, call your husband, and come here."
John 4:16

Before Jesus could minister to the needs of the woman at the well (John 4:1–42), he had to make her aware of what those needs really were (4:16–19). So after their talk about water, he said to her quite abruptly and with an apparent change of subject, "Go, call your husband, and come here." Why did Jesus say this? Because he knew the woman's heart and history, and he knew what would result from this question.

At once the Samaritan woman, till now quite chatty, clams up. "I have no husband," she says tersely. In personal evangelism you will find this same reaction when people's consciences are touched: guilt puts them on the defensive.

Jesus then tells her that she has spoken truly and discloses what, as the Son of God, he knows about her: she has lived with several different men and is a kept woman, not a wife. He is showing her that he knows her through and through, as she later acknowledges: "Come, see a man who told me all that I ever did. Can this be the Christ?...He told me all that I ever did" (vv. 29,39).

In our personal evangelism, we must tell people that Jesus knows them through and through. The Spirit of God can help us to develop discernment so that by listening to them and watching them we perceive what they are covering up and what their real needs are.

Someone has said that the most universal experience in this world is a bad conscience. Jesus had led her from her general sense of need to a particular awareness of particular sins and therefore to her need for forgiveness. In personal evangelism we need to learn from him and act on this same principle.

How would you answer the criticism that Christians go around trying to make everyone feel guilty?
Lord, how we need your sensitivity!

The woman said to him, "Sir, I perceive that you are a prophet. Our fathers worshipped on this mountain; and you say that in Jerusalem is the place where men ought to worship." Jesus said to her, "Woman, believe me, the hour is coming when neither on this mountain nor in Jerusalem will you worship the Father...God is spirit, and those who worship him must worship in spirit and truth."
John 4:19–21,24

As you read the story of Jesus and the woman of Samaria, you might feel that Jesus allowed the woman to go off on a tangent just when he had brought her to a realization of her sin, and wonder why he did so. I believe the answer is that he trusted the Holy Spirit to do the work of conviction and conversion and so he didn't press for a decision but let the conversation take its course. In this way he allowed the woman's spiritual interest to grow.

The woman wanted to start a discussion about the proper place for worship. Sometimes people start discussing issues to avoid the arrow of conviction, but I don't think this woman was doing that or Jesus would have handled her differently. I think there was genuine interest behind her question. Certainly Jesus took it seriously and answered it directly, telling her something quite new: that the time was coming when neither "on this mountain nor in Jerusalem" would people worship the Father. He went on to tell her that God is spirit (and therefore by implication present everywhere and not to be thought of as localized) and that those who worship him must worship him in spirit (from the heart through the Holy Spirit) and in truth (according to the truth of the gospel).

In this, Jesus was disclosing more about what he had to give: namely, the knowledge of God as Father—something that neither Jew nor Samaritan had at that time.

Am I willing to hear and stay with people's genuine questions?
Lord, help me not to rush things in this situation...and risk a setback.

In the world you have tribulation; but be of good cheer, I have overcome the world.
John 16:33

I quote this testimony at random from a Christian newspaper: "My husband . . . and I were youth directors in our church . . . when our two-and-a-
half-year-old son accidentally drowned. We had lived for the Lord and
never lost anyone. *We thought we would be spared such things.* I went
through four years numb, not understanding, not accepting my anger, continuing to try to be strong. I really was not talking to anyone about the pain
and finally went into deep depression."

The nurture that leaves Christians with false expectations of this kind,
and with no resources except the stiff upper lip for coping when trouble
strikes, is defective to the point of cruelty. Where do these expectations
come from? Are they just wishful thinking, or have they been induced by
external factors? It seems very plain that the salesmanlike man-centeredness
of so much of our evangelism that exalts the benefits, minimizes the burdens of the Christian life, and thereby fixes the thought patterns of converts, is one root cause of such false expectations.

How could we purge evangelism of its excessive and damaging subjectiv-
ity? The short answer is by learning to keep in step with the Spirit's New
Covenant ministry and to focus more directly on Jesus Christ himself as
Savior God; model human being; coming judge; lover of the weak, poor,
and unlovely; and leader of cross-bearing along the path that he himself
trod.

What are the benefits and burdens of the Christian life? Are people in your church
being presented with the truth about Christian commitment?
Pray for someone going through a death experience to be led out into resurrection.

*I am not ashamed of the gospel: it is the power of God for salvation to everyone who
has faith.*

Romans 1:16

We need to bring under review all our evangelistic plans and practices—our
missions, rallies, and campaigns; our sermons, talks, and testimonies; our
big meetings, our little meetings, and our presentation of the gospel in personal dealing; the tracts we give, the books we lend, the letters we write—
and to ask about each of them questions like the following:·

Is this way of presenting Christ calculated to impress on people that the
gospel is a *word from God?* Or is its tendency rather to distract attention
from the author and authority of the message to the person and performance of the messenger?

Is this way of presenting Christ calculated to promote or impede the
work of God in people's *minds?* Is it going to make people think and think
hard about God and about themselves in relation to God?

Is this way of presenting Christ calculated to convey to people the *doctrine* of the whole gospel? Or will it hurry people on to the demand for faith
and repentance without having made it clear just what they need to repent
of or what they ought to believe?

Is this way of presenting Christ calculated to convey to people the *application* of the whole gospel? Or is it likely to give an inadequate, distorted
impression of what the gospel requires?

Is this way of presenting Christ calculated to convey gospel truth in a
manner that is appropriately *serious?* Or is it so light, fun, and casual that
hearers will have a hard time taking it seriously and will regard it as a pick-
me-up for life's misfits?

How is our church presenting Christ through its regular and special programs?
*Lord, help us to present the gospel in such a way that all will feel that they and their
gifts are welcome—whether they are cerebral/academic/emotional/sporty/creative/
practical/imaginative/down-to-earth/serious-minded/humorous . . .*

Men of Athens, I perceive that in every way you are very religious.
Acts 17:22

The crucial difference between Christianity and other religions is that Christianity is a religion of revelation received; all other faiths are religions of revelation denied.

Christianity is a religion of faith in a special revelation, given through specific historical events, of salvation for sinners. Non-Christian religions, on the other hand, spring from the suppression and distortion of a general revelation given through man's knowledge of God's world concerning the being and Law of the Creator (Rom. 1:18–32; 2:12–15). Yet common grace prevents the truth from being utterly suppressed. Flashes of light break through which we should watch for and gratefully recognize, as did Paul at Athens (Acts 17:28).

Hence we find in non-Christian religions a restless sense of the hostility of the powers of the universe; an undefined feeling of guilt, and all sorts of merit-making techniques designed to get rid of it; a dread of death, and a consuming anxiety to feel that one has conquered it; forms of worship aimed at once to placate, bribe, and control the gods, and to make them keep their distance, except when wanted; an alarming readiness to call moral evil *good*, and good *evil*, in the name of religion; an ambivalent attitude of mind which seems both to seek God and to seek to evade him in the same act.

Therefore in our evangelistic dialogue with people of non-Christian religions, our task must be to present the biblical revelation of God in Christ—not as supplementing them but as explaining their existence, exposing their errors, and judging their inadequacy.

Do I need to be more aware of flashes of common grace in my dialogue with non-Christians?
Father, help me to understand where people are so I can point them to a true knowledge of you.

August 1

Fear not, Abram, I am your shield; your reward shall be very great.
Genesis 15:1

I am God Almighty; walk before me and be blameless.
Genesis 17:1

Abraham was capable of repeated shabby deceptions which actually endangered his wife's chastity. By nature a man of little moral courage, he was altogether too anxious about his own personal security. Also, he was vulnerable to pressure. At his wife's insistence, he fathered a child with Hagar, his wife's maid, and when Sarah reacted to Hagar's pride in her pregnancy with hysterical recriminations, he let Sarah drive Hagar out of the house (Gen. 12:10-20; 20:1-18; 16:1-16).

Plainly, then, Abraham was not by nature a man of strong principle and his sense of responsibility was somewhat deficient. But God in wisdom dealt with this easy-going, unheroic figure to such good effect that he not only faithfully fulfilled his appointed role on the stage of church history as the pioneer occupant of Canaan, the first recipient of God's covenant, and father of Isaac, the miracle-child, but also became a new man.

What Abraham needed most of all was to learn the practice of *living in God's presence*, seeing all life in relation to him, and him alone, as commander, defender, and rewarder. This was the great lesson which God in wisdom concentrated on teaching him. Again and again God confronted Abraham, and so led Abraham to the point where his heart could say with the psalmist, "Whom have I in heaven but thee? And there is nothing upon earth that I desire besides thee...God is the strength of my heart and my portion for ever" (Ps. 73:25-26).

Lord, I'm so encouraged to be reminded that Abraham was not always the giant of faith which he later became; he was frail and fallible just as I am, yet you molded him just as you can mold me and are molding me. Thank you.
Pinpoint the times in your life when God has confronted you with himself.

He (Abraham) said, "Oh, let not the LORD be angry, and I will speak."
Genesis 18:30

From being a man of the world, Abraham becomes a man of God. The old weaknesses sometimes reappear, but alongside these a new nobility and independence emerges, the outworking of Abraham's developed habit of walking with God. We also observe in him a new meekness as he declines to claim his due precedence over his nephew Lot (Gen. 13:8-13), and a new courage as he sets off with a mere three hundred men to rescue Lot from the combined forces of four kings (14:14-16). We see a new dignity as he deprecates keeping the recaptured booty, lest others think that the king of Sodom, rather than God Most High, had made him rich (14:17-24). We see a new patience, as he waits a quarter of a century, from the age of seventy-five to a hundred, for the birth of his promised heir (12:4;21:5).

We see him becoming a man of prayer, an importunate intercessor burdened with a sense of responsibility before God for others' welfare (18:23-33). At the end he is so utterly devoted to God's will, and so confident that God knows what he is doing, that he is willing (at God's command) to kill his own son, the heir for whose birth he had waited so long (22:1-19). How wisely God had taught him his lesson! And how well Abraham had learned it!

Think of anyone in the Bible or someone you know whom you believe "walks with God" or is a "friend of God." What are the characteristics of that person which lead you to this conclusion?
Lord, what does "walking with you" and "being your friend" mean in practice for me today?

In hope he believed against hope, that he should become the father of many nations;
as he had been told, "So shall your descendants be."
Romans 4:18

Abraham's life is an illustration of what true faith is. In his tenacious, God-
honoring adherence (against all reason and probability) to the divine
promise—in this case the promise that he should have an heir—he is the ex-
emplar and pattern for the justifying faith which the gospel calls us to exercise (Rom. 4:18–22).

Another New Testament illustration of faith in action is in the book of
Hebrews. The writer is seeking to stabilize troubled and distracted believers.
He writes: "Be content with what you have; for he has said, 'I will never fail
you nor forsake you.' Hence we can confidently say, 'The Lord is my helper,
I will not be afraid; what can man do to me?' " (Heb. 13:5–6).

God has spoken in the words of the biblical promise; we respond by taking the promise, believing it, resting on it, and adjusting our outlook on life
accordingly. That is faith; that is what it means to *stand* on the promises of
God.

Do I make a practice of responding to the promises of God in the way suggested
above? How can I *take, believe, rest on,* and *adjust to* a promise of God?
Lord, here is my need and here is your promise . . .

Jacob said to his father, "I am Esau your first-born. I have done as you told me; now sit up and eat of my game, that you may bless me."
Genesis 27:19

God dealt with Jacob, Abraham's grandson, in quite a different way than he dealt with Abraham. First, over a period of some twenty years, God let Jacob weave complex webs of deceit with their inevitable consequences — mutual mistrust, friendships turned to enmity, and the isolation of the deceiver. The consequences of Jacob's cleverness were themselves God's curse upon it.

When Jacob stole Esau's birthright and blessing, Esau turned against him (naturally!), and Jacob had to leave home in a hurry. He went to his uncle Laban, who proved to be as tricky a customer as Jacob himself. Laban exploited Jacob's position and bamboozled him into marrying not only his pretty daughter, whom Jacob wanted, but also the plain one with bad eyes, for whom he would otherwise have found it hard to get a good husband.

Jacob's experience with Laban was a case of the swindler swindled; God used it to show Jacob what it was like to be at the receiving end — something that Jacob needed to learn if he were ever to fall out of love with his own previous way of life. But Jacob was not cured yet. His immediate reaction was to give tit for tat; he manipulated the breeding of Laban's sheep so astutely, with such profit to himself and loss to his employer, that Laban grew furious, and Jacob felt it prudent to leave with his family for Canaan before active reprisals began. And God, who had hitherto borne Jacob's dishonesty without rebuke, encouraged him to go, for he knew what he would do before the journey ended.

Look back over God's dealings with you, remembering the times when he let you have your way and when he let you "taste" what you "dished out."
Father, thank you for being patient while I learn by trial and error.

Jacob said, "I will not let you go, unless you bless me." And he said to him, "What is your name?" And he said, "Jacob." Then he said, "Your name shall no more be called Jacob, but Israel, for you have striven with God and with men, and have prevailed."
Genesis 32:26–28

When Jacob learned that Esau was bringing an armed force against him to avenge the stolen blessing of twenty years before, he was thrown into complete despair. And now God's time had come. That night, as Jacob stood alone by the river Jabbok, God met him (Gen. 32:22–32). There were hours of desperate, agonized conflict: spiritual and, as it seemed to Jacob, physical.

Jacob had hold of God; he wanted a blessing, an assurance of divine favor and protection in this crisis, but he could not get what he sought. Instead, he grew ever more conscious of his own state—utterly helpless and, without God, utterly hopeless. He felt the full bitterness of his unscrupulous, cynical ways now coming home to roost. He had been hitherto self-reliant, believing himself to be more than a match for anything that might come, but now he felt his complete inability to handle things. He knew, with blinding, blazing certainty, that he would never again dare trust himself to look after his own life and to carve out his destiny. To make this doubly clear to Jacob, God lamed him as a perpetual reminder of his own spiritual weakness and his need to lean upon God always.

The nature of Jacob's prevailing with God was simply that he held on to God while God weakened him and wrought in him the spirit of submission and self-distrust; that he desired God's blessing so much that he clung to God through all that painful humbling until he got low enough for God to raise him up.

Why must God humble us?
Am I living by my wits or by God's wisdom?

I was with you in weakness and in much fear and trembling; and my speech and my message were not in plausible words of wisdom, but in demonstration of the Spirit and of power, that your faith might not rest in the wisdom of men but in the power of God.
1 Corinthians 2:3–5

Paul knew he was going to look silly in the eyes of the Corinthians. All right! He was prepared for that. He was going to rely on the Lord to honor his own Word. He told the Corinthians that he deliberately turned his back on philosophical and oratorical fireworks, resolving to speak plainly and simply and trust the Holy Spirit to demonstrate, confirm, and authenticate the divine truth of the message that he had brought. He was trusting God's power, not his own cleverness.

But Paul did feel a bit of a fool. That is what the words *weakness* and *fear* point to. Knowing that he would offend the Corinthians by not pandering to Greek intellectual conceit, he felt vulnerable and expected ridicule, and the expectation gave him no pleasure. Yet, he did not flinch. He knew that faithfulness required this of him, and he knew that he could trust God to honor that faithfulness. So Paul looked to the Holy Spirit to validate the Word.

And the Spirit did as Paul had hoped. The result was the Corinthian church! God does honor faithfulness to his truth—faithfulness both in adhering to its given content and also in presenting it in God's chosen way, as a testimony which can only be received through the enlightening that the Spirit gives. On occasion we are all called to faithful witness of this kind.

Is God's message to Paul: "Do not be afraid, but speak and do not be silent; for I am with you, and no man shall attack you to harm you; for I have many people in this city" (Acts 18:9–10) a message for you today?
Lord, help me to demonstrate in my life that however weak and inadequate we are, humanly speaking, we may be powerful through your Spirit.

*Work out your own salvation with fear and trembling; for God is at work in you,
both to will and to work for his good pleasure.*

                                                      Philippians 2:12–13

It is very important that we remove from our minds any conceited notion
which suggests that as we grow in holiness we shall need the cleansing
blood of Christ less. We shall never get beyond our need for the blood of
Jesus. The context of our sanctification is justification by the blood of
Christ.

The source of our sanctification is union with Christ. We are united with
him at the point where our first life (our old life) ends and the new life begins. The beginning of the new life means the renewing of our hearts so that
now we love God and his will, ways, and purposes, and discover our deepest desire—to know, love, get and keep close to, serve, please, and praise
him all our days. The summons to be holy is simply the call to be natural as
a Christian and let those new instincts, impulses, and longings express
themselves in the way we live.

The agent of sanctification is the Holy Spirit who works in us to make us
will and act according to God's good pleasure. Again and again we need to
go down on our knees and admit our helplessness and ask to be empow-
ered. Then, believing that God has heard and answered us, we need to
move into action, attempting to do the very thing about which we have
prayed.

If all this sounds easy, it shouldn't, because sanctification is a battle (Gal.
5:17). We never have our hearts entirely set on the things of God, so that
even if our actions are right by external standards, our hearts are never
quite right. It is struggle and conflict all the way.

What are we to grow out of as we grow in holiness? What will we never grow out
of?
Lord, I realize I can call nothing "growth" that takes me away from the cross.

I will run in the way of thy commandments when thou enlargest my understanding!
Psalm 119:32

I took about twenty years to get into the Psalms—partly because I was so concerned in the early years of my Christian pilgrimage to get clear on correct notions. And the Psalms, of course, don't analyze notions.

They jump from one topic to another; they're meditative and exclamatory. The format usually does not follow a line of expository argument (as Paul does, for instance). When we're worshipping, we're not concerned with expository argument. But that made it hard for me to tune into this book of the Bible.

The other thing that threw me was that the Psalms are simple and so exuberant. Much of our culture, both Christian and secular, conditions us not to favor the uninhibited expression of ourselves before God that the Psalms model. And as long as a person feels that the psalmists were rather uncivilized fellows because they expressed themselves so wholeheartedly and even fiercely, he will find it hard to identify with them. That was a problem for me at one time.

I am thankful to say that as the years go by I feel more in tune with the Psalms and I am sure that is how it ought to be. Living in the Psalms helps to turn little souls into big ones, and that is something we should all covet for ourselves.

As part of your own time with God, sing one or two of the many psalms that have been set to music; many are excellent for leading people into worship.
Lord, enlarge my understanding through this part of your Word.

The words of Amos, who was among the shepherds of Tekoa... Thus says the LORD.

Amos 1:1,3

The hallmark of Old Testament prophecy was the "Thus saith the Lord" formula preceding it. This formula proclaimed the source and authority of the prophets' messages: it told the world that their words were to be heard and received as God's royal announcements, and not just as the pious productions of man. The prophets' messages correspond not to editorials in *The Times* but to proclamations from Buckingham Palace.

Commonly, the prophets spoke in God's own person: the "I" of their oracles is more often than not Jehovah himself. The psychology of prophetic inspiration, involving auditory, visionary, intuitive, and reflective factors, is necessarily mysterious to us who do not share it. But both Testaments tell us that prophetic inspiration, however mysterious, was a recurring fact in Israel's history from Moses on and that this inspiration had definite and characteristic effects. It was more than natural insight, even more than spiritual enlightenment; it was a unique process whereby the human messenger was drawn into such complete identification with the message God had given him to deliver that what he said could be and indeed had to be treated as wholly divine.

Though the prophet's own powers of thought and craftsmanship were fully exercised in apprehending God's disclosures and, so to speak, in preparing them for publication (oral or written), the resulting product was uniformly and uncorruptedly "the Word of the Lord."

Could modern preachers and others who exercise teaching roles learn something from the Old Testament prophets' methods, skill, and craftmanship?
Lord, help me to identify with the message you want me to pass on to others.

To all to whom I send you you shall go, and whatever I command you you shall speak. . .I have put my words in your mouth.
Jeremiah 1:7,9

The nature of the prophet's task is crystallized in these words to Jeremiah. To put words into someone else's mouth is to tell him exactly what to say. This is what God did with the prophets. As they repeatedly tell us, the Word of the Lord came to them and told them what they must say to others in God's name.

Amos describes the prophets as mediators of revelation in two consecutive verses (Amos 3:7,8). "Surely the Lord GOD does nothing without revealing his secret to his servants the prophets." There the prophet is seer and hearer, the recipient of revelation. Then Amos says, "The lion has roared; who will not fear? The Lord GOD has spoken; who can but prophesy?" There the prophet is speaker and messenger, constrained to declare the secret that God has shown him.

Essentially, therefore, the prophets were forthtellers of God's Word, human agents who made his statements public and relayed them to the people to whom they were addressed. But because God's secret often included his secret plans, as well as the meaning of his present actions, the forthtellers of God's Word often appeared as foretellers of things to come. That is how the idea of prophets as predictors fits in.

Do you know any modern prophets—persons, that is, who apply God's Word in God's name to you and others? Do you pray for preachers to show themselves prophets in this sense?
Pray for any discouraged, isolated prophets whom you know.

He made known his ways to Moses, his acts to the people of Israel.
Psalm 103:7

The idea of revelation as essentially verbal communication does not imply that God is a celestial rabbi who does nothing but sit and talk. What it does imply is that no historical event in itself can make God known to anyone unless God himself discloses its meaning and place in his plan. Providential happenings may serve to remind us more or less vividly that God is at work, but their link (if any) with his saving purpose cannot be known until he himself informs us of it. No event is self-interpreting at this level.

The Exodus, for instance, was only one of many tribal migrations in history. Calvary was only one of many Roman executions. Who could have guessed the unique saving significance of these events if God had not spoken to tell us?

In one sense, all history is God's deed, but none of it reveals him unless he himself talks to us about it. God's revelation is not through deeds without words (a dumb charade) any more than it is through words without deeds. God speaks to us through deeds or, more biblically, through words which his deeds confirm and fulfill. The fact we must face is that if there is no verbal revelation, there is no revelation at all, not even in the life, death, and resurrection of Jesus of Nazareth.

How do you understand Psalm 19:1–4 in the light of what has been said above? Is there general and special revelation just as there is common and special grace? *Lord, thank you for your deeds in my life and the words you have given to help me have the right viewpoint on them.*

*Remember your leaders, those who spoke to you the word of God; consider the out-
come of their life, and imitate their faith. Jesus Christ is the same yesterday and today
and for ever.*
Hebrews 13:7-8

Receiving God's revelation is not simply a matter of sitting down and learning biblical doctrines. No modern theologian could make the point more
forcibly than the writer of Hebrews chapter 11 that faith is not orthodoxy
alone but existential trust in the living God. In fact, as Hebrews 11:7-8,11,
13 show, such trust is only possible on the basis of verbal communication
from God—divine commands and promises—that is recognized as such.

The belief that revelation is essentially verbal communication from
heaven doesn't militate in any way against the New Testament identification
of Jesus himself as the Word of God (John 1:1-14) who discloses the Father
(John 1:18; 14:9). To argue otherwise (as some do) is like arguing that because "Flying Scotsman" is the name of a locomotive, it cannot be the name
of a train. "Word" (*logos*) denotes the expression of mind in reasoning and
speech. God's Son is called his Word because in him God's mind, character,
and purposes find full expression. God's revelation is called his Word because it is reasoned verbal discourse which has God as its subject and
source. The verbal word bears witness to the personal Word and enables us
to know the latter for what he is, which otherwise we could not do.

Although Hebrews begins by hailing God's Son as the perfect image of
his Father, three times out of four the phrase "the word of God" is used to
denote not Christ but the divine message concerning him (Heb. 1:3; 4:12;
6:5; 13:7).

Study all the references to the Word of God in Hebrews.
Father, for all that the Word of God means—thank you with all my heart.

Flesh and blood has not revealed this to you, but my Father who is in heaven.
Matthew 16:17

Since the New Testament represents an advance on the Old, may we speak of revelation as "progressive"? It all depends on what we mean by that word. If our meaning is simply that God's Old Testament utterances, however diverse, all contributed in one way or another to his build-up for the coming of his Son, the word is acceptable enough. But much liberal theology has used the word "progressive" to express the idea that the history of revelation is really the history of how Israel's thoughts of God evolved from something very crude (a tribal war-god) through something more refined (a moral Creator) to the conception of God taught by Jesus (a loving Father); and has set forth this idea in such a way as to imply that Christians need not bother with the Old Testament at all, since all that is true in its view of God can be learned from the New Testament, and all the rest of what it says about him is more or less false.

But this is not so. God was certainly amplifying men's knowledge about himself throughout the revelatory process, but the idea that what was revealed later contradicts and cancels what was revealed earlier is wrong. So is the widespread neglect of the Old Testament to which this idea has led. The New Testament revelation always rests on the Old as its foundation, and to remove the foundation once the superstructure is in place is the surest way to dislodge the superstructure itself. Those who neglect the Old Testament will never make much of the New.

Later revelation, far from conflicting with what had gone before, presupposed and built on it at each stage. This idea is best expressed by calling the revelatory process cumulative rather than progressive.

Can parents learn anything from God's cumulative revelation to his people about the way to bring up their children?
Lord, help me to keep building a true picture of you from your revelation.

We impart this in words not taught by human wisdom but taught by the Spirit, interpreting spiritual truths to those who possess the Spirit.
1 Corinthians 2:13

Inspiration took many psychological forms. Here as elsewhere God showed himself a God of variety. The basic form of the process was *dualistic* inspiration, in which the recipient of the revelation remained conscious throughout of the distinction between himself and God. The inspiration that produced the Old Testament prophetic oracles, the Mosaic laws, and the apocalyptic visions of Daniel and John (in Revelation) was of this kind.

Lyric inspiration was that in which the inspiring action of God fused with, concentrated, intensified, and shaped the mental processes of the poet. This produced the Psalms, the lyrical drama of Job, the Song of Solomon, and the many great prayers that we find scattered throughout the historical books.

In *organic* inspiration, the inspiring action of God coalesced with the mental processes—inquiring, analytical, reflective, interpretive, applicatory—of the teacher, seeking to distill and pass on knowledge of the facts and right thoughts about them. This type of inspiration produced the historical books of both Testaments, the apostolic letters, Proverbs, and Ecclesiastes.

There was nothing to prevent the same man from being the medium at different times of different forms of divine inspiration, and it seems clear that all three were combined in the highest degree in the inspiration of Jesus himself.

Why is it important to understand the different forms of inspiration?
Thank you, Lord, that you used unique individuals with their God-given gifts to be the human agents of your divine inspiration of the Bible, your written Word.

Vanity of vanities, says the Preacher, vanity of vanities! All is vanity.
Ecclesiastes 1:2

Look, says the preacher, at the sort of world we live in. Take off your rose-colored spectacles, rub your eyes, and look at it long and hard. What do you see? You see life's background set by aimlessly recurring cycles in nature. You see its shape fixed by times and circumstances over which we have no control. You see death coming to everyone sooner or later, but coming haphazardly, seemingly without distinguishing between good and evil. Men die like beasts, good men like bad, wise men like fools. You see evil running rampant; swindlers and liars get ahead in business, good men don't. Seeing all this, you realize that God's ordering of events is inscrutable; as much as you try to discover it, you cannot.

But once you conclude that there really is no rhyme or reason in things, what profit (value, gain, point, purpose) can you find in any sort of constructive endeavor? If life is senseless, then it is valueless, and in that case, what use is it working to create things, to build a business, to make money, even to seek wisdom? For none of this can do you any obvious good; it will only make you an object of envy; you can't take any of it with you; and what you leave behind will probably be mismanaged after you have gone.

What point is there, then, in sweating and toiling at anything? Must not all man's work be judged "vanity and a striving after wind"? It is to this pessimistic conclusion, says the preacher, that optimistic expectation of finding the divine purpose of everything will ultimately lead us. Be realistic, says the preacher; face these facts; see life as it is. You will have no true wisdom till you do.

Facing facts can either lead us to pessimism or deeper trust in God—depending on what?

Lord, thank you that the facts I face are not just what I see and hear all around me, but also what you are doing and going to do.

I said to myself, "Come now, I will make a test of pleasure; enjoy yourself." But behold, this also was vanity.
Ecclesiastes 2:1

The writer of Ecclesiastes tested the pleasures of life by tasting them (Eccles. 2:1–11).

He tried fun and games and drink (vv. 1–3); then he went into construction, home building, and estate management (vv. 4–6). Next he piled up possessions—male and female slaves, herds and flocks, silver, gold, and other treasures (vv. 7–8); whatever he wanted he took. But he still remained unsatisfied in the end, although the work had been enjoyable while it lasted. (vv. 9–11).

This is surely true of many lives. We enjoy doing things so we respond to a challenge and work hard and perhaps we make money, build up a firm, and acquire a mansion for ourselves. It's fun doing it but when it's over we discover that it was only "a striving after wind." It has not brought us joy. It has brought us comfort, certainly, but there's more to joy than not suffering discomforts; there needs to be the sense that life in itself is worthwhile, that we are significant.

If we look for meaning and significance in the pleasures of life, we shall be disappointed because we'll be looking in the wrong place. Pleasures promised by achievement cheat us: we think we're going to get endless satisfaction out of them once we've "made it"—but we don't. Instead we find that, as Marie Antionette said, when you have everything nothing *tastes*. The more you have of this world's delights, the less delightful you find them when you stop and think.

What gives my life meaning and significance?
Turn your thoughts into praise and ask God to help you to go more confidently about your daily life as you remember how significant you are in God's eyes.

I saw all the oppressions that are practiced under the sun.
Ecclesiastes 4:1

In Ecclesiastes chapter 4, the writer looks around God's world and reports what he sees.

First he sees the miseries of oppression (vv. 1–3). On one side there are the oppressed—crying and in pain, with no one to comfort them; on the other are the oppressors who have power on their side and are able to treat others like dirt—so much that the powerless and crushed might feel it would be better never to have lived.

Then he sees the rat race of life (vv. 4–8). "I saw that all toil and all skill in work comes from a man's envy of his neighbor." One of the great motivations in life is envy, jealousy, pride, and the resolve to do better than someone else. But a life full of energetic activity motivated by jealousy will never lead to satisfaction.

Next he sees loneliness in God's world (vv. 9–12). The central thought of the paragraph is the sadness of the person who's alone: when he falls, there's no one to pick him up (v. 10). When he's in trouble, there's no one to stand by him. There are people like this in God's world and in his family, the Christian church.

Finally, he sees the miseries of life's ups and downs (vv. 13–16). The writer is probably referring to an actual incident when he speaks of the "old and foolish king, who will no longer take advice, even though he had gone from prison to the throne or in his own kingdom had been poor." When he rose to power, he became proud and pig-headed. What will happen? In due course he will be displaced by a poor wise youth who in turn will be displaced and forgotten too. Life has its ups and downs for everyone, and the higher they rise, the harder they fall.

What are your feelings and thoughts about what you see of the problems of life? *Lord, not a lot has changed since the days of Ecclesiastes. There's still oppression, loneliness, the rat race, ups and downs. . . How can I be in but not of all this?*

All the toil of man is for his mouth, yet his appetite is not satisfied.
Ecclesiastes 6:7

In chapter 6 of Ecclesiastes the writer says first that a man who lives long and well but does not enjoy life's good things is worse off than an unborn child. Both he and the unborn child go to the same place, but he goes less happy (vv. 3–6).

Then he makes the generalization that even a person who works hard to feed himself will still have an unsatisfied appetite (v. 7). So "what advantage has the wise man over the fool?" (v. 8). He then comments that realism is better than fantasy; living on fantasies is another example of "vanity and a striving after wind" (v. 9).

Now comes a sort of summary. "Whatever has come to be has already been named, and it is known what man is, and that he is not able to dispute with one stronger than he. The more words, the more vanity, and what is man the better? For who knows what is good for man while he lives the few days of his vain life, which he passes like a shadow? For who can tell man what will be after him under the sun?" (vv. 10–12). In other words: What's the use of wisdom if life's like this? We can't make sense of it. These are the bitterest verses in Ecclesiastes, pulling together all the feelings of futility that the first half of the book has laid out for inspection and treatment.

But now, in the second half, this writer will tell his readers: Seek wisdom, value wisdom, and you'll be on the road to joy, however bitter and pessimistic the feelings you may have as you start the journey, and however many more miseries you may meet en route. It is to joy, not gloom that he aims to lead us.

Be on the lookout for this bitter mood either in yourself or in the people you meet, read about in books and newspapers, hear on the radio, or watch on television. *Pray for these people, that God will guide them to the path of wisdom and joy.*

Remember. . . your Creator in the days of your youth.

Ecclesiastes 12:1

The writer of Ecclesiastes answers his basic question, "How can life be joy?" in the last chapters of the book. He hints at three secrets of joy which are spelled out more fully in the New Testament. The secrets of joy are to love yourself, your neighbor, and your God. Loving our neighbor as we should is not possible until we have learned to love ourselves; loving ourselves as we should is not possible until we have learned to love our God; and love for God would not be possible except that God in the first place loves us and set value on us as those whom he made and redeemed and brought into his family.

So the first secret of joy is to love God. This is the thought that the writer, in his low-key way, is expressing when he says, "Remember. . .your Creator in the days of your youth." In other words: Right now, while you've still got all your energy and strength, be energetic in serving God who has done so much and given so much to bless you. There are conversions late in life, but it's sad when a person has to live his last days in regret that he didn't come to love the Lord sooner so that he might have served him with the energy of his youth. In both Old and New Testaments serving God was a part of loving him—as was fearing him: "Fear God, and keep his commandments" (v. 13). This is a fear that has nothing to do with being frightened. It is an expression of the love which adores, worships, and stands in awe, remembering the greatness of God and the smallness of ourselves.

Old Testament Israelites loved the Lord because he loved them and brought them out of captivity in Egypt. Christians love the Lord because he loved them and redeemed them from captivity to sin and from that eternity without God toward which we were all heading.

Is my life lacking in joy? How much am I loving God?
Lord, show me day by day what it means to love you with all my heart, soul, mind, and strength (Mark 12:30).

Cast your bread upon the waters... Give a portion to seven, or even to eight.
Ecclesiastes 11:1–2

The second secret of joy is to love your neighbor (Ecclesiastes 11:1-6). The key verses in this passage are quoted above. They picture open-handed generosity which sees need all around and takes risks in trying to meet it. You cast your bread on the waters. You give to the needy from which you can't by any human standard of calculation expect any return. Remember the parable of the talents and the man who was so afraid of ending up empty-handed that he did nothing, except bury his talent in the ground? When his master returned, he was not commended, as he had expected to be, but severely censured and told that he had been unfaithful. By doing nothing, so that he risked nothing, he had achieved nothing; and our Lord cares nothing for do-nothing disciples.

There ought to be real exuberance, real willingness to take risks, in the way that we labor to help and serve others. True Christians will be found constantly doing things which seem imprudent in the service of others. The worldly-wise will warn: "You do that and you'll go bankrupt. You do that and what's going to happen to your home? Or your reputation?" But that's not the spirit of the free-hearted, open-handed, risk-taking generosity to which we are called (Luke 6:30). We shouldn't ask whether there is enough in the fridge to warrant our feeding the hungry. We should do it because the need is there, even if we then have to go hungry ourselves, for that is the spirit we are to catch and express: the spirit that's willing to take the risk of extending and even over-extending ourselves to meet our neighbor's need. The first Christians had that spirit (Acts 2:44–45; 4:34–35). We must have it too.

For meditation and possible action: "The best thing to do is to burn your bridges behind you, make things inevitable, and then go ahead. That's how you catch the spirit of risky, audacious, enterprising love."
Lord, help me today to be liberal, open-handed, generous, and free in loving my neighbor.

Light is sweet, and it is pleasant for the eyes to behold the sun.
Ecclesiastes 11:7

The third secret of joy is to love yourself, in the sense of allowing yourself to enjoy life's enjoyable things (Eccles. 11:7–10). In these verses the writer throws light on how we can be happy with our lot each day, despite its particular strains and pains. We should practice enjoyment and be enthusiastic about everyday delights. It's better to be alive than not. In the earlier part of the book the writer, modeling the man who had done and tried everything, said that he hated life because none of his achievements had brought him any satisfaction and he felt cheated. But the right-minded person, the writer now tells us, doesn't hate life. He remembers that "light is sweet, and it is pleasant for the eyes to behold the sun. For if a man lives many years, let him rejoice in them all" (vv. 7–8).

When the writer says, "All that comes is vanity," he means that life will likely not be quite as you expected nor bring you all that you hoped for. Nonetheless we can and should rejoice as we live the life that God gives us. For life is good. There is color, light, warmth, and beauty in God's world; there are people who say and do kind things; life brings many delightful moments if we're on the lookout for them.

It is part of Christian wisdom to live enthusiastically, realistically expecting that much will go wrong and feel pointless, but at the same time heartily enjoying every delight that God gives us each day. This is good advice for all of us, but the writer particularly applies it to young people (vv. 9–10).

Do you agree that you should love yourself? If so, in what sense and on what grounds?

Lord, open up and quicken all my senses and my heart and mind to perceive and respond to everything and everyone that reflects in any way your love, truth, or creativity.

Seek first his kingdom and his righteousness, and all these things shall be yours as well.
Matthew 6:33

Jesus tells his disciples that he doesn't want them to be anxious or over-occupied about material possessions (Matt. 6:25–34). This does not mean we're to be lazy: elsewhere in the New Testament we are told to work hard and honestly and provide for those who depend on us (2 Thess. 3:10; Eph. 4:28; 1 Tim. 5:8). But it does mean that these things must not take priority over our relationship with God.

Martha lost sight of this priority. When Jesus and his disciples came to visit, she as hostess wanted to put on a good show and cook them a lovely meal. There was nothing wrong with that, but it forced her to postpone her own top priority. Mary pursued that priority as she sat and listened to Jesus. When Martha was annoyed and asked Jesus why he didn't tell Mary to come and help her, Jesus answered that while she (Martha) worried about many things (i.e., the routines of hospitality), Mary chose the one thing which takes priority over everything else. Martha should be glad to shoulder the kitchen work and allow Mary that privilege rather than try resentfully to deprive her of it.

It's easy to fall into the trap of constant busyness and to tell ourselves that other things are more important than our communion with God. Actually, nothing is more important. William Temple said that we tend to think that conduct is the most important thing and prayer is an aid to acting right, whereas in truth prayer is the most important thing and our conduct is an index to the quality of our praying. We are to put first things first, trusting God to take care of our needs, refusing to let anxiety about them occupy the forefront of our lives, and making the quest to know and please God our first concern.

What I really want above all else for myself and those whom I love is...(finish the sentence honestly).
Ask God to help you keep/choose the right priorities.

Jesus said . . . "My food is to do the will of him who sent me, and to accomplish his work."

John 4:34

At the level of motivation and attitudes, Jesus is a yardstick of what it means to be fully human. There is something really sub-human about failure to love God and other people as he did. Only as we set ourselves to imitate Christ at this level are we fulfilling and developing—as distinct from violating and diminishing—our own human nature, which is already much diminished through sin; and only in this way can we find true joy, which is always integrally bound with a sense of fulfillment. When Jesus said that his food was to do the will of him who had sent him and to accomplish his work, he was testifying to the joy which he found in his Father's service—service which was the fulfilling of his nature as the Son, and also and equally the fulfilling of his nature as man.

For us, as for Jesus, full realization of all that potential which is distinctively human (a realization which is both the heart of freedom and the height of joy) is found not in self-will, but in service to God (which for us means serving the Son with the Father, and others for the Lord's sake). Other paths may bring temporary pleasure but they lead neither to fulfillment nor to freedom nor to joy; and enlargement of our experience will be little enough compensation for the shrinkage of our real humanity.

Can I echo Jesus' words at all?
Lord, enlarge my experience of you so that I may grow in true humanity.

Do not grieve the Holy Spirit of God.
Ephesians 4:30

Be filled with the Spirit.
Ephesians 5:18

The plea against grieving the Spirit is a witness both to the Spirit's personhood and to the fact that divine holiness is his nature. As with the first and second person of the Godhead so with the third: some ways of behaving please him and others distress and offend him. In the second category come bitterness, wrath, anger, clamor, slander, malice, and stealing (Eph. 4:28,31), and in fact any other transgressions of moral law. For Christians to fall into these sins directly thwarts his purpose and spoils his work of making us Christlike. Knowledge that our bodies are temples of the Spirit and that this "gracious, willing guest" is hard at work in our hearts to sanctify us should induce reverent awe and quickly shame us out of all moral laxity (1 Cor. 6:19; Phil. 2:12).

To dissuade us against grieving the Spirit, the Bible calls us to the positive counterpart—to be filled with the Spirit. The words imply a constant obligation. "Filled" conveys the thought of being wholly concerned with and wholly controlled by the realities which the Spirit makes known, and the ideal of life to which he points us. From what source should satisfaction be sought? Not from indulgence to alcohol (the worldly person's way of raising his enjoyment level), but from being occupied entirely with the Spirit's concerns. Then we shall have something to sing about, for the gratified Holy Spirit will sustain in us a joy which the worldly person never knows (Eph. 5:18–20).

Are the Christians in your church fellowship noted for their joy? It's all very well to claim deep inner joy but no one will believe us if our faces habitually show tension, strain, and discontent.
Lord, my flesh is weak but my spirit is willing for your Spirit to fill every part of my being.

When I am afraid, I put my trust in thee.
Psalm 56:3

Fear takes many forms. There is fear of the consequences of the past. There is fear of the unknown future. There is fear of the relationships in which we are involved and of the people to whom we have to relate. And some are afraid of what it will cost them to follow God. They realize that God is calling them and that his call requires them to break with the way they have been living. They see that they are going to lose on the deal, at least in human terms, and they are not quite sure that they can face that.

What people facing the problem of fear need to know is the adequacy of God to support, to help, to strengthen them for his service, to carry them through pressures, strains, pains, and to turn their material loss to spiritual gain.

Paul preached the adequacy of God from the cross. "He who did not spare his own Son but gave him up for us all, will he not also give us all things with him?" (Rom. 8:32).

The fact that he has given us the greatest gift at the cross, his own Son to die for us, guarantees that he will give us "all things"—everything else we need and everything he can devise that makes our ultimate happiness.

The most fearful people are usually the most imaginative ones. Have you ever sought for God to be Lord of your imagination and restore it, along with the rest of your personality, to healthy and creative functioning?
Lord, I have this problem with fear... How can I trust you when I'm afraid? It's a human impossibility. But with you all things are possible.

I honor my Father. . .I do not seek my own glory.
John 8:49–50

Godliness is the quality of life which exists in those who seek to glorify God. The godly man does not object to the thought that his highest vocation is to be a means of God's glory. Rather, he finds it a source of great satisfaction and contentment. His ambition is to follow out the great formulas in which Paul summed up the practice of Christianity: "Glorify God in your body"; "whether you eat or drink, or whatever you do, do all to the glory of God" (1 Cor. 6:20; 10:31). His dearest wish is to exalt God with all that he is, in all that he does.

Like God himself, the godly man is supremely jealous that God, and God only, should be honored. Indeed this jealousy is a part of the image of God in which he has been renewed. There is now a doxology written on his heart, and he is never so truly himself as when he is praising God for the glorious things that he has done already and pleading with him to glorify himself further.

We may say that it is by his prayers that he is known—to God, if not men. Prayer in secret is the mainspring of the godly man's life. And when we speak of prayer, we are not referring to prim, proper, stereotyped, self-regarding formalities which sometimes pass for the real thing. The godly man does not play at prayer, for his heart is in it. Prayer to him is his chief work. And the burden of his prayer is always the same, the expression of his strongest and most constant desire: that God will be glorified.

Look up Psalm 21:13; 57:5; John 12:28; Matthew 6:9.
Make these verses the basis of your prayer and worship.

*Be fruitful and multiply, and fill the earth and subdue it; and have dominion over
the fish of the sea and over the birds of the air and over every living thing that moves
upon the earth.*

Genesis 1:28

The Manichean idea was that the material world is evil and worthless. Our
dealings with it should therefore be cut down to a bare minimum. True spirituality means living as much out of the world as possible; holiness is to be
defined in terms of abstinence from needless traffic with created things.
Nothing is gained from the study of anything here below, and the less interest we have in the world around us, the better for our souls.

Such "spirituality" is in no way Christian, yet it constantly appears in the
Christian church. Some people still cherish the idea that constructive
thought about the world's contents and problems is no part of a Christian's
business; or they keep their Christian faith and their secular studies locked
up in separate compartments in their minds, seeing no need or obligation to
bring the two together for their mutual enrichment. The zeal of Christians
who have such negative attitudes is undoubted but it is no wonder if they
strike others as queer fish, only half-alive and oddly under-developed.

The Manichean attitude is altogether wrong. God forbids Christians to
lose interest in his world. He made people to rule the created order; we are
to have dominion over it and to use it for God's glory, and therefore we may
and must study its contents and problems. This belongs to our vocation
both as humans and Christians.

Isn't it vital (especially for young people) to discover what lines of approach Scripture takes to history, natural science, philosophy, psychology, and other "secular"
studies? Are we doing anything about this?
*Pray for any young people you know who feel split in two, asking that they will be
encouraged to press on and develop a Christian worldview.*

Do not be anxious about your life, what you shall eat or what you shall drink, nor about your body, what you shall put on.
Matthew 6:25

Read again Jesus' words about anxiety concerning material things (Matt. 6:24–35) and note the reasons he gives why we should not and need not adopt such an attitude.

Anxiety about such things destroys a sense of proportion. While we are worrying about food and clothing, we cannot be appreciating and revelling in God's great gift of life.

Anxiety also destroys spiritual perception. While we are absorbed with our worries, we cannot be conscious of the value which God places on us. If he cares for the birds, can't we trust our heavenly Father to provide for our needs?

Next comes a commonsense argument. You can't change the situation by worrying ("Which of you by being anxious can add one cubit to his height, or span of life?") (v. 27), so what's the point of doing it?

Finally—and this is the clincher—as well as being pointless, worry over things is needless. The same God who clothes the flowers and the grass with glory will surely give us, his children, the clothing, food, and drink that we need.

Jesus calls his disciples "men of little faith" and this indicates what the anxiety stems from: namely, unbelief. If we really believed in God's promises and his relationship to us as a loving, generous, caring father, we wouldn't be full of anxious thoughts. Instead we would seek first his kingdom (the life of salvation, obedience, and fellowship) and his righteousness (his daily will), and trust God for all our needs. He wants us to do that and get on with each day's business, rejoicing in the knowledge that he will be looking after us throughout our life in this world until he takes us home to glory.

What are you anxious about now?
Hand each anxiety to God in words and perhaps in some symbolic way too.

You shall love the Lord your God. . . with all your mind.
Matthew 22:37

When Christ enjoins us, as part of the first commandment, to love God with all our minds, he is telling us to use our minds not merely to study biblical doctrine by itself in a vacuum, as it were, but to apply that doctrine to the facts of God's world as we know them so that we may interpret them rightly and in all things discern the mind and will of God.

Christians are forbidden to lose interest in God's world. The biblical faith is given to us not merely to show us how to secure heaven but also to provide us with the principles of creative and imaginative living here and now. We are to use the minds he gave us in applying revealed truth to the whole of life, in order that all may be sanctified.

We are certainly to be detached from the world in the sense that we are not to regard it as our true home nor to look to it for our true reward. That is the genuine Christian "other-worldliness" of the person who can say, "For me to live is Christ" (Phil. 1:21). But equally, we must not turn our backs on the world and lose interest in it. God cares about it and so must we.

This will mean being prepared to think about the pressing problems of our time—race relations, industrial relations, the world food supply, and the threat of nuclear war. It will also mean that as we seek to win others for Christ we will need to face their individual difficulties. Christian witness involves more than throwing clumps of prearranged texts at unbelieving heads; it means sitting down beside those whom we want to help and thinking through their problems with them.

Am I prepared to love God with my mind in these ways?
Lord, make me both unafraid to think and concerned and involved enough to do so.

Blessed are the poor in spirit, for theirs is the kingdom of heaven.
Matthew 5:3

The word translated as "poor" is a good deal stronger in the Greek: it means, literally, "beggars." A beggar is bankrupt, destitute, and beyond self-help; he has no resources, no prospects, and no hope in and of himself. What Jesus is saying is: "Blessed (happy, fortunate, to be envied, and regarded as privileged) are the spiritual beggars; those so aware of and humbled by their own spiritual destitution that they're prepared to admit their need openly." Here Jesus is challenging the idea prevalent in Judaism that a Jew, as one of God's covenant people, would be in a position to earn God's favor. The truth is that none of us has any plea, anything in our favor, anything to commend us, anything to offer. We are all "guilty, vile, and helpless."

The kingdom of heaven is a new life, a new order of things, a new lifestyle. We come into the kingdom by receiving Jesus as both Savior and King of our lives. Life in the kingdom is a life of sustained repentance, just as it's a life of sustained faith and joy in our new relationship with God. Sometimes Jesus talks about the kingdom as a present reality (Matt. 5:3,10); sometimes as a future reality (Matt. 5:20). But the relationship which makes us partakers of the kingdom is the same, although it will be a marvelously enriched one in heaven. And this relationship is for none other than the poor in spirit, the spiritual beggars, who respond to Jesus as their divine Savior and Lord and are accepted by God the Father for Jesus' sake.

For meditation/thanksgiving: Beggars *can* be choosers. They can remain sitting by the roadside or they can come to Jesus as they are at any moment.
Lord, are you, through my present experiences, wanting me to realize my own spiritual bankruptcy—apart from you—in every area of my life?

Blessed are the meek, for they shall inherit the earth.
Matthew 5:5

The meek are those who know themselves to be poor in spirit, who have
learned, honestly and from their hearts, to regret all the dehumanizing and
subhuman things in which they have been involved as wanderers in this lost
world, and who now in humility want only the will of God. "Moses was
very meek, more than all men that were on the face of the earth" (Num.
12:3). His meekness was shown in his acceptance of what God ordained,
including endless battles with those recalcitrant and disappointing people
whom he was trying to lead from Egypt to Canaan, including, even, the
enormous disappointment of himself not getting into the Promised land.

Moses was a man with a fierce temper—it was this which had betrayed
him during the time in the wilderness—but when God said, in effect, "Now
look, Moses, in order to teach the whole world how much loss sin can
bring, I'm not going to let you enter the land; the people will go in, but you
won't," he did not curse God in furious protest; quietly, if sadly, he accepted
God's decision. That's meekness. Meekness, for a child of God, means accepting uncomplainingly what comes, knowing that it comes from the
hand of God who orders all things. What he sends, we accept in faith even
if it hurts, knowing that it's for our and others' good.

Those who are meek—that is, prepared to forego their rights in this
world, if that's what God requires of them—will inherit the earth: they will
be made infinitely rich in the future. I think Jesus was referring to the riches
of heaven more than to earthly blessings when he spoke, echoing Psalm
37:11, of inheriting the earth. Mercies promised in earthly from in the Old
Testament regularly turn out to have celestial content in the New.

Meekness is not a form of weakness; it consists of a willingness to accept whatever
God sends—and this calls for the strength that comes from God. Can you agree,
both in theory and from experience?
Is there anything I need to accept instead of resisting?

In the year that King Uzziah died I saw the Lord sitting upon a throne.
Isaiah 6:1

Read the whole of Isaiah chapter 6. Today and in the next four days we will
focus particularly on the truths about God which Isaiah shows us. Holiness, which in the broadest sense signifies all that distinguishes God from
men, is the proper biblical term for the blend of these truths.

First, God is the Lord. Isaiah saw a visual symbol of lordship: God
seated on a throne. It must have been a vast throne because Isaiah tells us,
"His train filled the temple," and the holy place of the temple was approxi-
mately sixty feet by thirty feet and forty-five feet high.

The vision of God as King, whether perceived visually or only with the
mind's eye, recurs frequently in the Bible. Psalm after psalm proclaims that
God reigns. John saw "a throne...in heaven, with one seated on the
throne" (Rev. 4:2). Micaiah "saw the LORD sitting on his throne" (1 Kings
22:19) and was therefore not cowed when he saw kings Ahab and Je-
hoshaphat sitting on their thrones in the gate of Samaria (1 Kings 22:10).
The vision of God on the throne had made plain to Micaiah who was in
charge.

This vision of God's sovereign providence is enormously strengthening.
To know that nothing happens in God's world apart from God's will may
frighten the godless, but it stabilizes the saints, assuring them that God has
everything worked out and that everything that happens has a meaning,
whether or not we can see it at the time. Peter, speaking of the cross, told
his hearers that they were guilty of putting Christ to death and needed to
repent of that, but he left them in no doubt that it would not have happened apart from the will of God (Acts 2:23). Knowing that God is on the
throne upholds us under pressure and in the face of bewilderment, pain,
hostility, and events that seem to make no sense.

Before you pray, alone or with others, focus on some verse or passage that highlights God as Lord and King.
Pray, remembering that you are coming to a king and may bring "large petitions."

I saw the Lord. . . high and lifted up. . . Above him stood the seraphim; each had six
wings: with two he covered his face, and with two he covered his feet, and with two
he flew.

                                                        Isaiah 6:1–2

The second truth about God in this chapter, and a second aspect of his holiness, is his greatness. The vision was of God "high and lifted up," with the six-winged seraphs hovering before him in worship. Every bit of the description of each has something to teach us.

To start with, two wings covering each angel's face is a gesture that expresses *reverent restraint* in God's presence: the attitude of being content not to pry into what God has chosen to keep secret but to live by what one has heard him say. Reverence includes unwillingness to go a single step beyond what Scripture says. When we reach the outer limits of what Scripture tells us, it is time to stop arguing and start worshipping.

Two wings covering each angel's feet expresses the spirit of *self-effacement* in God's presence. This is also an aspect of true worship. Genuine worshippers want to blot themselves out of the picture, calling no attention to themselves, so that every mind and heart, starting with their own, can concentrate without distraction on God exclusively.

The third element in the angels' posture was that each hovered on two wings as humming-birds, ready to dart away—to go for God, to run his errands—just as soon as the command was given. That *readiness* also belongs to the spirit of true worship: we acknowledge the greatness of God by putting ourselves at his service.

Irreverence, self-assertion, and inaction frequently disfigure worship. Is my/our worship disfigured in any of these ways?
Lord, I want to forget about myself, concentrate on you, and worship you. . .

Holy, holy, holy, is the LORD of hosts; the whole earth is full of his glory.
Isaiah 6:3

Here is a third truth about God and a third aspect of his holiness: his near-ness or, to say it in long words, his omnipresence in manifestation.

"The whole earth is full of his glory." *Glory* means God's presence shown forth. Angels and also spiritually alert humans see God shining forth in every place and in every process. Nowhere can one escape from his pres-ence. For those who love to be in God's presence and have no desire to get away from it, this is good news; it is only bad news for those who would rather that God did not see or notice the things that they do.

Psalm 139 starts by celebrating God's nearness and his inexhaustive knowledge of who and what each believer is and ends with a plea that God, the searcher of hearts, would show the psalmist any sin that was in him so he might put it away. "Thou knowest when I sit down and when I rise up; thou discernest my thoughts from afar. Thou searchest out my path and my lying down, and art acquainted with all my ways . . . Search me, O God, and know my heart! Try me and know my thoughts! And see if there be any wicked way in me, and lead me in the way everlasting!" (Psalm 139:2–3,23–24).

This aspect of God's holiness will be an uncomfortable truth to anyone who is not willing to pray that prayer.

Meditate on Psalm 139.
Turn the psalm into prayer—praising God for his detailed knowledge of you and sharing honestly your feelings about this precious, awesome, humbling truth.

I said: "Woe is me! For I am lost; for I am a man of unclean lips, and I dwell in the
midst of a people of unclean lips; for my eyes have seen the King, the LORD of hosts!"
Isaiah 6:5

The fourth aspect of God's holiness in this chapter, the aspect that we often think of in isolation when his holiness is mentioned, is his purity. Isaiah perceived this purity, and the sense of being defiled and unfit for God's fellowship overwhelmed him. Sin is uncleanness in relation to God's purity, and just as Isaiah felt unclean before God when he thought of his sins, so will every right-minded person.

"I am a man of unclean lips," Isaiah said. He was thinking of his particular sins of speech. The Bible has much to say about such sins, for they show what is really going on in a person's heart (Luke 6:45). We use God's gift of speech to express malice and cut others down; we gossip (a practice which has been defined as the art of confessing other people's sins); we deceive and exploit, fool and betray people by lying to them; we cheapen life and ruin relationships by disgraceful, demeaning talk. Perhaps in delivering God's message, Isaiah the prophet had up to this point been more concerned to make a reputation as a preacher than to glorify God. If so, his lips were unclean because his heart had been wrong.

"I dwell in the midst of a people of unclean lips," Isaiah continued. In those words, perhaps, he was acknowledging that he had gone with the crowd, talked as they talked, been foul-mouthed and irreverent with others who were foul-mouthed and irreverent, and been led astray by bad examples. For the first time, maybe, he saw himself as the hypocritical conformist to the world's ways which he really was. In these words he expressed his shame at what he could now see.

Do you daily ask God to be Lord of your speech? Should you? It might be helpful to study the Bible passages about words, speech, and the tongue.
Lord, am I tolerating things your purity cannot tolerate? Show me . . .

*Then flew one of the seraphim to me, having in his hand a burning coal which he
had taken with tongs from the altar. And he touched my mouth and said: "Behold,
this has touched your lips; your guilt is taken away, and your sin forgiven."*
Isaiah 6:6–7

The fifth truth about God, and the final strand in the totality of his holiness, is his mercy—the purifying, purging mercy that Isaiah experienced
when he confessed his sin. The altar was the place of sacrifice and the coal
pictures the application of sacrifice—in New Covenant terms, the application of the shed blood of Jesus Christ to the guilty conscience. The initial
application is to the sore places of conscious guilt. Isaiah felt most keenly
his sins of speech, and therefore his lips were touched specifically. But just
as true conviction of sin is of general sinfulness as well as particular wrongdoing, so the angel's words meant that all Isaiah's sin, known and unknown, was atoned for (literally, taken out of God's sight).

The initiative here was God's, as it always is when people come to know
his grace. P.T. Forsyth used to insist that the simplest, truest, profoundest
notion of God's nature is *holy love*: the mercy that saves us from our sin,
not by ignoring it but by judging it in the person of Christ and so justifying
us justly. Isaiah, from his standpoint, would undoubtedly agree. Mercy acts
through the arranging, accepting, and applying of an atoning sacrifice. It is
almost unbelievably marvelous: it sounds too good to be true! But it is
really the deepest truth of all.

Have you ever experienced the purifying, purging mercy of God? Would you be
able to explain this in non-theological terms to someone else?
Pray for an opportunity to speak to someone in need of God's mercy.

*The grace of the Lord Jesus Christ and the love of God and the fellowship of the
Holy Spirit be with you all.*

2 Corinthians 13:14

It's loose and a bit dangerous to speak of God as a person. Jesus claimed to
be God the Son and prayed to a God in heaven whom he called Father. He
promised to send a second comforter or a paraclete (advocate, counselor,
friend, enabler, assistant, supporter): namely, the Holy Spirit who came at
Pentecost. So it might be more accurate to think of God as a tri-personal
person!

It would be a mistake to think that you cannot be a person unless you
have a body. There is a sense in which my body is me but there is also a
sense in which my body is not me. All sorts of things can go on in my active imagination which have nothing to do with my body, for instance. And
if *I* can have a personal life without a body, so can God.

We need to beware of any suggestion that God is less personal than we
are. C.S. Lewis tells the story of a girl who was brought up to believe that
personal images of God were crude and primitive and taught to think of
God as higher substance. Later she began to reflect on this and discovered
she was actually thinking of God as an infinitely extended rice pudding.
What was more, she detested rice pudding! If we don't think of God as fully
personal, we think of him as inferior to ourselves. The truth is that he is
more personal than we are, for personal existence is realized in personal relationships, and the mutual love-relationships between Father, Son, and
Holy Spirit are richer than any relationships that you and I ever know.

When you think of God, what do you have in your mind? A blank? An artist's impression of Jesus while he was on earth? Or what?
Lord, may your Spirit fill my mind with biblical, true images of you.

The Son of God... loved me and gave himself for me.
Galatians 2:20

God's love for sinners involves his *identifying himself with their welfare.*
Such identification is involved in all love: it is, indeed, the test of whether
love is genuine or not. If a father continues cheerful and carefree while his
son is getting into trouble, or if a husband remains unmoved when his wife
is in distress, we wonder at once how much love there can be in their relationship. For we know that those who truly love are only happy when
those whom they love are truly happy also. So it is with God in his love for
human beings.

God's end in all things is his own glory—that he should be manifested,
known, admired, adored. This statement is true but it is incomplete. It
needs to be balanced by a recognition that by giving his love to us, God has
voluntarily bound up his own final happiness with ours.

God was happy without man before man was made. He could have continued happy had he simply destroyed man after man had sinned. But he
set his love on particular sinners, and thus, by his own free voluntary
choice, he will not know perfect and unmixed happiness again till he has
brought every one of them to heaven. He has in effect resolved that henceforth for all eternity his happiness shall be conditional on ours. Thus God
saves not only for his glory but also for his gladness. This helps to explain
why there is joy (God's own joy) in the presence of the angels when a sinner
repents (Luke 15:10), and why there will be "rejoicing" when God sets us
faultless at the last day in his own holy presence (Jude 24).

Perhaps you've sung, "He has made me glad," but have you ever pondered the staggering truth that I can make him glad?
*"I cannot tell why he whom angels worship should set his love upon the sons of
men"—including me—but I'm so thankful that you do this, Lord!*

The people who know their God shall stand firm and take action.
Daniel 11:32

The action taken by those who know God is their *reaction* to the anti-God trends which they see operating around them. While their God is being defied or disregarded, they cannot rest. They feel they must do something; the dishonor done to God's name goads them into action.

This is exactly what we see happening in the narrative chapters of Daniel, where we are told of the exploits of Daniel and his three friends. They were men who knew God, and who in consequence felt compelled from time to time actively to stand out against the conventions and dictates of irreligion and false religion. Daniel in particular appears as one who would not let a situation of that sort slide, but felt bound to challenge it openly. Rather than risk possible ritual defilement through eating palace food, he insisted on a vegetarian diet, to the consternation of the prince of the eunuchs (Dan. 1:8–16). When Darius suspended the practice of prayer for a month (on pain of death), Daniel not merely went on praying three times a day, but did so in front of an open window, so everyone might see what he was doing (Dan. 6:10).

It is not that Daniel was an awkward, cross-grained fellow who luxuriated in rebellion and could only be happy when he was squarely against the government. It is simply that those who know their God are sensitive to situations in which God's truth and honor are being directly or tacitly jeopardized and, rather than let the matter go by default, will force the issue on people's attention and thereby seek to compel a change of heart about it— even at personal risk.

Are there any matters on which, for God's sake, I ought to stand firm and take action?
Lord, you know whether by nature I am a "Hamlet"—"thinking too precisely on the event"—or someone who is over-hasty. Guide and shape me.

I love thee, O LORD, my strength.
Psalm 18:1

Let Israel be glad in his Maker. . . Let them praise his name with dancing, making melody to him with timbrel and lyre! For the LORD takes pleasure in his people.
Psalm 149:2-4

There is an emotional element in the makeup of each human individual which calls to be expressed in any genuine appreciation and welcoming of another's love, whether it be the love of a friend or a spouse or the love of God in Christ. Charismatics understand this and their provision for exuberance of sight, sound, and movement in corporate worship caters to it. In the interests of decency, order, and perhaps social respectability, dead-pan physical restraint has long been the conventional way to express reverence in worship, at least in the English-speaking world; and any breach of this norm becomes at once suspect.

What makes charismatics more demonstrative, however, is not lack of reverence for God, but fullness of happy love for Jesus Christ and Christian people. Anyone who has shared in the holy hugging of charismatic congregations or seen, as I have, charismatic bishops dancing in church knows that.

Granted, charismatic forms of emotional expression can easily become an exhibitionist routine, but then cool bodily stillness, with solemn fixity of face, can equally easily be the expression of a frigid, heartless formalism. Between these two you may make your choice, but by scriptural standards there is no doubt that a disorderly liveliness, the overflow of love and joy in God, is preferable to a tidy deadness that lacks both. A living dog, after all, really is better than a dead lion (Eccles. 9:4).

What are the differences between emotion and emotionalism in worship?
I love you, Lord.

Who shall separate us from the love of Christ?...For I am sure that neither death, nor life...nor anything else in all creation, will be able to separate us from the love of God in Christ Jesus our Lord.

Romans 8:35,38–39

Nothing in creation can separate us from God's love: that is a permanent and eternal fact. Whatever may come our way, whether the heavens fall and the earth dissolves, or the bomb goes off, or the Lord returns, God will still be loving us and we shall still be enjoying that love.

Just as we shall never, not even in heaven, be more justified than we are on earth as believers in Christ, so we shall never be more secure—grasped as we are by the almighty, sovereign love of God, now and forever.

When a Christian slips into sin, does that separate him from the love of God? In the fundamental sense, the answer is no, because the Christian who is justified by faith has been accepted by God for all eternity into the divine family. So if he sins, he doesn't stop being a child of God; he just starts behaving like a bad child rather than a good one. His relationship with his father isn't destroyed, but it is spoiled until the wrong is acknowledged, forgiven, and set right. Bad children miss out on the good things that their parents are planning for them and need to be disciplined so that they may learn to be better children. So it is with God's children. But Christian prodigals, miserable as they make themselves, don't cease to be children of God or to be loved by him.

Have I really grasped this one unshakable ground of security and responded by being a loving, grateful child in the family of God?

Praise God in song or spoken words that "Things future, nor things that are now, nor all things below or above, can make him his promise forego, or sever my soul from his love."

The love of Christ controls us.
2 Corinthians 5:14

Paul is telling his readers that Christians are different from what other people are and from the way they themselves once were because the love of Christ controls them. He spells out this difference in 2 Corinthians 5:14–6:2.

First, our *motivation* in life has become different (5:14–15). We have been loved and claimed. Christ died for all so all must see themselves as having died—finished with the old life for good. The way of the world cannot be our way any longer. Christ must be Lord of our lives from now on.

Second, our *vision* of life has become different (5:16–17). We see people in a new way. Now we see Jesus, not as a human oddity, or only a figure in Palestinian history, but as a divine Savior, and we see other people as lost sinners.

Third, our *relation to God* has become different (5:18–19). Once we were at odds with God and he with us. But now God has reconciled us to himself and taken us into his service, giving us "the ministry of reconciliation" and "entrusting to us the message of reconciliation."

Fourth, our *relation to others* has become different (5:20–21; 6:1–2). Nobody ever approaches others in the way that we do. For we go to them as ambassadors for Christ, workers with God, God's persuaders, messengers from heaven, "God making his appeal through us." God has sent us to speak to others in his name and on behalf of his Son and it is as his spokesmen that "we entreat you not to accept (mentally) the grace of God in vain (without the active faith and repentance that saves)."

For thought: Lost sinners may not understand what I say, especially if I use Christian jargon such as "lost sinners," but they will watch what I do.
Lord, may your love affect my motivation, vision, and all my relationships today.

This is my commandment, that you love one another as I have loved you. Greater love has no man than this, that a man lay down his life for his friends.
John 15:12–13

Love in the Spirit (Col. 1:8) is surely the gratitude to God and the goodwill toward men by knowing the love of the Father, who gave the Son, and of the Son, who gave himself for our salvation.

Modeling itself on this divine love, love in the Spirit becomes a habit of self-giving service in which some element of a person's life is constantly being laid down for someone else's sake. Paul draws its profile in his letter to the Corinthians (1 Cor. 13:4–7). It has as its heart an ongoing altruism, a desire to see others made great, good, holy, and happy—a passion that this fallen world finds incomprehensible and which in itself is altogether supernatural. *Agapē* the regular New Testament word for it, was not used in this sense before Christianity appeared, and no wonder: the thing itself became known only through Christ. Now *agapē* is the identifying mark of those who, among the many who claim to know God, really and genuinely do (1 John 3:14–16; 4:7–11). It is no natural gift or development, but the supernatural fruit of the Spirit (Gal. 5:22), issuing from a heart that sees and knows the love of God through the Spirit.

Make a list of all the people whom you really desire to be "made great, good, holy, and happy."
Talk to God about some of these people and work out a time and place for regularly naming all these people, and your heart's desire for them, before God.

When I could bear it no longer, I sent that I might know your faith, for fear that somehow the tempter had tempted you and that our labor would be in vain.
1 Thessalonians 3:5

Pastoral love whereby an older Christian feels and carries responsibility for others (particularly younger Christians) is one of the costliest forms of Christian fellowship. Paul's pastoral love and what it cost him are seen in 1 Thessalonians 2:17–3:10. Such love is required of all of us, not just of Christian ministers. It brings deep concern and makes us deeply vulnerable: not being able to meet those whom we love, not knowing how they are managing under pressure, not knowing even whether our love is returned, hurts. As a rule, those who love most are hurt most.

There is, of course, another side. Pastoral love blossoms into joy and pride when the loved ones make progress, and the more love, the more joy. Paul knows that it is God, not himself, whom he must thank for his converts' faith and faithfulness, but the joy he has through knowing that he has not, under God, labored in vain, is real and honest and nothing to be ashamed of before God. To know that God has used you to bless others in a decisive way is joy indeed.

Far from exploiting the loved ones in its own interest, pastoral love identifies with their interests and is at their disposal. So Paul prays and is ready to work again for his converts' spiritual welfare. He encourages them when he tells them how the news of their steadfastness had ministered encouragement to him.

Do I have this kind of concern about those who come into the Christian family through me or my church?
Lord, help me to care for others way beyond my own self-interest or any desire to prove anything about myself to myself or to anyone else.

If we walk in the light, as he is in the light, we have fellowship with one another.
1 John 1:7

Christian fellowship is an expression of both love and humility; it springs from the wish to help and the wish to be helped; it is a corporate seeking by Christian people to know God better through sharing with each other what individually they have learned already. And here are three further truths about fellowship.

First, it is *a means of grace.* Through and in fellowship, our souls are refreshed and fed by the effort to communicate our knowledge of divine things, to help and pray for others, and to receive from God through them.

Second, fellowship is *a test of life.* Fellowship means opening our hearts to our fellow Christians. The person who discards pretense when talking with his fellow believers is the one who is being open and honest in his daily dealings with God. He is the one who is walking in the light.

Third, fellowship is *a gift of God.* "The grace of the Lord Jesus Christ and the love of God and *the fellowship of the Holy Spirit* be with you all" (2 Cor. 13:14). It is only where the Holy Spirit has been given, where we are spiritually alive to God and anxious to grow in grace ourselves and help others do the same, that true fellowship will be a possibility. It is only as the Spirit enables us that we shall actually be able to practice it.

Such fellowship can happen in preaching; as we pray together; in group Bible study; in talk between friends over a meal; in talk between husband and wife at home in the evening. But in every case, the Lord's presence and power will be realized through the words, attitudes, actions, and love of a fellow Christian (Matt. 18:20).

Lord, may the fellowship of the Holy Spirit be realized in my life and relationships today.
What sort of "marks" would my church fellowship get in this "test of life"?

The Son of man goes as it has been determined; but woe to that man by whom he is betrayed!
Luke 22:22

Scripture teaches us that as king, God orders and controls all things—human actions included—in accordance with his own eternal purpose. Scripture also teaches us that as judge he holds every person responsible for the choices he makes and the courses of action he pursues. Thus hearers of the gospel are responsible for their reaction. If they reject the good news, they are guilty of unbelief (John 3:18). Paul, entrusted with the gospel, is responsible for preaching it; if he neglects his commission, he is penalized for unfaithfulness (1 Cor. 9:16).

God's sovereignty and human responsibility are taught side by side in the same Bible. Sometimes, as in the verse at the beginning of this reading, they occur in the same verse.

What are we to do about this antinomy, this apparent incompatibility between two apparent truths?

We must accept it for what it is and learn to live with it. We must refuse to regard the apparent inconsistency as real and put down the semblance of contradiction to the deficiency in our own understanding. We must not think of the two principals as rival alternatives, but as, in some way which at present we do not grasp, complementary. We must be careful not to juxtapose them nor to make deductions from either that would cut across the other. We must use each within its own sphere of reference. We must note what connections exist between the two truths and their two frames of reference and teach ourselves to think of reality in a way that provides for their peaceful coexistence, remembering that reality itself actually has proved to contain both.

How does/should God's sovereignty and human responsibility affect our evangelism?

Lord, if I did not believe in your sovereignty, I might go frantic; if I did not believe in human responsibility, I might be feckless, cynical, defeatist.

The body does not consist of one member but of many.
1 Corinthians 12:14

Do not quench the Spirit.
1 Thessalonians 5:19

There are many hindrances to body life. We need to search our hearts to see if these are impeding the reality of body life in our churches.

Among the clergy, clericalism can impede body life. Clericalism is a conspiracy. It is a state of affairs in which the minister says, "You leave the spiritual ministry to me; that's my job." And the congregation says, "Yes, that's absolutely right, and so we will." Or the congregation may say to the minister, "We hired you to do the spiritual ministry. Get on with it." And the minister says what he should never consent to say: "I accept that, and so I will!" For those who serve God as clergy and pastors, it is necessary to challenge that conspiracy and decline to be a party to it—to insist on the principle of every-member ministry.

We should aim at the state of affairs reflected by a letterhead I once received. It stated first the name of the church, second, "ministers: the congregation," and third, "assistant to the ministers": the name of the pastor! That is how it should be in every church.

In another church I saw on the vestry door a little plaque saying, "Head Coach." That was right also!

Another hindrance to body life is formalism: the supposition that if you are doing things correctly, then all is well. That formal correctness will be an empty shell of church life, a barren sham, if the realities of body life are not there to back it up.

Self-sufficiency on the part of any in the congregation, standoffishness which is unwilling to open up to brother Christians, complacency within the church—these too will hinder body life. Be warned!

What is hindering me (us) from fully enjoying body life?
Meditate on the staggering concept that your church is Christ's body—his mouth, his hands, his feet—to its members and to a lost, needy world.

We are his workmanship, created in Christ Jesus for good works.
Ephesians 2:10

Just as God works to make a perfect whole out of his church (Eph. 5:25–27), so he is at work in the life of every individual Christian.

Imagine a site occupied by a functioning business. The buildings in which the firm works are being pulled down, one by one, and new and better buildings are being put up in their place, using materials that originally belonged to what was demolished. While this goes on, business continues as usual, except for various temporary arrangements which call for patience. The constant changes are wearisome to those who have to keep the business going and who are not always told in advance about each successive disruption.

But in fact the architect has a master-plan for all stages of the rebuilding and a most competent manager directs and oversees every step. On a day-to-day basis there always proves to be a way of keeping the business going. Thus each day those involved in the business can truly feel that they have fulfilled their responsibility to serve the public, even though it wasn't as perfect as they would have wanted it to be.

The site and the business that goes on there represent our lives. God is constantly at work on the site, demolishing our bad habits and forming Christlike habits in their places. The Father has a master-plan for this progressive operation. Christ, through the Spirit, is executing this plan on a day-to-day basis. Though it involves frequent disruptions of routine and periodic bewilderments as to what God is up to, the overall effect of the work continues to increase our capacity for serving God and others.

Can you personalize this general picture by filling in what bad habits God is demolishing in you and what disruptions and bewilderments you are facing?
Jesus, universe-creator, once carpenter of Nazareth, I trust you and put the building of my life and our church into your skillful, loving hands.

The thing that David had done displeased the LORD.
2 Samuel 11:27

The story of David and Bathsheba (2 Sam. chapters 11–12) has a very modern ring to it. David, we are told, was at home, although it was the time when kings went out to war. The implication there is that David ought not to have been taking things easy. As it was, Satan, who finds mischief for idle hands to do, found an object for David's idle eyes to light on. The king, from the roof of his palace, saw Bathsheba washing, liked what he saw, and wanted what he saw, thus breaking the tenth commandment ("You shall not covet your neighbor's wife"—Exod. 20:17).

So David sent for Bathsheba and very soon was breaking the seventh commandment ("You shall not commit adultery"—Exod. 20:14). Bathsheba became pregnant and David tried to cover up what he had done. He recalled Uriah, Bathsheba's husband, from the battlefield and tried to get him to sleep with his wife so that he would assume that the child was his. Uriah, being a faithful Israelite, committed to his friends in the field, declined to do this; he did not feel it right to have fun with his wife while his colleagues camped out, having no fun at all.

So David arranged for his murder, thus breaking the sixth commandment ("You shall not kill"—Exod. 20:13). Then, after all that, David apparently forgot what he had done. But "the thing that David had done displeased the LORD," and he sent Nathan the prophet to make David sharply aware of his guilt. And David, who was a real man of God, although a dreadfully backslidden one just then, responded with deep repentance (Ps. 51).

For thought: If a great man of God like David could be caught unaware and fall so deeply into sin, so could any of us.
Lord, I cannot trust myself in this situation. . . Deliver me from it or in it, I pray.

Beware of false prophets, who come to you in sheep's clothing but inwardly are ravenous wolves.
Matthew 7:15

In Matthew 7:15–20, Jesus warns his disciples against the false teachers who will surely come; they will seem harmless or even attractive, but inwardly they will be like wolves—savage, wild, and destructive.

The mark of the false prophet or teacher is self-serving unfaithfulness to God and his truth. It may be that he says what he shouldn't; but it is far more likely that he will err by failing to say what he should. He will gloss over all the tough questions and issues as did the false prophets in the Old Testament who went around saying, "Peace, peace," when there was no peace (Jer. 6:14). They wouldn't speak the tough word calling for repentance nor suggest that Israel was out of sorts spiritually. Instead they brought groundless comfort, lulling people into a false sense of security so that their hearers were totally unprepared for the judgment which eventually came on them.

There are teachers in the church today who never speak of repentance, self-denial, the call to be relatively poor for the Lord's sake, or any other demanding aspect of discipleship. Naturally they are popular and approved, but for all that, they are false prophets. We will know such people by their fruits. Look at the people to whom they have ministered. Do these folks really know and love the Lord? Are they prepared to take risks, even hazard their lives, for Jesus? Or are they comfortable, inactive, and complacent? If so, they are self-deceived, and those who have irresponsibly encouraged their self-deception will have to answer for it.

Anyone who is in a position of spiritual leadership who fails to teach the more demanding, less comfortable, "narrow gate" and "rough road" side of discipleship becomes a false prophet.

Are you/Is anyone you know in danger of turning into a false prophet? Pray very hard for yourself/that person. What action can you take?

Worthy art thou, our Lord and God, to receive glory and honor and power, for thou didst create all things, and by thy will they existed and were created.
Revelation 4:11

What is God's ultimate end in his dealings with his children? It is the glory of God himself. There is nothing morally dubious about this: if we believe that man can have no higher end than the glory of God, how can we say anything different about God himself? The idea that it is somehow unworthy to represent God as aiming at his own glory in all that he does, seems to reflect a failure to remember that God and man are not on the same level, and to show lack of realization that whereas a man who makes his own well-being his ultimate end does so at the expense of his fellow creatures, God has determined to glorify himself by blessing his creatures. He wills to display his resources of mercy in bringing his saints to their ultimate happiness in the enjoyment of himself.

How does this bear on the problem of providence? It gives us insight into the way God saves us and suggests the reason why he does not take us to heaven the moment we believe. We see that he leaves us in a world of sin to be tried, tested, belabored by troubles that threaten to crush us—in order that we may glorify him by our patience under suffering, and in order that he may display the riches of his grace and call forth new praises from us as he constantly upholds and delivers us. Psalm 107 is a majestic declaration of this.

Are there people who need to hear from me that the way they are handling their suffering is bringing glory to God's name from me and others who are observing them?

Lord, give me sensitivity toward anyone whom I may meet today who is feeling tried, tested, belabored, and maybe crushed.

Commune with your own hearts on your beds, and be silent.
Psalm 4:4

This is eternal life, that they know thee the only true God, and Jesus Christ whom thou hast sent.
John 17:3

The journey of our lives is a double journey. There is an outward journey into external confrontations, discoveries, and relationships, and there is an inner journey into self-knowledge and the discovery of what constitutes my individual self-expression, self-fulfillment, freedom, and contentment within. For the Christian, the outward journey takes the form of learning to relate positively and purposefully to the world and other people (to all God's creatures) for God the Creator's sake, and the inward journey takes the form of gaining and deepening our acquaintance with God himself and with Jesus the Son.

In the hustling, bustling West today, life has become radically unbalanced with education, business interests, the media, the knowledge explosion, and our go-getting community ethos all uniting to send people off on the outward journey as fast as they can go, distracting them from ever bothering about its inward counterpart.

Today in western Christianity the story is the same, so that most of us (without realizing it) are unbalanced activists, conforming most unhappily in this respect to the world around us. Like the Pharisees who were also great activists (Matt. 23:15) we are found to be harsh and legalistic, living busy complacent lives of conforming to convention, and caring much more, as it seems, for programs than for people.

Are my inward and outward journeys more or less balanced or are some adjustments needed? Do I need to reach *out* more or reach *in* more?
Lord, help me to rearrange my activities and priorities in the light of what I have learned from answering those questions.

Father, I desire that they also, whom thou hast given me, may be with me where I am, to behold my glory.

John 17:24

The experience of heaven will be a family gathering, as the great host of the redeemed meet together in face-to-face fellowship with their Father-God and Jesus their brother. This is the deepest and clearest idea of heaven that the Bible gives us. Many Scriptures point to it (Matt. 5:8; 1 John 3:2; Rev. 22:4; 1 Cor. 13:12; 1 Thess. 4:15).

It will be like the day when the sick child is at last able to leave the hospital and finds his father and the whole family waiting there to greet him—a family occasion, if ever there was one. "I see myself now at the end of my journey," said Bunyan's Mr. Stand-fast, as he stood halfway into Jordan's water. "The thoughts of what I am going to, and of the conduct that waits for me on the other side, doth lie as a glowing coal at my heart...I have formerly lived by hearsay and faith, but now I go where I shall live by sight, and shall be with him in whose company I delight myself."

What will make heaven *heaven* is the presence of Jesus and a reconciled divine Father who loves us for Jesus' sake no less than he loves Jesus himself. To see and know and love and be loved by the Father and the Son, in company with the rest of God's vast family, is the whole essence of the Christian hope. If you are a believer, and so a son or daughter, this prospect satisfies you completely. If it does not strike you as satisfying, it would seem that as yet you are neither.

Have you ever thought about heaven in terms of a joyous family gathering? Add that to your other "pictures" of heaven and think about it like that today as you go about your business.

Father, I praise you that as your adopted child, I can look forward to heaven as a completely happy family gathering.

To them (the saints) God chose to make known how great among the Gentiles are the riches of the glory of this mystery, which is Christ in you, the hope of glory.
Colossians 1:27

Man was made for hope and he withers and perishes without it. But there is no real hope apart from the knowledge of God through Jesus Christ. To have all one's hopes anchored in this passing world is pitiful, according to Scripture. To be worthwhile, our hope must be set on joys that last forever. Now Christ's Second Coming was the focus of hope for the early Christians. It is our own ultimate hope too, for it will mark our entry into fullest fellowship with him—which is heaven. We know very little about heaven, but I once heard a theologian describe it as "an unknown region with a well-known inhabitant," and there is not a better way to think of it than that.

Richard Baxter expresses the thought in these lines:

My knowledge of that life is small,

The eye of faith is dim,

But it's enough that Christ knows all,

And I shall be with him.

To those who have learned to love and trust Jesus, the prospect of meeting him face to face and being with him forever is the hope that keeps us going, no matter what life may throw at us.

Many people today ask in agony: What is life for? What meaning can it have when death ends it and may strike at any time? To these the Christian can and must answer: life was always intended to be a journey into joy, and death is just a stage in that journey. Faith in Jesus brings us into a relationship with God which makes it possible for us to face death with confidence and a glad heart because we know that being absent from the body means being present with the Lord (2 Cor. 5:8). To realize the meaning of death is to discover both life's meaning and hope's power.

Think of those you know or know about whose life in this world is such that their greatest longing is to be delivered from it.
Pray especially for those who do not yet have faith in Jesus and therefore have no hope in heaven. Lord, today I pray especially for...

Of that day or that hour no one knows, not even the angels in heaven, nor the Son, but only the Father.

Mark 13:32

The New Testament assures us that Jesus comes for all Christians at their time of death, to receive them to himself (John 14:3; Acts 7:55–60). But when the inspired writers look ahead, their eyes are not on this, but on Jesus' personal public return to judge the world, destroy death, and make all things new. It is a striking fact that this event (called the *parousia*, meaning "royal visit") is referred to on an average in every thirteenth verse of the New Testament and every tenth verse of the Epistles. "He shall come," says the creed, "to judge the living and the dead." The event is no doubt unimaginable but human imagination is no measure of divine power.

The time of Jesus' coming is hidden and the surrounding circumstances are left obscure, but what is certain is that we shall meet Jesus face to face and find, if our faith is real, both that we know him and that he knows us.

Meanwhile it is for us to "watch"—to be alert and ready (Mark 13:33–37)—and to let the prospect of one day standing before the Savior, whom we love without having seen (1 Pet. 1:8), spur us to holy living and faithful service. "Every one who thus hopes in him purifies himself as he is pure" (1 John 3:3).

If your first thought on waking each day were to be, "Jesus might come back to earth today," would it make a difference to the way you live? Try it and see.
Lord, help me to strike the balance of enjoying my present life (because it comes from your hand and you are with me in it) while "waiting for and hastening the coming of the day of God" (2 Pet. 3:12).

He who hears my word and believes him who sent me, has eternal life; he does not come into judgment, but has passed from death to life.
John 5:24

We must all appear before the judgment seat of Christ.
2 Corinthians 5:10

How can these two statements be fitted together? How does free forgiveness and justification by faith square with judgment according to works? The answer seems to be as follows.

First, the gift of justification shields believers from being condemned and banished from God's presence as sinners. This is made clear in the vision of judgment where alongside "the books" recording each man's works, the "book of life" is opened, and those whose names are written there are not "thrown into the lake of fire" (Rev. 20:11–15).

Second, the gift of justification does not at all shield believers from being assessed as Christians, and from forfeiting good which others will enjoy if it turns out that as Christians they have been mischief-makers or slack or destructive. This is made clear in Paul's warning to the Corinthians to be careful what lifestyle they build on Christ, the one foundation. "If anyone builds on the foundation with gold, silver, precious stones, wood, hay, stubble—each man's work will become manifest; for the Day will disclose it, because it will be revealed with fire...If the work which any man has built on the foundation survives, he will receive a reward. If any man's work is burned up, he will suffer loss, though he himself will be saved, but only as through fire" (1 Cor. 3:12–15). "Reward" and "loss" signify an enriched or impoverished relationship with God, though in what ways it is beyond our present power to know.

Study the Bible teaching about judgment according to *works* (e.g., Matt. 12:33–37;16:27; Rev. 20:11–15; Rom. 2:6–11; 2 Cor. 5:10; Luke 12:48).
Reflect on the truth that words and works are indices to a person's heart. Pray about your own area of weakness.

September 26

The family's future
A God who rewards

Your Father who sees in secret will reward you.
Matthew 6:4

Some people are surprised at Christ's teaching about rewards; they think it makes the Christian life sound mercenary. But we must not be super-spiritual about this; Jesus wouldn't! The reward motive is powerful, and he appeals to it. To understand his mind, however, we must remember that the rewards belong within the context of the family relationship between Christians and their heavenly Father.

Parents often reward children for doing things they ought to be doing anyway. They love to encourage and help the child. The reward comes as a gift, not a merit-badge. The child may not, strictly speaking, deserve it, but it will surely help him to go on doing what he should be doing (and that is why it is given). In the same way, we don't deserve rewards as Christians, but God knows our nature and generously encourages us.

C.S. Lewis differentiates between rewards that are of a different character from the activity which brought them about and those which consist in the perfection of that activity. If a man marries a woman for money, he is seeking the first sort of reward and we call him money hungry. But in a good marriage, the reward which the man has sought and found is simply that of being able to spend the rest of his life with the lady he loves.

The activity of which Matthew chapter 6 speaks is the service of God: looking toward him, reaching out to him, praising, praying, worshipping, adoring, loving, and obeying him, and thus enjoying fellowship with him. The reward for that is an ever-closer relationship with God himself. Hereafter we will not literally be walking around a place called heaven wearing heavy, jewel-studded gold bracelets: that picture is a pointer to something else. Our reward will be that for which we have been qualifying throughout our discipleship on earth: God's welcome, his "well done!" and the communication to us of his love in his immediate actual presence.

When Jesus speaks of rewards he is referring both to that final blessing and also to all the kindnesses and encouragement which our Father gives to his children as they seek him day by day (Heb. 11:6).

Think of Jesus "who for the joy that was set before him endured the cross" (Heb. 12:2).
What is my attitude to rewards? What rewards am I openly or secretly seeking right now?

*We must all appear before the judgment seat of Christ, so that each one may receive
good or evil, according to what he has done in the body.*
2 Corinthians 5:10

When I speak of our eternal destiny, I'm referring to that state of joy or grief
beyond death which I have learned from Jesus Christ, God's incarnate Son
who rose from the dead, and about which the authors of the New Testament all agree. I am not talking of survival as such but of a state in which
we consciously reap what we have actually sown.

The New Testament makes it plain that this life, in which bodies grow
old and wear out while characters get fixed, is an ante-chamber, dressing
room, and moral gymnasium where, whether we know it or not, we all
prepare ourselves for a future life which will correspond to what we have
each chosen to be, and will have in it more joy for some and distress for
others than this world ever knows.

When the world to come becomes a reality, the abiding consequences of
choices and commitments made here will be revealed and received. "He
(God) will render to every man according to his works: to those who by patience in well-doing seek for glory and honor and immortality, he will give
eternal life; but for those who . . . obey wickedness, there will be wrath and
fury" (Rom. 2:6–8). The wise person will keep in view this truth which his
own conscience will confirm to him if he lets it speak, and will not let himself fall victim to reactionary skepticism, even if others around him do so.

Am I aware enough of the world to come and of the sowing/reaping principle?
Lord, help me today and always to sow for the Spirit.

The words of the wise heard in quiet are better than the shouting of a ruler among fools.

Ecclesiastes 9:17

Oswald Chambers's exposition of Ecclesiastes (actually a set of transcribed talks) bears the title "Shade of His Hand," a phrase that comes from Francis Thompson's poem "The Hound of Heaven":

Halts by me that footfall:
Is my gloom, after all,
Shade of his hand outstretched caressingly?

The title is perfect for what the book contains. The hand of God is a very big one and when it's stretched over you, even with a purpose of protection, it may look and feel like a great black cloud, hiding the sun. Then your mood may well be one of darkness. The earlier part of the book of Ecclesiastes sets forth a classic sequence of such moods. In dark moods it's good to ask: "Is my gloom, after all, Shade of his hand outstretched caressingly?"—for frequently it is! Sometimes God lets moods of gloom come upon us for our good so that we may be brought to our senses, led to review our lives, and make some necessary changes. Self-absorption always produces gloom, and pleasure-keeping ends in disgust. Maybe we need to start living on a different basis. By loving our Creator and our neighbors more selflessly, we thereby find our own daily joy.

Oswald Chambers never finished his exposition. A few days after he uttered those gorgeous words (to troops in Egypt in 1917), he died of pneumonia. He was forty-three. Right at the end of his treatment of Ecclesiastes 11, he spoke of looking forward "to that great hour when we shall pass from beneath the shade of his hand into the full shine of his face."

The last word of wisdom and pointer to joy in this world is the realization that here God is preparing us for another world where his light will shine on us as it never did in this one. We need to remember that when we see the unfinished business and apparent wastage of potential all around us.

Is the place I'm in shaded in order to teach me something, or is it simply a protected place?
Lord, I feel exposed and unprotected. Shield me, I pray.

They will go away into eternal punishment, but the righteous into eternal life.
Matthew 25:46

We are told in the parable of the sheep and goats (Matt. 25:31–46) that those whom the judge rejects go away into *kolasis* (punishment) *aionios* (a final state). The phrase is balanced by the reference to *zoe aionios* (eternal life) which is also a fixed and final state. Even if this word *aionios* is believed to mean only "belonging to the coming *aion*," and not to imply endlessness in the sense of perpetual continuity, the thought of endlessness is certainly bound up in the phrase "eternal life," and can hardly therefore be excluded from the corresponding and balancing phrase "eternal punishment." The idea that in this text *aionios* as applied to *kolasis* must imply everlastingness seems to be unbreakable.

The New Testament always conceives of this eternal punishment as consisting of an agonizing knowledge of one's own ill desert, of God's displeasure, of the good that one has lost, and of the irrevocable fixed state in which one now finds oneself. The doctrine of eternal punishment was taught in the synagogue even before our Lord took it up and enforced it in the Gospels. All the language that strikes terror into our hearts—weeping and gnashing of teeth, outer darkness, the worm, the fire, gehenna, the great gulf fixed—is all directly taken from our Lord's teaching. It is from Jesus Christ that we learn the doctrine of eternal punishment.

Study the following Bible passages and any other relevant ones on this topic, and reach your own conclusions, prayerfully: Luke 16:26; John 3:18–19,36; 5:29; 12:32; Acts 3:21,23; Rom. 1:16; 5:18–21; 1 Cor. 15:25–28; 2 Cor. 5:10,19; 6:2; Gal. 1:4; Eph. 5:25; Phil. 2:9–11; 1 Tim. 2:4; Titus 2:11; Heb. 2:9; 9:27; 1 Pet. 3:19; 2 Pet. 3:9; 1 John 1:5; 2:2; 4:8.

Ask God to lay on your heart a few people for whom you should pray regularly that they will enter into eternal life.

I looked, and behold, a great multitude which no man could number, from every na-
tion, from all tribes and peoples and tongues, standing before the throne and before
the Lamb, clothed in white robes, with palm branches in their hands, and crying in a
loud voice, "Salvation belongs to our God who sits upon the throne, and to the
Lamb!"

Revelation 7:9–10

Revelation 7:9–17, a passage often read at funerals, gives us a heart-
warming picture of heaven and tells us a great deal about the international
community that is found there.

Who are they? They are the Lord's people who have now arrived home.
They have been brought together and welded into a single community by
their shared knowledge of the salvation for which they are now praising
God. Loving the Father and the Son, they love each other too.

Where did they come from? "Out of the great tribulation" (v. 14). I don't
think this is a reference to one terrible happening at the end of the age; it is,
rather, a description of world history in which things are always rough for
the people of God because the world is against them.

How did they get there? First, through justification, deriving from
Christ's cross ("They have washed their robes and made them white in the
blood of the Lamb"—v. 14). Second, through preservation by the indwelling Holy Spirit. The seal on the foreheads of the servants of God (v. 3) is
surely a reference to the Holy Spirit given to God's people as a sign of ownership, means of protection, and mark of authentication.

Where are they now? They are with the Father and Son in pain-free
peace (vv. 9,15,17). What are they doing? They are singing Christ's praises
and serving him day and night because they love him. How are they feeling? They are experiencing what C.S. Lewis describes as a delight compared
with which all the raptures of earthly lovers are mere milk and water. They
are realizing the joy and fulfillment of being in the Savior's presence with no
distractions or distresses or anything else that would make their fellowship
less than perfect.

Do I need to look up and look forward to heaven more than I do?
Lord, I do ask you for patience, stability, and steadiness as I look up and ahead.

Let your requests be made known to God.
Philippians 4:6

When I was seven years old I ran under a bread truck, thereby proving to my parents that I wasn't to be trusted on the road. When I was almost eleven, my friends were being given bicycles, and I boldly asked for a bicycle for my next birthday.

On my birthday morning, I came down to breakfast, eagerly wondering what the bicycle would look like and saw, beside my place at the table, a typewriter. Perhaps you're thinking, "What's this? A boy of eleven who had asked for a bicycle being given a typewriter? Poor lad! What a pain for him!" But no! My parents knew me better than I knew myself. That typewriter was the best present I ever had. No single object has given me more pleasure over the years than that typewriter and its successors. You'd better believe it—it's true! And I learned to honor my parents for their loving wisdom in giving me something better for me at that time than a bicycle.

Our heavenly Father is a good and wise parent too, in just the same way. In foolishness and ignorance, albeit with total sincerity and the best motives, we ask him for the wrong thing. He doesn't slap us down. Instead he lets us tell him why we want it. He waits to see if we will work through it and find out what we ought to be asking for, and then, supposing that that has not happened, he gives us something better—the thing that we would have asked for had we been perfectly wise and our hearts entirely right. If we have confidence in his fatherly goodness and thereby trust what he is doing, we learn something from each such experience. The assumption we must *not* make is that God does not hear our requests or want us to have the best. He does!

Reflect on your life and identify the times when you have had the experience of receiving from God something better (seen in perspective, with hindsight, taking the long view) than the thing you were asking him for. Is there something you need to accept today as God's "something better"?
Thank God for all the "something betters" that he's given you.

Have mercy on me, O God, according to thy steadfast love; according to thy abundant mercy blot out my transgressions.

Psalm 51:1

I find it easy to believe the tradition that Psalm 51 was written by David after Nathan the prophet had reproved him for his sin in relation to Bathsheba.

The psalm begins by presenting to us David's petition: his cry for mercy which is the basic theme of this song of prayer (vv. 1–2). Then comes David's *confession:* his acknowledgment of ill-desert (vv. 3–6); David's *remission:* the hope of cleansing from sin's guilty stain, on which he lays hold (vv. 7–9); David's *restoration:* the plea for spiritual quickening which he makes (vv. 10–12); David's *dedication:* his purpose of going out, now that he's been humbled and has received forgiveness, to spend the rest of his life offering worship for, and telling the world about, God's amazing grace (vv. 13–17); and finally David's *intercession:* a prayer for the blessing of the whole church (vv. 18–19).

This is a wonderful pattern of prayer for anyone made aware of his sin and need of forgiveness, whether he's an unbeliever coming in repentance and faith to God for the first time, or a child of God coming to his father for forgiveness day by day. Such a prayer may be a part of a person's conversion or an expression of his convertedness. Either way, the plea is for mercy on the basis of God's steadfast love. God has promised to forgive and restore those who come to him hating their sins and wanting to be saved from them. He did it for David; he will do it for us, too.

What can you learn from this psalm about prayer, repentance, faith, and sin?
Lord, help me to keep remembering that I shall never stop needing your mercy and that I can never come before you on my own merits.

How long, O LORD? Wilt thou forget me for ever?
Psalm 13:1

The Bible contains many recorded models of prayer—150 psalms, the Lord's Prayer, and the prayers of saints from Abraham to Paul. They are like big clothes which parents buy for their children to grow into.

The Lord's Prayer in particular shows the pattern of goals and desires to which all truly Christian praying conforms, and I find it salutary to ask myself again and again, "Have my prayers spelled out what is in the Lord's Prayer?" Also I have found amplifying and specifying each clause in the Lord's Prayer is an infallible way to restart when I get stuck or when I am struck dumb by the feeling that all I have to say to God is empty and meaningless.

As for the Psalms, I am always intrigued to find how Christians relate to them, for it took me years after my conversion to feel at home in them. Why? Partly, I think, because the view of life as a battle which the Psalms embody took longer to root itself in my heart than in my head; partly because the middle-class misconception that tidiness, self-conscious balance, and restraint are essentials of godliness—a misconception which makes most of the Psalms seem uncouth—possessed both my head and my heart for longer. More and more, however, the psalmists' calls for help, their complaints, confessions of sin, depression, celebrations of God, cries of love for him, challenges and commitments to him, and hopes placed exclusively in him, have become the emotional world of my prayers and I think this is how it should be.

Try reading the Psalms and using them as model prayers—one a day for the next 150 days perhaps!
Lord, help me to keep talking to you throughout each day, as though you are a close-at-hand but awesome friend.

Pray then like this.
Matthew 6:9

There have been those who have doubted whether the Lord's Prayer ought ever to be used word for word as Jesus gave it, because he said, "Pray like this"—meaning that what followed was to be a model for praying rather than an actual prayer. I think that's reading into the verse more than can be read out of it. Besides, when the disciples said, "Lord, teach us to pray," Jesus said, "When you pray, say: 'Father, hallowed be thy name...' " (Luke 11:1–4). So there's no doubt that Jesus intended his people to use the Lord's Prayer as their own prayer.

At the same time, the fact that Jesus says, "Pray then like this," means that he intends us also to treat this prayer as a pattern for all our praying. This form maps out the kind of prayer that God always longs to hear from his children. Every prayer of ours, whether for ourselves or for others, ought to reflect in some way the pattern of desire, purpose, and concern in the Lord's Prayer.

Let's look now at the pattern. First comes the word of address or invocation; this tunes us into the person ("Our Father...in heaven") to whom we are praying and helps us to get his identity and dignity clear in our minds.

Then come two trios of prayers—the first having at its center our Father (his name, kingdom, and will) and the second having ourselves (our need of provision, pardon, and protection) at its center. Think of these as two concentric circles—a bigger one representing the first trio and a smaller one the second. Both circles have the same central focus—the God who gives what we ask—but the second circle must be looked at in terms of the first. We are to ask that God will meet our needs not for our own selfish purposes, but as part of his glorifying of himself.

Examine some of your own prayers in light of the model prayer. Do you have the right trust? Are your priorities comparable?

Lord, teach me to pray the kind of prayers that bring you joy, and myself and others your many kinds of blessings.

Our Father who art in heaven...
Matthew 6:9

Our *Father*, who art in heaven: The very fact that we call God *father* should remind us of three truths. First, we must come to God through Christ, for it is only through him that we become children of God and can call God our father at all (John 1:12). Second, we should come to God in a spirit of obedience. Throughout the Bible, fatherhood, both human and divine, implies authority—authority which requires obedience and submission. Third, we can come to God with confidence. "If you then, who are evil, know how to give good gifts to your children, how much more will your Father who is in heaven give good things to those who ask him!" (Matt. 7:11). God is the perfect father whose goodness we can trust absolutely and so we can come to him with full assurance that he will hear, care, and give the best.

Our Father, who art in *heaven*: Jesus tells us to call God our father in *heaven* not because he wants us to think of him as remote (when in fact, God is near to us all the time), but because he wants us to realize that God exists on a higher plane than we do. To declare that God is in heaven is to remind ourselves that he is not like us—weak and changeable. Instead he is strong and steady. His love is constant and his power infinite. Children have to adjust, sometimes painfully, to the fact that their human fathers are not God and can't do absolutely everything, but our heavenly Father really is omnipotent. There are no limits to the good he is able to do for us.

Our Father, who art in heaven: Saying *our* reminds us that we don't pray in isolation. We are members of a family, and we talk to our father along with the rest of his family, asking him to do things for them as well as for us.

Is there anything in my relationship with my father on earth that is blocking me in my relationship with my Father in heaven?
Father, show me how to clear these blockages... Thank you for every way in which my human father has shown me something of your fatherhood.

Hallowed be thy name. Thy kingdom come, Thy will be done, on earth as it is in heaven.

Matthew 6:9–10

Hallowed be thy name: This tests our motives. When the Lord declared his name to Moses, he "passed before him, and proclaimed, 'the LORD, the LORD, a God merciful and gracious, slow to anger . . . keeping steadfast love . . .' " (Exod. 34:6–7). God's name is a setting forth of his nature. Thus, when we pray that God's name will be hallowed, we are praying that the truth about his nature, character, and ways may be known and that he will be worshipped, glorified, and praised for all that he is and all that he does. Jesus meant this when he prayed, "Father, glorify thy name" (John 12:28). The honor and praise of God's name should be the motive in all our praying. If we ask for the right and necessary thing only for the sake of our own advantage or comfort, as the Israelites in the desert did, God may send us a judgment along with what we have asked for, as he did to the Israelites (see Num. 11).

Thy kingdom come: This tests our submission to God. When Jesus prayed that God's will would be done, he was in Gethsemane. Being truly human, he shrank from the idea of the cross and began to pray, "My Father, if it be possible, let this cup pass from me." Then he added, "Nevertheless, not as I will but as thou wilt" (Matt. 26:39).

How well do you know God's nature? Write down, perhaps with the help of a concordance or Bible dictionary, the words which describe God's nature.
Father, may people glorify, praise, and honor you for your . . . (supply the characteristics from your list).

Give us this day our daily bread; And forgive us our debts, as we also have forgiven our debtors; And lead us not into temptation, But deliver us from evil.
Matthew 6:11–13

The first three petitions in the Lord's Prayer center on the greatness of God; these three highlight our smallness and dependence.

Give us this day our daily bread: We pray first for provision, reminding ourselves that none of the things we need, not even the most routine and basic, ever do or can come to us without God.

Forgive us our debts: Then we pray for pardon, asking God to forgive our shortcomings. Elsewhere in Scripture sin is pictured as uncleanness, rebellion, missing the mark, straying off the path. Why is it described as a debt here? Because this is a prayer the children of God can use. We owe our Father a debt of unlimited love and obedience, and we continually need to ask his forgiveness for failing to pay it; that is, for not loving and obeying him as perfectly as we should. People have wondered why believers need to pray this since God as our judge has already justified us and will not now hold our sins against us. The reason is that our constant sins of omission and commission strain and spoil the parent-child relationship between him and us. Just as the prodigal could not enjoy his relationship with his father until he came home and asked for forgiveness, neither can we. Pardon in God's courtroom is once for all, but forgiveness in God's family needs to be renewed over and over again. And those who know that they live by God's pardoning mercy will show it by conscientiously forgiving others.

Lead us not into temptation: Lastly we pray that God will not put us in situations where we will be too hard-pressed by the tempter or by trying circumstances; but rather we ask him to deliver us from the Evil One and the evil thing (the Greek can be translated either way and both thoughts are there). Conscious of our weakness, we beg God to keep us from spiritual disaster and collapse.

How can we be delivered from the Evil One and evil circumstances (1 Pet. 5:8–10; 1 Cor. 10:13)?
Lord, show me how to resist in faith or escape from this situation. . .

Blessed are those who mourn, for they shall be comforted.
Matthew 5:4

I don't want to narrow the exposition of "those who mourn" but I'm sure the central thought is that of mourning for our sins and for the way in which we have messed up our lives by our own folly (and perhaps the lives of others), and certainly obstructed God's purpose for us. Our lives are twisted, our outlook distorted. We are constantly off-center and off-key: morally and spiritually, we have much to mourn about.

Changing the metaphor, we can say we are like a ruined building. God has to demolish and rebuild us. We do well to mourn for all that has happened to make such a reconstruction job necessary. But, says Jesus, blessed are those who mourn for they shall be comforted.

This comfort and encouragement comes from God's willingness to do the work of renewing us and to go on doing it until it is finished. "I am sure that he who began a good work in you will bring it to completion at the day of Jesus Christ" (Phil. 1:6).

How comforting and encouraging it is to know that we are fully pardoned (when God forgives, he forgets) and that the renewal of our lives already in progress will not stop until we perfectly bear the Savior's image and are fully and truly human in the way God meant us to be!

Think of God's work in your life or someone else's life as a massive reconstruction job. Sometimes it may be necessary to say to yourself or someone else: "Be patient. God has not finished with me (him/her) yet!"
Lord, I need your patience.

*Blessed are those who hunger and thirst for righteousness, for they shall be satisfied.
Matthew 5:6*

It is only those who are born of the Spirit of God who hunger and thirst for righteousness. Natural man in his fallen state has no passion to please God. He may know that God requires righteousness but he rather resents and regrets that, and the pious morality that perhaps he pursues is somewhat reluctant, and certainly far less than whole-hearted.

But for the person who has been born by the Spirit into the kingdom, righteousness is a natural disposition; he sincerely and spontaneously wants to please and honor and show his gratitude to the God who created and redeemed him. He truly longs to be holy and can honestly say, "I delight in the law of God, in my inmost self" (Rom. 7:22).

The passion of that person will increasingly be satisfied. God will give him what he seeks, leading him onto the path of holiness in this world and perfecting him in sanctity in the world to come. Holiness is the highway to happiness for Christians.

What are the things you really crave in your life? Search your heart before God and let him speak to you. If you don't hunger and thirst for righteousness, is it because you are confusing true righteousness with self-righteousness? To see righteousness in its most attractive form, look at Jesus.

I hunger and I thirst;
Jesus, my manna be:
O living waters, burst
Out of the rock for me.
(J.S.B. Monsell, 1866)

My soul is cast down within me... Hope in God.
Psalm 42:6,11

Have you ever heard of the spiritual disease which people in medieval times called *accidie*? It is something that threatens all Christian workers after the first flush of enthusiasm has worn off. It's a form of sloth but not at the physical level. It is apathy of the soul. It shows in a certain toughness of mind and weariness of spirit which often results from hurt and disillusionment.

People with *accidie* in this sense have grown cynical about ideals, enthusiasms, and strong hopes. They look pityingly at young people and say, "They'll learn," taking it for granted that when they've learned, they'll become tough inside too. Once upon a time these leather-souled people were keen, hopeful, and expectant. But nothing happened, or they got hurt, and now they protect themselves against further pain by adopting cynical, world-weary attitudes.

If these people are ministers of churches, they work mechanically, merely going through the motions because their light has really gone out and they're no longer expecting anything exciting to happen. They feel that they know from experience that exciting things don't happen, and that's an end of it. So they merely plod on, expecting nothing and receiving nothing.

But the Lord does not send us out on his work in order that nothing may happen. His word is intended to have impact; it's sent out to accomplish something. We ought never to settle for a non-expectant, defeated attitude. Rather we should be asking and expecting great things from God.

God has given each of us a ministry. What is yours? What are you expecting and asking from God in relation to it?
Pray for defeated Christians (maybe yourself included) and work out possible antidotes to your/their attitudes.

Since we are justified by faith, we have peace with God through our Lord Jesus Christ.
Romans 5:1

There is no peace like the peace of those whose minds are possessed with the full assurance that they know God and God knows them, and that this relationship guarantees God's favor to them in life, through death, and forever. This is the peace which Paul analyzes in full in Romans chapter 8.

"There is therefore now no condemnation for those who are in Christ Jesus... It is the Spirit himself bearing witness with our spirit that we are children of God, and if children, then heirs... We know that in everything God works for good with those who love him... Those whom he justified he also glorified... If God is for us, who is against us?... Who shall bring any charge against God's elect?... Who shall separate us from the love of Christ?... I am sure that neither death, nor life, nor angels, nor principalities, nor things present, nor things to come...will be able to separate us from the love of God in Christ Jesus our Lord" (Rom. 8:1,16–17, 28,30,31,33,35,38–39).

This is the peace which Shadrach, Meshach, and Abednego knew; hence the calm contentment with which they stood their ground in the face of Nebuchadnezzar's ultimatum: "If you do not worship, you shall immediately be cast into a burning fiery furnace; and who is the god that will deliver you out of my hands?" (Dan. 3:15). Their reply is classic: "O Nebuchadnezzar, we have no need to answer you in this matter. If it be so, our God whom we serve is able to deliver us...and he will deliver us out of your hand, O king. But if not, be it known to you, O king, that we will not serve your gods" (Dan. 3:16–18). It doesn't matter! It makes no difference! Whether they live or die, they are content.

Lord, how I long to experience more of your supernatural peace.
Do I need to rearrange my day so that I can be unhurriedly quiet before God?

You are not your own; you were bought with a price.
1 Corinthians 6:19–20

We all have a problem with plain, straight, ornery self-will: the inclination to do what I feel like doing, whether right or wrong. Again, Paul takes this problem to the cross of Christ and deals with it there.

C.T. Studd, great missionary of two generations ago, once said, "If Jesus Christ be God and died for me, no sacrifice is too great for me to make for him." The logic is plain: sacrifice must answer sacrifice, love must answer love.

But it's also plain that none of us can evade the constant problem of self-will. Solve it in the only place where it can be solved—at the foot of Christ's cross.

Paul knew that the message of Christ and him crucified has *power*: power to touch the human heart at its deepest need; power to provide a new dynamic for a new kind of living; power to evoke loyalty and commitment; power to make people new.

Paul wanted to see lives transformed by that power. He knew that was what God purposed. So, understanding these things, he formed the policy of preaching only Christ and him crucified, testifying rather than debating, and never getting away from the theme of redemption.

True wholeness, which none of us experiences fully in this life, only comes about when pleasing God and pleasing ourselves amount to the same thing.
Lord, only you can set me free from wanting to please my fallen self and give me the desire and the power to please you and so be true to my truest and best self.

If they were wise, they would understand this, they would discern their latter end!
Deuteronomy 32:29

A wise man listens to advice.
Proverbs 12:15

If we want God to guide us, our attitude needs to be right. Here are some guidelines as to how we can play our part in arriving at right decisions.

First, we must be willing to *think*. It is false piety, super-supernaturalism of an unhealthy pernicious sort that demands inward impressions with no rational base, and declines to heed the constant biblical summons to consider. God made us thinking beings, and he guides our minds as we think things out in his presence.

Second, we must be willing to *think ahead* and weigh the long-term consequences of alternative courses of action. Often we can only see what is wise and right, and what is foolish and wrong, as we dwell on the long-term issues.

Third, we must be willing to *take advice*. It is a sign of conceit and immaturity to dispense with taking advice in major decisions. There are always people who know the Bible, human nature, and our own gifts and limitations better than we do, and even if we cannot finally accept their advice, nothing but good will come to us from carefully weighing what they say.

Fourth, we must be willing to *be ruthlessly honest with ourselves*. We must suspect ourselves: ask ourselves why we feel a particular course of action will be right and make ourselves give reasons.

Fifth, we must be willing *to wait*. "Wait on the Lord" is a constant refrain in the Psalms and it is a necessary word, for the Lord often keeps us waiting. When in doubt, do nothing, but continue to wait on God.

Have you grasped these guidelines in such a way that you would be able to pass them on clearly? Perhaps someone needs to hear what you have just understood. *Father, please take away the "guidance is so hard" block from my mind.*

What sort of persons ought you to be in lives of holiness and godliness, waiting for and hastening the coming of the day of God!

2 Peter 3:11–12

In 2 Peter 3:11–18, Peter has four very important things to say about the way we should think and act in relation to Christ's return.

Hold fast to the certainty of Christ's coming. God's time scale is not ours; God has merciful reasons for delay; Christ's coming will be unexpected, but it is a certainty because God has promised it; and Christians must live in the light of this knowledge.

Live in readiness for Christ's coming. Those who expect it should get ready for it, pursuing holiness, avoiding this world's entanglements and all that is disruptive among men and blameworthy before God. In this, as in cultivating Christlikeness and seeking assurance, zeal must be shown and effort exerted; apathy and half-heartedness will not do.

Understand the delay in Christ's coming. Peter juxtaposes two startling thoughts: first, that God delays the day out of compassionate patience so that more may be saved; second, that Christians hasten on the day by the quality of their lives. Prayer with "holiness and godliness" may be included; both contribute to making the day dawn.

Grow spiritually while waiting for Christ's coming. Knowledge about Christ and first-hand experience of his grace should increase daily. Christians must not stand still.

Make a list of what you need to do today. In the light of the possibility that Christ may come, rearrange your priorities or rewrite/revise the list.

Lord, I pray for your peace as well as a sense of urgency as I go into this day with all its possibilities, including the possibility of your return.

*In many and various ways God spoke of old to our fathers by the prophets; but in
these last days he has spoken to us by a Son.*
Hebrews 1:1–2

Basic to the New Testament is the claim that Christianity is a revealed religion. The Greek word translated "reveal" means to unveil something that
was previously hidden or bring into view something that was out of sight
before. Christianity rests on the unveiling of the hidden Creator himself;
Christians enjoy "the light of the knowledge of the glory of God in the face
of Christ" (2 Cor. 4:6). The process whereby God revealed himself to men
and women through his dealings with a single national family—Israel—
reached its climax in the person, words, and works of Jesus of Nazareth,
God's incarnate Son. So the Christian revelation-claim finds its final statement in the majestic opening words of the Epistle to the Hebrews.

Revelation is a divine activity, not a human achievement. It is not the
same thing as discovery or the dawning of insight or the emerging of a
bright idea. Revelation does not mean people finding God, but God finding
us, God sharing his secrets with us, God showing us himself. In revelation,
God is the agent as well as the object. It is not just that we speak about God
or for God; God speaks for himself and talks to us in person. The New Testament message is that in Christ God has spoken a word for the world, a
word which all people in all ages should hear and respond to.

Why is it important to establish that Christianity is a revealed religion? Is there no
room for discovery, insights, and bright ideas?
Lord, continue to reveal yourself to me and to my church family.

Say among the nations, "The LORD reigns! Yea, the world is established, it shall never be moved; he will judge the people with equity."

Psalm 96:10

From Genesis to Revelation, the Bible's dominant conviction about God is that behind and beneath all the apparent confusion of this world lies his plan. That plan concerns the perfecting of a people and the restoring of a world through the mediating action of Christ. God governs human affairs with this end in view, and human history is an outworking of his purpose: history is his story.

The Bible details the stages in God's plan. God visited Abraham, led him into Canaan, and entered into a covenant relationship with him and his descendants (Gen. 17:7-8). He gave Abraham a son and turned Abraham's family into a nation which he led out of Egypt into a land of their own. Over the centuries he prepared them and the Gentile world for the coming of the Savior-king (1 Pet. 1:20). At last, "when the time had fully come, God sent forth his Son, born of a woman, born under the law, to redeem those who were under the law, so that we might receive adoption as sons" (Gal. 4:4-5). The covenant promise to Abraham's descendants is now fulfilled to all who put faith in Christ (Gal. 3:29).

The plan for this age is that the gospel should go through the world and "a great multitude...from every nation, from all tribes and peoples and tongues" (Rev. 7:9) be brought to faith in Christ; after which, at Christ's return, heaven and earth will in some unimaginable way be remade; and where "the throne of God and of the Lamb" is, there "his servants shall worship him; they shall see his face...they shall reign for ever and ever" (Rev. 22:3-5).

Do I need to take time to read the Bible straight through as one story and summarize in my own words its main plot?
Lord, thank you that you do have a plan for the world and for me.

I came that they may have life, and have it abundantly.
John 10:10

God in redemption finds us in our sinful, fallen state: all of us more or less disintegrated personalities, largely out of control of ourselves and also out of touch with a great deal of ourselves, including most of what is central to our real selves. His gracious purpose is to bring us into a reconciled relationship with himself through Christ and to reintegrate us and make us whole beings through the outworking of that relationship.

The relationship itself is restored once and for all through Christ being made sin for us so that we in consequence could be made the righteousness of God in him. Justified and adopted into God's family through faith in Christ, Christians are immediately and eternally secure.

But the work of recreating us as psychophysical beings, on whom Christ's image is to be stamped, is a lifelong process of growth and transformation. Indeed, it extends beyond this life because the basic disintegration—that between the psychic (conscious personal) life and the physical life—will not finally be healed until the redemption of our bodies. Not until then shall we know all that is now shrouded in the mysterious reality of the unconscious or reach the end of the split-self dimension of Christian experience whereby those whose hearts delight in God's Law nonetheless find in themselves allergic, negative reactions and responses to it. Still, however, the indwelling Holy Spirit abides and works in us to lead us toward the appointed goal, and he deals with each one's broken and distorted humanity as he finds it.

Try to summarize in your own words, on paper, or out loud as though to an inquirer, the gist of the Good News.
Praise God for each aspect of the gospel now being experienced by you.

The grace of God has appeared for the salvation of all men.
Titus 2:11

When I was an undergraduate, I used to punt on the river. One day I suddenly found myself upside down in the water with strands of green weeds around my head and the light up at my feet.

Imagine the following situation. A person has fallen into the water. He can't swim. The weeds are entangling him; he is thrashing around but he cannot get free and is desperate. Three people come along on the bank.

One looks at him and says, "He's all right; if he struggles he'll get out: they always do. It's even good for his character that he has to struggle like this. I'll leave him." The second person looks at the poor struggling man and says, "I'd like to help you. I can see what you need. You need some tips about swimming. Let me tell you how to swim." Then there is the third man who comes along. He sees the situation and jumps in, overcomes the man's struggles, gets him free from the weeds, brings him back to the shore, gives him artificial respiration, and puts him back on his feet.

Which of those three men is the truest illustration of what God does to save us? The first corresponds to a message of self-help: a hard, unfeeling, and really sub-Christian form of Christianity. The second pictures someone telling us how to be saved but doing nothing more. The third is a picture of God taking the initiative: Christ coming right down to where we are, entering our trouble, and doing all that has to be done. He breaks the bonds of sin and guilt that bind us, brings us to land (that is, to God), restores life, and makes us believers—all this by his sovereign grace which saves wonderfully and absolutely from first to last.

Have I been taking this amazing salvation for granted?
Lord, thank you for all that you did to save me and for all that you are doing to set me free to be your person.

In him all the fulness of God was pleased to dwell, and through him to reconcile to himself all things, whether on earth or in heaven, making peace by the blood of his cross.
Colossians 1:19-20

Most human problems have a dimension dealing with our relationship with God, and we cannot get the human part of the problem right until the relationship with God has been put right as well.

Guilt is a very fundamental problem, and people who deny God are still hung up with it today. The psychiatrists tell us that. Paul knows that the problem of spiritual guilt finds its solution at Calvary in the knowledge of the Christ who made "peace by the blood of his cross." This is the only way into God's peace.

Then there is the pervasive problem of forlornness or loneliness: the feeling that in this great bustling world I am on my own and I am lost. I have no one to turn to, no one to help me, and I don't know where I'm going. To know that God loves us personally brings healing and hope to those experiencing this forlornness.

Such people need to grasp what the cross was all about: "God shows his love for us in that while we were yet sinners Christ died for us" (Rom. 5:8). They need to be told in one way or another that God loves them and did all that for them. He wants them as his children. He adopts them into his family by virtue of what Christ has done for them. He will be with them and love them forever. Now they are no longer lost—they are found.

Guilty, forlorn people need to experience the love of God in Christ. But how does this love reach them initially? Isn't it usually through someone who cares enough about them to turn them from self and sin and lead them to God?
Pray for some guilty, forlorn Christian or non-Christian, asking God to show you if you should be helping to meet his or her needs.

Christ redeemed us from the curse of the law, having become a curse for us.
Galatians 3:13

Commenting on this verse Martin Luther wrote: "All the prophets did foresee in Spirit that Christ should become the greatest transgressor, murderer, adulterer, thief, rebel, blasphemer, etc., that ever was or could be in all the world. For he, being made a sacrifice for the sins of the whole world is not now an innocent person and without sins...but a sinner." He was, of course, talking about the imputing of our wrongdoing to Christ as our substitute.

Luther continues: "Our most merciful Father...sent his only Son into the world and laid upon him...the sins of all men saying: Be thou Peter that denier; Paul that persecutor, blasphemer and cruel oppressor; David that adulterer; that sinner which did eat the apple in Paradise; that thief which hanged upon the cross; and briefly be thou the person which hath committed the sins of all men; see therefore that thou pay and satisfy for them. Here now comes the law and saith: I find him a sinner...therefore let him die upon the cross. And so he setteth upon him and killeth him. By this means the whole world is purged and cleansed from all sins."

The presentation of the death of Christ as the substitute exhibits the love of the cross more richly, fully, gloriously, and glowingly than any other account of it. Luther saw this and gloried in it. He once wrote to a friend: "Learn to know Christ and him crucified. Learn to sing to him, and say, 'Lord Jesus, you are my righteousness, I am your sin. You have taken upon yourself what is mine and given me what is yours. You became what you were not, so that I might become what I was not.' "

What a great and wonderful exchange! Was there ever such love?

Have I really grasped what it meant for Christ to be our (my) substitute? *Worship him with your words and life today.*

Repent, and believe in the gospel.
Mark 1:15

Repentance and faith are a pair. They belong together like husband and wife. They are the two key words for the proper response to the gospel. In the New Testament, the word *repent* sometimes comes first and the word *faith* second; at other times the order is reversed. In some passages only one of the words is used, but the other is implied (Matt. 4:17; Mark 6:12; Luke 24:47; Acts 2:38; 11:18).

We must be clear about what these words mean in the Bible. When we are summoned to repent, we are not being asked to feel bad about something for awhile and then forget it and carry on as before. Many people have fits of remorse, but this doesn't necessarily mean that they have repented in the biblical sense of the word. Repentance must include the idea of turning and changing, of being different.

Faith in the biblical sense also means more than most people seem to appreciate. "You've got to have faith," people say—meaning that we must keep looking on the bright side. But in Scripture faith is far more than having a generally hopeful attitude; it's a matter of responding to a person who is addressing you and to truths which you have grasped. God promises forgiveness through Jesus Christ and faith responds, "Thank you for that word of forgiveness. I accept it and take Jesus to be my Savior and you to be my Father. From now on I want to live as your child." Faith says, "Yes" to the Father's love and sees itself as bound to God henceforth in gratitude.

For thought: "A forgiveness which bypasses the need for repentance issues not from love but from sentimentality" (J.R.W. Stott).
Lord, may repentance and faith be constant realities in my daily life; may my turning from sin and my unbelief be more and more decisive and may my trust in you grow stronger and deeper.

Every man did what was right in his own eyes.
Judges 21:25

Judges is the book of the permissive society. It tells us in painful, spine-chilling detail what happens when people do what is right in their own eyes. It's the story of Israel at a time when God's laws had been forgotten and unfaithfulness and apostasy summed up the lifestyle of most Israelites. The country had drifted into a state of disorder, and in the book of Judges we see the cost of this in human terms. It's a book about violence, looting, rape, murder. It's also a book in which the heroes—the people whom God uses—are victims of their society just as many people today are victims of ours. These heroes are, to a greater or lesser extent, flawed and mixed-up personalities. Samson was perhaps the most obvious example of this. We need to understand that he and others were like that because God's people corporately were in a mixed-up state morally and spiritually, and this affected everyone.

We see how God reacted to this permissive society. "The people of Israel again did what was evil in the sight of the LORD; and the LORD gave them into the hand of the Philistines for forty years" (Judg. 13:1). And we can expect him to react similarly in judgment to the permissive society in our days. God is not like Father Christmas. He has a moral character; there are things that he loves to see and things that he hates to see in the lives of human beings whom he made to bear his image; when we do what he hates, sooner or later, he will respond in judgment.

What should the people of God in general and my church in particular be doing about the permissive society all around us?
Lord, show us if we need to find ways of leavening the community in which we live. Give us grace and humility so that we don't cause unnecessary offense.

*My thoughts are not your thoughts, neither are your ways my ways, says the LORD.
Isaiah 55:8*

Ever since the seventeeth century in the world of western thought, the God-shrinkers have been busy. In the seventeenth century the deists taught that God is very remote from his world. He set it going and no doubt watches it, but he does not directly control the things that happen in it. He is like a clockmaker who makes a clock, sets it ticking, and then sits back with folded arms. This view effectively barred God out of his world.

In the eighteenth century, Kant, the philosopher, taught that it is unphilosophical to imagine a God who communicates with people; so the Bible isn't God's living Word. This view silenced God completely.

In the nineteenth century various theologians and philosophers argued that there's no more to God than the idea of him that we happen to have in our minds. God corresponds to our highest thoughts about him: in other words, man by thinking makes and shapes God.

The result of three centuries of speculative theology along these lines is that many in the twentieth century who have inherited this legacy of bad thinking cannot bring themselves to trust the Bible as God's Word and to believe that God is a living, speaking, active Lord who really is in charge of the world. So the tendency is to think of man as very great and God as rather small—a vague, remote influence who doesn't matter too much (although it's certainly nice to be in touch with him and to think of him as on the edge of our world if we want him).

How would you counteract this bad thinking if someone were to express it to you? Meditate on some Bible passages which emphasize God's greatness and his detailed involvement with and care of his creation.

As the heavens are higher than the earth, so are my ways higher than your ways.
Isaiah 55:9

Along with much bad thinking that has come down to us from the last four hundred years, goes split living.

Do you know people who live their lives in separate compartments? Do you perhaps do this yourself? People who live compartmentalized lives worship God and go to church and do their "religious" bit on Sundays; then they switch that off and pursue their professions, weekday work, weekend hobbies, and all their relationships as though these were matters entirely separate from their Christian commitment. They don't even try to see their lives as a whole in terms of God and his Word. Instead they slip into their religious compartment on Sundays and their secular compartment on the other days of the week and allow no communication between the two.

This joins a further great evil of our times: mental sleep. Christians who are mentally asleep are those who are happy with a Christianity that doesn't demand hard thinking about anything. As long as they are singing choruses and enjoying Christian fellowship, they are perfectly happy, and are simply not interested in learning the works, ways, and will of God as set forth in the Bible—which is what we call theology. As children of God, we should be interested in theology—interested to find out from the Bible what our heavenly Father is up to. If we don't give ourselves to serious thinking and reading and study about our faith, we will have weak, small, inadequate ideas of God, and our worship and service will be impoverished as a result.

Am I belittling God by my split living and lazy thinking? Is there a Christian education course I could enroll in?

Lord, there's so much I need to learn, so much I haven't thought through. Make me willing to spend the necessary time and effort.

If anyone loves the world, love for the Father is not in him.
1 John 2:15

Worldliness is not a matter of having, using, and enjoying the good things of this world. If it were, only the destitute could be spiritual! True, Jesus told the rich young man to sell all his possessions (Matt. 19:16–22), but this was because he could see that this man's wealth was the most important thing to him. It would be wrong to infer that Jesus calls everyone to sell all that they have. Elsewhere in the New Testament we are taught the right way to handle wealth (1 Tim. 6:17–19). We are to be good stewards of it, yet never to put our trust in it or allow it to possess us. Some, no doubt, are still called to abandon it, but not all.

Worldliness is a matter of the heart—that is, of what one loves and lives for. "Do not love the world or the things in the world. . . For all that is in the world, the lust of the flesh and the lust of the eyes and the pride of life, is not of the Father but is of the world" (1 John 2:15–16). We are told not to treat the pleasures, profits, and honors after which others run as our final goals, but to love and serve the Father and make pleasing him our total business.

In other words, we must make the right priority decisions. The child of God must not make choices which give pleasure, profit, position, or anything else that belongs to this life only, priority over the claims of God, his glory, his work, and his people. Paul wrote: "Demas, in love with this present world, has deserted me" (2 Tim. 4:10). There are many like Demas today. They may not be completely out of the church or out of Christian service, but they've left someone else carrying the heavy end and making the sacrifices, and have moved into things they can do while continuing their love affair with this present order of things.

How would you define worldliness? What is your weakest point in this area?
Lord, keep renewing my mind so that I may be transformed (Rom. 12:1).

The heart is deceitful above all things, and desperately corrupt; who can understand it?

Jeremiah 17:9

Blind spots are danger spots. Accidents happen because of blind spots in the motorist's field of vision. In cricket, the batsman's blind spot makes him vulnerable to leg-spinners. Strategic oversights lose wars. Hidden flaws cause airplanes to crash. Unrecognized gaps in knowledge mean disaster in examinations. Our blind spots are hard to detect and eliminate simply because *we do not know what and where they are.* Until we are made aware of their existence, we can do nothing about them.

In the church's spiritual warfare against the world-rulers of this darkness, we have to realize that the devil, like any good general, exploits his opponents' blind spots as much as he can.

Think, for instance, how he plays on them in the sphere of Christian morality. Here he has an invaluable ally in the limitless capacity of the fallen human heart for self-deception. "The heart is deceitful above all things"— not because it was created so but because it has fallen under the power of indwelling sin; and one of its characteristics is deceit, which creates blind spots on the conscience (Heb. 3:13).

So we find nothing easier than to fool ourselves about our spiritual condition, to occupy our minds with watching against small, superficial sins while overlooking great, deep-seated ones like hypocrisy and pride, which actually grow fat on theatrical self-abasement and exaggerated carefulness about trifles. Christ warned his disciples against moral blind spots (Matt. 7:3-5). It is always easier to detect small sins than big ones in anyone, most of all ourselves.

Am I concentrating on trifles while missing something big and serious in the area of my own flawed character?
Lord, show me if there's any bad attitude or habit which has been part of my character and conduct for so long that I have gotten used to its company.

He (the devil) was a murderer from the beginning, and has nothing to do with the truth, because there is no truth in him.
John 8:44

It is easy to have intellectual as well as moral blind spots. Scripture speaks of the devil as the enemy of truth as well as godliness. He leads Christians into unconscious falsifications of God's truth as eagerly as into unconscious transgressions of God's Law.

Intellectual blind spots spring from the uncritical assimilation of prejudices. These act on the mind like a blindfold, drastically reducing the field of vision, or like tinted spectacles, imparting a color of their own—by objective standards a false one—to everything in sight. Prejudices are simply tradition swallowed wholesale: tradition in the sense of those opinions and viewpoints which confront us unchallenged and unquestioned, claiming to be authoritative and therefore normative for our own thought.

Once we have reached the necessary intellectual maturity and independence, we need to stand back from all this tradition which we have absorbed in order to test and evaluate it, so that we may, if necessary, correct it and escape its limitations.

In theology the criterion for testing and correcting traditional ideas is God's written Word, and it is the church's constant duty to reform its tradition by this inspired norm. Tradition of one sort or another has a great deal to do with determining the content and outlook of our own present-day faith. And each bit of our heritage, including the evangelical tradition, needs to be tested and reformed by the Scriptures.

Do I need to spend more time reading the Bible for myself and less time reading books about the Bible?
Lord, as I read your Word, show me if any traditions are blinding me.

Put on the whole armor of God, that you may be able to stand against the wiles of the devil.

Ephesians 6:11

Roman soldiers were given full armor to go into battle and Paul has this in mind when he speaks of the armor which God gives to us his soldiers in our war against Satan. When we become Christians, we find ourselves at war with the devil, for the devil is now at war with us. Prior to conversion we were in his power and for that reason he didn't need to take any special steps against us. But the moment we receive God's pardon and are taken into his family as adopted children, Satan is after us to recapture us.

"Satan" is the Hebrew for adversary, and Satan is the adversary first of God and then of God's people. "Devil," from the Greek *diabolos*, has the sense of slanderer, one who speaks evil because he thinks evil, and the devil thinks evil against God and Christians. He is also full of wiles (deceitful ways). So we have against us an infinitely mean, smart, devious, malicious, evil, personal intelligence.

What are we to do? Panic? No. We can and must put on the whole armor of God, make use of all the resources he provides, and withstand Satan whenever he attacks. Then we may hope to find ourselves standing triumphant in the field of battle with our enemy fled. "Take the whole armor of God, that you may be able to withstand in the evil day, and having done all, to stand" (Eph. 6:13). "Resist the devil and he will flee from you" (James 4:7).

Am I conscious of being engaged in a battle? How well equipped am I for it? *Lord, open my eyes to see the enemy so I can fight properly instead of thrashing about blindly.*

Stand. . . having girded your loins with truth, and having put on the breastplate of righteousness, and having shod your feet with the equipment of the gospel of peace.
Ephesians 6:14–15

A good belt is an essential requirement for the well-equipped soldier. The Christian soldier must have a good belt too—the belt of truth. By "truth" Paul means "divine truth known as a guide to life." The ignorant Christian is a vulnerable one. We must know our Bibles and be clear on God's works, will, and ways, or we shall fail in our spiritual warfare.

Second we are to put on the breastplate of righteousness. A breastplate guards the vital organs of lungs and heart. Righteousness here means practical holiness and daily obedience. The person of conscious integrity who is all out for God and goodness and doesn't compromise is the one who has on the breastplate of righteousness. The breastplate then shields him against all Satan's devices for inducing moral defeat, disaster, and consequent despair.

Then come shoes. Paul tells us to have our feet shod with the equipment (or readiness to maneuver) that the gospel of peace provides. Readiness to deal with Satan's undermining and often unnerving suggestions springs from knowing the peace of Christ—the pardon, self-acceptance, contentment, and inner tranquility that flow to us through the gospel. If we don't know that we're at peace with God, Satan will be able to say, "Look at the mess you're making of your life. God will never accept you," or "Look at the trouble that's coming your way. You'll never make it," and we won't have any answer. But if we have come as sinners to Jesus and received his gift of peace, we can withstand Satan and throw his accusations and insinuations back in his face.

Think more about what it means to be armed with truth, righteousness, and the gospel of peace.
Lord, I come to you for my lack in this area. . .

*Stand . . . taking the shield of faith, with which you can quench all the flaming darts
of the evil one.*

Ephesians 6:14,16

A Roman infantryman would carry a huge shield in front of him to deflect
any arrows as he advanced across open country into battle. Those arrows
might have flaming flax fastened to their points, to do double damage if
they struck. The Christian warrior has to face "flaming darts" from Satan
and for this he needs the shield of faith.

"Faith" here has two aspects. First, it is our trust in God's promises. God
has said he will never leave or forsake his people; faith means grasping firm
hold of that promise and holding it up against Satan when he comes and
says (prompts us to say to ourselves), "It's too hard. You'll never make it.
Give up now."

Also, faith is our focus on God's Son. The author of Hebews urges us to
look to "Jesus the pioneer and perfecter of our faith, who for the joy that
was set before him endured the cross, despising the shame, and is seated at
the right hand of the throne of God" (Heb. 12:2). Jesus pioneered the way
we have to go, and is now with the Father in glory. That is where we too
shall finally be if we look to him who knows what we are going through
and is beside us all the way, helping us along. We shall advance, and Satan
will not be able to stop us.

Is my faith a shield to me day by day? Am I depending on God's promises and
looking to Jesus?
*Lord, help me consider you who endured from sinners such hostility against yourself,
so that I might not grow weary or faint-hearted (Heb. 12:3).*

*Take the helmet of salvation, and the sword of the Spirit, which is the word of God.
Ephesians 6:17*

The helmet protects the head against stunning, crushing blows. For the
Christian soldier, God provides the helmet of salvation, which I believe
means assurance of salvation, present and future. We can't be knocked out
by Satan if we are sure that now, tomorrow, and for all eternity we are safe
in the hands of God who holds us securely and will keep us forever by his
power.

The helmet and the other pieces of armor which Paul has mentioned so
far (belt, breastplate, shoes, shield—Eph. 6:14–16) are defensive weapons.
Now Paul names an offensive weapon: "the sword of the Spirit, which is
the word of God." We are to take this and use it as Jesus used it when he was
tempted. Satan made suggestions and each time Jesus quoted Scripture and
said in effect: "It is by this word of my Father, not by any of your words,
that I am going to live. So get away from me, Satan." Thus he resisted the
devil, using the sword of the Spirit, and the devil retreated. That is how we
are to use the Word of God when Satan comes to tempt us: we are to set it
like a brandished sword between him and ourselves.

Determine to allow time to memorize Bible verses and passages so that you can resist the devil with this sword of the Spirit. If Satan is accusing you falsely about
anything, tell him to get behind you in Jesus' name, quoting the appropriate word
(promise) of God.

*Lord, thank you for the power of your name and person and the truth of your Word.
I go forward trusting you and it for victory.*

*The Spirit helps us in our weakness; for we do not know how to pray as we ought,
but the Spirit himself intercedes for us with sighs too deep for words.*
                                                                    Romans 8:26

It is easy to fear that circumstances will be too much for us—that we will
fail to cope as Christians. Paul's answer is that the Spirit helps us in our
weakness. Again and again in our praying we have the experience of knowing and feeling a need and wanting to tell God about it, but we find either
that words will not come at all or else that the words we use seem to not
convey what is really in our hearts. It can be a very distressing and frustrating experience.

At such times we need to remember that "the Spirit himself intercedes for
us with sighs too deep for words" (v. 26)—literally, "groanings which cannot be expressed." It was he who stirred up our desire to pray about these
needs in the first place, and when we run out of words, he "intercedes for
the saints according to the will of God" (v. 27). So we need not think: Because I haven't been able to pray about this as I should have and wanted to,
I must expect trouble. Instead we should feel assured that the Lord will hear
the words the Holy Spirit has been praying in our hearts. So we may expect
to receive all the help we need in order to cope with each situation, despite
our weakness. Prayer has been made for us, and that prayer will be answered.

Learn Romans 8:26–27 and remind yourself of these words every time you are
overwhelmed by needs and pressures and disgusted at the weakness and inadequacy of your own prayers.
*Father, write this truth on my heart and help me to pray to my limits and beyond
them through the power of your Holy Spirit each day.*

Abide in me, and I in you.
John 15:4

The pace and preoccupations of urbanized, mechanized, collectivized, sec-ularized modern life are such that any sort of inner life is very hard to main-tain. To make prayer your life priority, as countless Christians of former days did outside as well as inside the monastery, is stupendously difficult in a world that runs you off your feet and will not let you slow down. And if you attempt it, you will certainly seem eccentric to your peers, for nowa-days involvement in a stream of programmed activities is decidedly "in" and the older ideal of a quiet, contemplative life is just as decidedly "out."

That there is a widespread hunger today for more intimacy, warmth, and affection in our fellowship with God is clear from the current renewal of in-terest in the experiential writings of the Puritans and the contemplative tra-dition of prayer as expounded by men like Thomas Merton. But the concept of the Christian life as sanctified rush and bustle still dominates, and as a result the experiential side of Christian holiness remains very much a closed book.

Why? Partly because of the observable unorthodoxy, or at least doctrinal indifference, of some of its exponents; partly because it sometimes opened the door to fanatical and antinomian attitudes; partly because it was thought to be anti-intellectual; partly because it was viewed as a Roman Catholic preserve and likely therefore to be unhealthy; and partly because evangelical devotion is so firmly oriented to listening for God to speak in and through the text of Scripture that anything beyond this is at once sus-pect. The plain fact is that today's biblical Christians, wherever else they are strong, are weak on the inner life—and it shows.

Spend time thinking out the meaning and implications of today's verse.
Lord, show me my false attitudes in this matter and help me to give them up.

Barnabas wanted to take with them John called Mark. But Paul thought best not to take with them one who had withdrawn from them in Pamphylia, and had not gone with them to the work.

Acts 15:37–38

In trying to choose the greater of two goods or the lesser of two evils, we must attempt to calculate results; for the best course, other things being equal, will always be that which promises the most good and the least harm. But since our capacity to foresee results is limited, differences of opinion are inescapable, and so the most devoted Christians will not always see eye to eye on policy decisions.

For example, Paul and Barnabas differed as to whether to take with them on missionary service John Mark, Barnabas's nephew. Barnabas knew his record but clearly believed he would be a help on their trip. Paul thought it best not to take with them someone who had withdrawn from them in Pamphylia. Each of them insisted on making the best decision and was not prepared to settle for anything less, but they differed as to what the best decision was. Being in disagreement as to whether Mark was likely to prove an adequate colleague, they concluded that the best decision open to them was to split up and each take the associate he judged best for the task. So Barnabas took Mark to Cyprus and Paul went with Silas on a trip that ended in Europe.

Some are embarrassed that Paul and Barnabas should ever have been involved in passionate disagreement but there is no reason to regard this as moral failure, any more than there is to see their parting as strategic disaster. We can be sure that God being who he is, no Christian forfeits blessing for parting company with his brother when both want the best, and only calculation of consequences divides them.

Because others make different choices from those I make, am I inclined to attribute baser motives to them?
Lord, help me to keep remembering that the Christians with whom I disagree are brothers and sisters and that we have (or should have) the same ultimate objectives.

God sent me before you to preserve for you a remnant on earth, and to keep alive for you many survivors. So it was not you who sent me here, but God.
Genesis 45:7–8

Young Joseph's brothers sold him into slavery in Egypt where, traduced by Potiphar's venomous wife, he was imprisoned—though afterwards he rose to eminence. For what purpose did God in his wisdom plan that?

So far as Joseph personally was concerned, the answer is given in a psalm: "The word of the LORD *tested* him" (Ps. 105:19). Joseph was being tested, refined, and matured; he was being taught during his spell as a slave, and in prison, to focus on God, to stay cheerful and charitable in frustrating circumstances, and to wait patiently for the Lord.

Very frequently God uses sustained hardship to teach these lessons. So far as the life of God's people was concerned, Joseph himself gave the answer to our question when he revealed his identity to his distracted brothers (Gen. 45:4–15). Joseph's theology was as sound as his charity was deep. Once again, we are confronted with the wisdom of God ordering the events of a human life for a double purpose: the man's own personal sanctification, and the fulfilling of his appointed ministry and service in the life of the people of God.

Pray for yourself or someone else who is enduring "sustained hardship"—that the outcome will be good and as soon as possible.
Make a list of the times when God and his Word have tested you. What have you learned from them? Have you thanked God for the good that came out of them?

Use a little wine for the sake of your stomach and your frequent ailments.
1 Timothy 5:23

Is any one among you suffering? Let him pray.
James 5:13

It's true that salvation embraces both body and soul. And there is indeed, as some put it, healing for the body in the atonement. But perfect physical health is not promised for this life but for heaven, as part of the resurrection glory that awaits us. Full bodily well-being is a future blessing of salvation rather than a present one.

It is also true that blessing is missed where faith is lacking. But even in New Testament times, among leaders who cannot be accused of lacking faith, healing was never universal.

So what are we to do when we are ill? We should certainly go to the doctor and use medication and thank God for both. But equally we should certainly go to the Lord (Doctor Jesus, as some call him) and ask what message of challenge, rebuke, or encouragement he might have for us regarding our sickness. Maybe we shall receive healing in the form in which Paul asked for it; maybe however we shall receive it in the form in which Paul was given it (2 Cor. 12:7–10). We have to be open to either.

How would you answer someone who felt that going to the doctor showed lack of faith?

Pray for doctors, especially any you know—that they will use their skill and knowledge well and that when they don't know where to turn, they will be helped to make the best possible decisions.

Happy is the man who finds wisdom, and the man who gets understanding.
Proverbs 3:13

What steps must a man take to lay hold of the gift of wisdom? There are two prerequisites according to Scripture.

First, one must learn to *reverence God.* "The fear of the LORD is the beginning of wisdom" (Ps. 111:10). Not until we have become humble and teachable, standing in awe of God's holiness and sovereignty, acknowledging our own littleness, distrusting our own thoughts, and willing to have our minds turned upside down, can divine wisdom become ours. It is to be feared that many Christians spend all their lives in too unhumbled and conceited a frame of mind ever to gain wisdom from God at all. Scripture says: "With the humble is wisdom" (Prov. 11:2).

Then, second, one must learn to *receive God's Word.* Wisdom is divinely wrought in those, and those only, who apply themselves to God's revelation. "I have more understanding than all my teachers"—why?—*"for thy testimonies are my meditation"* (Ps. 119:99). So Paul admonishes the Colossians: "Let *the word of Christ* dwell in you richly, as you teach and admonish one another in all wisdom" (Col. 3:16).

How are we to do this? By soaking ourselves in the Scriptures, which, as Paul told Timothy (and he had in mind the Old Testament alone!), "are able to instruct you for salvation" through faith in Christ, and to perfect the man of God "for every good work" (2 Tim. 3:15-17).

How long is it since you read straight through the Bible? Do you spend as much time each day with the Bible as you do with, for example, the newspaper?
Lord I need your wisdom for this situation. . . Help me to take the necessary steps for receiving it.

When Paul perceived that one part were Sadducees and the other Pharisees, he cried out in the council, "Brethren, I am a Pharisee, a son of Pharisees: with respect to the hope and the resurrection of the dead I am on trial."

Acts 23:6

Scripture lays down guidelines as far as right conduct is concerned but there is still plenty of room for imagination and creativity, and a spirit of enterprise and even opportunism in serving God—the kind of spirit which characterized Paul (Acts 16:35–39; 17:22–31; 23:6–10). Within the boundaries set by God's specific commands, applications can vary and be better or worse, just as chess games vary within the limits set by the pieces' permitted moves.

And the best course will always be that which promises most in the total situation, just as the best first moves in a chess game will be those which promise most in the total situation, bearing in mind the game's importance; whether one is playing black or white; whether one should go for a win or a draw; the known strengths and weaknesses of one's opponents; one's own skill with this or that opening or line of offense, and so on.

Proper Christian obedience is thus as far away as possible from the treadmill negativism of the conscientious conformist, whose main concern is never to do anything wrong and who conceives the whole Christian life in terms of shunning doubtful things. To be sure, a tender conscience which trembles at God's Word (Isa. 66:2; Ezra 10:3) and fears to offend him (Jude 23) is a Christian grace and should never be frowned on as an introspective morbidity; but, just as we cannot maintain health on a diet of disinfectants only, so we cannot fully or healthily obey God by trying to avoid defilements and risks and by omitting to ask what is the *most* we can do to glorify God.

Do I tend to avoid evil rather than to be adventuresome in good and positive ways? *Lord, help me to be imaginatively and creatively (and therefore attractively) moral and right.*

We have the prophetic word made more sure. You will do well to pay attention to this as to a lamp shining in a dark place, until the day dawns and the morning star rises in your hearts.
2 Peter 1:19

The word "dark" is one which would be used for a dingy place like a cellar, cow shed, or mine. So Peter is picturing some dirty, murky place, perhaps filled with obstacles. We need the light in order to avoid the obstacles and see the way and perhaps also to clean up the place.

Why does he speak of the place where we are as dark? Because that's how the world is. It's dark through moral laxity (see the examples Peter pinpoints in 2 Pet. 2). And the church has been affected too.

We need to do as Peter suggests: pay attention to the Scriptures, for they are like a lamp shining in a dark place. The psalmist paints a similar picture: "Thy word is a lamp to my feet and a light to my path" (Ps. 119:105). When we're traveling along in the dark and we hold a lamp in front of us, it doesn't banish all the darkness but it does banish the bit ahead so that we can see where to tread. And thus we can keep going until the day dawns and the sun comes up.

Are there any dark places in my life or in the lives of those I care for which need to be exposed to the light of God's truth? How and when can this best happen? *Lord, I need more light in this situation... Show me if I am responding to all the light you have shown me so far. I long for more light.*

The ordinances of the LORD are true, and righteous altogether.
Psalm 19:9

For practical purposes the words *infallible* and *inerrant* are interchangeable. When we apply them to the Bible, what we are saying is that only those who accept as from God all that Scripture proves to tell us, promise us, or require of us, can ever fully please him. Both words thus have religious as well as theological significance; their function is to impose on our handling of the Bible a procedure which expresses faith in the reality and veracity of the God who speaks to us in and through what it says and who requires us to heed every word that proceeds from his mouth. This procedure requires us not to deny, disregard, or arbitrarily relativize anything that the writers teach or to discount any of the practical implications for worship and service which their teaching carries or to cut the knot of any problem of Bible harmony, factual or theological, by allowing ourselves to assume that the writers were not necessarily consistent with themselves or with each other.

For me to confess that Scripture is infallible and inerrant is to bind myself in advance to follow the method of harmonizing and integrating all that Scripture declares, without exception, I must believe that it is from God, however little I may like it, and whatever change of present beliefs, ways, and commitments it may require, and I must actively seek to live by it.

For thought: We can't prove all scriptural statements to be true but we can be certain that they can be trusted because they come from God.
Lord, when different parts of Scripture are hard to reconcile, help me not to make snap judgments or be afraid to face them and think hard about them.

They shall all be taught by God.
John 6:45

It is the promised privilege of all Christians to be taught by God, and it is the Spirit of God who teaches them. The Spirit who taught all things to the apostles is the anointing that teaches all Christ's people (1 John 2:27)—not by fresh disclosures of hitherto unknown truth, but by enabling us to recognize the divinity and bow to the authority of divine realities set before us.

But are we open to this working of the Spirit? As long as we approach the Scriptures with detachment, concerned only to appreciate them historically or aesthetically, and as long as we treat them merely as a human record, we scarcely are. We are only open to the Spirit's ministry to the degree we are willing to step inside the Bible and take our stand with the men to whom God spoke—Abraham listening to God in Ur, Moses listening to God at Sinai, the Israelites listening to God's Word from the lips of Moses and the prophets, the Jews listening to Jesus, the Romans and Corinthians and Timothy listening to Paul and so on— and to share joint tutorials with them, noting what God said to them and then seeking to see, in the light of that, what he would say to us.

Most of us are not that willing—we are prejudiced, lazy, and unprepared for the exercise of spirit and conscience that it involves. But greater willingness and increased receptiveness are themselves the Spirit's gifts. Therefore we must use the prayer, "Teach me thy statutes" (Ps. 119:12), as a plea not only for teaching but for teachableness.

How much am I prepared to work at and pray for an understanding of the Bible? *Lord, may your Spirit direct my imagination so that through this gift of yours I can understand your Word better.*

Of his own will he brought us forth by the word of truth that we should be a kind of first fruits of his creatures.

James 1:18

The point that James is making in this verse is that *God brought Christians to birth through the Word.* He uses it to illustrate the principle of the previous verse that all good things come from "the Father of lights," the unchanging Creator of sun, moon, and stars, whose ordering of the universe is the measure of his power to bless and who through Christ shows Christians a Father's love. As born-again children, Christians are the first fruits of creation—that part which is given to God to be his sole possession and to be partaker of his holiness. These are the dimensions of the new dignity and destiny into which the Word introduces us.

In verse 21 James goes on to say that *God brings people to glory through the Word.* Everything depends on our being "quick to hear" and receive the Word with meekness, so that it becomes "implanted" in the soil of our hearts. Our receptiveness, in turn, depends on our total moral state— whether we are willing to clamp down on our pride and other forms of natural nastiness or not (vv. 19–21). If we are, the Word can save us both here and hereafter.

In verse 25 we see that *God blesses those who are doers of the Word.* A religion of hearing and not doing is hypocrisy and self-deceit. To forget the needs which God's message exposes is frivolous, stupid, and inexcusable. To look at the Word closely, and to persevere in doing what it says, is the only way to be blessed.

Do I need to make written notes of what God says to me through his Word and spend time working out how to put this into practice?
Thank you for the life I already enjoy through your Word; may I know more of this life as I go on hearing and doing your Word, however you speak through it to me.

Blessed be thou, O LORD; teach me thy statutes!
Psalm 119:12

To the psalmists the Word of God meant a body of divine instruction, written indeed for reference but for the most part handed down orally; a body of instruction whose very existence was a sign of God's favor: Israel was privileged to enjoy both his grace and his teaching. God had declared his will in both purpose and command, and godliness meant precisely living by his Word.

In Psalm 119:1–16 the psalmist speaks of treasuring the Word in his heart and memory, dwelling on it and delighting in it, looking to it to keep him from sin and teach him the way of life. He longed to practice it fully.

Along with the *fact* of God's Word, this passage indicates its *forms*, viewing it from many angles. Word means message; law means instruction, as from a father to his family; testimonies, statutes, judgments or ordinances, precepts, and commandments are moral imperatives. References to the blessedness of those who walk in the Law, and the pinpointing of seeking God as the heart of law-keeping, are reminders that the Word includes promises and reveals God himself. The Word is God's medium of communication and communion with people in all the many-sidedness of his relationship with us.

Finally these verses show the *fruit* of God's Word. It elicits desire for obedience, prayer for instruction, and wholehearted seeking of God; it cleanses the way, diverting us from what defiles; it moves us to speak for God and find our joy in him. Thus through the Word of God, the work of God goes on in human lives.

Am I making sufficient use of God's Word—the main means of guidance, growth, and grace?
Make the passage the basis for your prayer.

My word and the Word

We heard this voice borne from heaven, for we were with him on the holy mountain. And we have the prophetic word made more sure.

2 Peter 1:18–19

Peter wants his readers to be sure of the reality, truth, and reliability of the things that he has taught them concerning Jesus Christ. The gist of what he says is: We didn't stuff you with stories that have no factual basis when we told you about the power and coming of our Lord Jesus Christ. No, we were eye-witnesses of his majesty. We saw and heard. He received honor and glory from God the Father; a voice came to him from the majestic glory saying, "This is my Son, whom I love; with whom I am well pleased." We saw it, we heard it. Take it from me.

But then he goes on: Don't *just* take it from me. We have a more sure, firm, reliable source of knowledge about Christ than even eye-witness testimony: namely, the prophetic Word (i.e., the Old Testament as a whole). Startlingly, Peter moves from his own personal testimony to Scripture. He tells his readers that the prophetic Word is more sure; that what God said confirms his experience, not the other way around.

The prophetic Word also covers apostolic writing for us: "Our beloved brother Paul wrote to you according to the wisdom given him . . . There are some things in them (i.e., in his letters) hard to understand, which the ignorant and unstable twist to their own destruction, as they do the other Scriptures" (2 Pet. 3:15–16). So Peter was already, in the apostolic age, comparing the letters of his brother Paul with other Scriptures, thus classifying them as Scripture too.

Is my church family marrying personal testimony and scriptural truth?
Lord, may I, like Peter, be able to say to others with authority, "Take it from me," because what God says in the Bible confirms my experience.

In the way of thy testimonies I delight as much as in all riches.
Psalm 119:14

Pleasure, unalloyed and unending, is God's purpose for his people in every aspect and activity of their fellowship with him. "In thy presence there is fulness of joy, in thy right hand are pleasures for evermore" (Ps. 16:11). I hold the heady doctrine that no pleasures are so frequent or intense as those of the grateful, devoted, single-minded, wholehearted, self-denying Christian. I maintain that the delights of work and leisure, of friendship and family, of eating and mating, of arts and crafts, of playing and watching games, of finding out and making things, of helping other people, and all the other noble pleasures that life affords are doubled for Christians, for they taste God in all their pleasures and this increases them, whereas for other people pleasure brings with it a sense of hollowness and reduces it.

Also, I believe that every encounter between the sincere Christian and God's Word, however harrowing or humbling its import, brings joy as its spin-off, and the keener the Christian the greater the joy.

But this joy does not come from seeking it through Bible study or any other activity. Bible study for our own pleasure, rather than for God's, ends up by giving pleasure neither to him nor us. It only gives enjoyment if conforming to our Creator in belief and behavior, through trust and obedience, is its goal. What brings joy is finding God's way, God's grace, and God's fellowship through the Bible, even though again and again what God tells us in the Bible knocks us flat.

Read Psalm 119 and note how often the writer speaks of God's laws being his delight, his joy, or something he loves.
Lord, I want to experience more and more what it means to delight in you. . .

If you are willing and obedient, you shall eat the good of the land.
Isaiah 1:19

There is such a thing as human nature, and true humanness and self-fulfillment, and that true humanness is true freedom. But freedom requires submission to an adequate external authority, otherwise integration of our life will never be achieved. Without an external principle of authority, each person's name becomes Legion, for he is many; a thousand different desires pull him different ways, and he goes through life literally distracted. He has no criterion for determining priorities; he never knows himself well enough to be sure what he really wants most, and is constantly being disappointed as expected delights turn to dust and ashes under his hand. He lives on the edge of nihilism, the denial of real value in anything.

Brave he may be (for it is not a nice place to live), but fulfilled and contented he is not. His so-called freedom is actually bondage to himself and he never understands the paradox that real freedom is only found under authority. In fact there is only one principle of authority that leads to the total fulfillment which is total freedom—namely, acceptance of the Creator's personal rule in and through our Lord Jesus Christ, a rule that is exercised by means of the Scriptures.

Christianity is thus the truest humanism for it brings us under the authority that truly fits our human nature and leads it to integration, and so brings us contentment. In commending the Christian gospel we should focus attention on Jesus Christ who is God's authority, law, gospel, and salvation in person. The essential verdict for which the gospel calls is not on Christianity as a system but on the Son; and the fundamental authority which the gospel proclaims is his personal rule over our lives via the Word, as our Savior and rightful Lord.

Do I have an attitude of willing obedience to God's authority?
Lord, as far as I know I am "willing and obedient" and yet I don't seem to be eating "the good of the land" in any sense. Show me if there's something I need to do or give me patience until your promise is fulfilled. (Alternatively, if you are eating "the good of the land," praise God.)

Blessed is the man who walks not in the counsel of the wicked.
Psalm 1:1

Psalm 1 sets the tone and focuses the outlook for the whole psalter. It's a meditation showing the profile of the godly person, comparing him with the ungodly. Try to read the whole psalm with this thought in mind.

The godly avoid and turn from the thoughts and plans, interests and attitudes of those who scoff at godliness and defy God. Instead they delight in God's Law. Why? Because they delight in God himself of whom the law testifies and from whom it derives. This is the *way* of the righteous, in contrast to the ungodly.

The *fruit* of the righteous is a matter of Godlikeness in conduct, influence for good, and positive contribution to others' welfare. In this sense the ungodly are conspicuously unfruitful; sin being a disintegrative force, its servants bring themselves and the world only misery. The godly man's fruit is consistent and regular, like that of a tree rooted by a river and fed by the water in the ground. The picture is of God supplying strength for all good works through the godly man's meditation on the Word. His universal prospering is inward; since he tries to do everything for God's praise, according to his Word, he is enriched by the inner contentment of a good conscience, even when his endeavors are outwardly frustrated and abortive.

His *stability* is due not only to his inner integration but to the fact that God knows his way, accepts, and watches over him. In the final judgment he will stand—confirmed in God's favor—while the ungodly, whose way is unacceptable, will fall. Scripture regularly evaluates ways of life by noting how they will fare at Judgment Day.

Has the New Testament affected any of the spiritual realities in this psalm?
Lord, if my conduct, influence, contribution are not pleasing to you, show me . . .

Remember the sabbath day, to keep it holy.
Exodus 20:8

The Puritans had helpful things to say about Sunday, which to them was the Christian sabbath and, as they constantly said, "the market-day of the soul." It was not, they said, a day for idleness, but a day for resting from the business of our earthly calling in order to pursue the business of our heavenly calling. Nor was it meant to be a tedious burden, but a joyful privilege; not a fast but a feast; not a useless labor, but a means of grace.

In order to get the most out of Sunday, they said, we need to prepare ourselves for it—freeing ourselves from distractions and encumbrances and spending time on Saturday in self-examination, confession, and prayer.

Public worship was to be central on the Lord's day, and Puritans had little sympathy with those who complained at the length of services, although Baxter did urge preachers to "preach with such life and awakening seriousness...and with such easy method and with such variety of wholesome matter that the people may never be weary of you."

The Puritans stressed that the family must function as a religious unit on the Lord's day, with the man of the house exercising his responsibility to care for the souls of his household. The Puritan pastor, unlike his modern counterpart, did not scheme to reach the men through the women and children but vice versa.

He also tried to avoid the pitfalls of legalism (putting all the emphasis on what one must *not* do on the Lord's day) and of Pharisaism (the habit of mind which is poised to censure others for their real or fancied lapses in this area).

The Puritans felt that joy should be the keynote of public worship. Is joy the keynote of your church services? If not, why not?
Lord, are we making the most of this means of grace which you have given us?

Fulfil the law of Christ.
Galatians 6:2

Situationists are right to stress that each situation is in some sense unique and that only by concentrating intensely on it shall we ever see what is the best we can make of it. Rightly too they stress that love always seeks the best for all parties and is betrayed if we settle for mere formal correctness or avoidance of wrongdoing without asking whether we could do something better. Insistence that real love is creative, enterprising, and unwilling to settle for second-best in relationships is a substantial grain of truth in situationism. Another is that the lovingness of loving action should be thought out and spelled out in terms of the relationship itself.

But situationism goes astray in its denial that any action is intrinsically immoral, evil, and forbidden. And this one mistake is ruinous.

The New Testament says that though our relationship to God is no longer determined by law because Christ freed us from law as a system of salvation, we are under the law of Christ as a standard of sanctification.

By denying that there are universal God-taught prohibitions, we enmesh love in perplexities. How am I to love my neighbor now? By attending to the situation, I am told. But how am I to define the situation? Any definition will be arbitrary and open to challenge. And having defined it, how can I be sure what is really the most loving thing to do? My built-in moral compass is not completely reliable, and I am hampered by sin and ignorance. I need God's laws to guide me; and there is no clash between keeping God's commandments and loving my neighbor: in fact they go together (1 John 5:2). Law is love's eyes; love is law's heart.

Think some more about the law and the Christian. (Starters: Rom. 6:14; 7:1-6; 10:4; 1 Cor. 9:21; Gal. 3:23–26.)
Lord, help me to be creative and enterprising in my loving of others—within the limits you have laid down.

Gird up your minds, be sober, set your hope fully upon the grace that is coming to you at the revelation of Jesus Christ. As obedient children, do not be conformed to the passions of your former ignorance, but as he who called you is holy, be holy yourselves in all your conduct.

1 Peter 1:13–15

In these verses we are warned against three evils which could blight our Christian lives. The first is being *slack*—so "gird up your minds," pull yourselves together, concentrate. The second is being *haphazard*, which is the way of the drunkard—so "be sober," discipline yourself, be purposeful and alert. The third is being *double-minded*, the evil that results from looking too hard at this world's attractions and not hard enough at the prospect being held out to us by God's promises—so "hope fully," fix your hope on what is to come.

Holy living is motivated by the hope of glory with Christ. To Christians who, like Peter's readers and those living under hostile regimes today, face hardship and ill treatment for Christ's sake for the remainder of their stay on earth, such a hope is supremely stabilizing and encouraging.

Hope is a powerful motive for holy living. Having said that, Peter invokes two more motives for holiness. The first is the Christians' sense of privilege (vv. 18–21) springing from the knowledge of three things: first, the *preciousness* of the blood of Christ which was shed for them; second, the *concern* God has shown for their redemption, designating his Son for this task before they ever existed; third, their *adoption* as God's sons and heirs through the new birth. The second motive is their sense of reverence for the God who is related to them as a just judge as well as a loving father. This filial reverence (not panic or terror) is the meaning of the fear of God (v. 17).

What steps am I taking to gird up my mind? Does our church program explain what this means and encourage the activity?
Lord, I encourage myself now with the thought of the new heaven and earth to come.

Whether you eat or drink, or whatever you do, do all to the glory of God.
1 Corinthians 10:31

In Christian obedience, the motive must be right as well as the action. Most motives are either reactions to situations or people determined from without (i.e., fear or gratitude), or they are personal goals determined from within (e.g., achieving wealth or reputation). Love however is a complex motive involving both these elements; it can be both a reaction of goodwill, occasioned and energized by appreciation of the beloved, and also a purpose of conferring benefit and happiness, irrespective of whether the recipients deserve it or what it costs.

The Christian's supreme motive must always be the glory of God, and seeking his glory is the truest expression of love for him. But love for people for the Lord's sake should motivate us also, and this has been an area of keen debate in recent years. How should love determine my behavior toward my neighbor?

It is necessary to reject the situationist idea that biblical rules of conduct are only rules of thumb, and that sound calculation of consequences can in principle make transgression of any of them right and good. At the same time it is important to realize that the more strongly neighbor-love operates as a motive (other things being equal), the more enterprising and skillful we are likely to be in devising, within the limits that the Law sets, the most fruitful ways and means of doing others good.

And when we find ourselves having to make "lesser-evil" choices, love for God and neighbor will enable us to see the best that can be made of a bad job, and to choose in the least destructive way. Love is like a good referee—applying the rules in a way that secures the best for everyone.

For thought: Doing good to others should involve us and not just our actions.
Lord, in whatever I may do for others today, help me to give something of myself.

You must not be like the hypocrites.
Matthew 6:5

The original meaning of the word *hypocrite* was play-actor. In the ancient theater, long before the days of makeup, actors would wear masks to represent the characters they were playing. Anyone watching such (or indeed any) actors would be mistaken if they supposed they were seeing real people or their real lives. All they were seeing would be people putting on a show playing different parts, in order to entertain, impress, and be applauded.

So Jesus tells his disciples not to be like hypocrites—in this case the Pharisees—in their giving, praying, and fasting (Matt. 6:1-18). The Pharisees, says Jesus, put on an act before an audience, hoping that people will think them wonderfully pious. If that happens, they receive their reward from men. But God will not be pleased with their performance. He, so to speak, will be watching but not clapping, knowing that they have done it for themselves, not for him.

Over against this hollow religiosity, Jesus holds up the standard set out in the sixth beatitude: "Blessed are the pure in heart, for they shall see God" (Matt. 5:8). Being pure in heart means much more than having a heart and mind free from thoughts and desires that might be called dirty; it's a matter of having God himself as our goal and wanting above all to please, honor, know, adore, and get close to him.

The whole first half of Matthew chapter 6 is a sermon on purity of heart, as illustrated by three of the activities of a disciple's life—giving, praying, and fasting. There must be no hypocrisy, phoneyness, artificiality, or showing off in these or any other areas of Christian worship and service.

Think about the kind of situations and occurrences which have made me feel pleased with myself. What does this show me about who I am really trying to impress or find favor with?
Lord, where my motives are mixed, help me to acknowledge this and not pretend otherwise.

Just as the body is one and has many members, and all the members of the body, though many, are one body, so it is with Christ.
1 Corinthians 12:12

The body was Paul's standard illustration for making clear the inner life of the church. There is one church universal which is invisible in its own nature. It is the company of those who have living faith in Christ and so are united to each other because they are united to him. But that church becomes visible wherever the people of God, either many or few, meet together to worship, pray, maintain the ministry of the Word, spread the gospel, have fellowship, celebrate the sacraments, and share the things of God. So Paul writing to the local church at Corinth says, "You are the body of Christ" (1 Cor. 12:27).

He would say the same thing, no doubt, to every congregation he was privileged to address. For each local congregation is a small-scale presentation and an authentic sample of the church universal. Therefore, when people look at any congregation, they should see the life of the world church concentrated in that one place.

What sort of life should it be?: Body life, the life in which all limbs are contributing to the welfare of the whole body. Our bodies give us trouble when any part is not working properly, but when the parts work properly, the body's life is a wonderful thing. In the same way Paul wants us to understand that the life of a church is a wonderful thing as, in the power of God's Spirit, each limb, unit, bit, piece, joint, and muscle does its best and contributes to the health of the whole (Eph. 4:16).

What kind of body life is my local church enjoying?
Pray for the health and vigor of your local church.

Once you were no people but now you are God's people.
1 Peter 2:10

In this fallen world where men and women are alienated through sin from both God and each other, God has acted to create for himself a new people who should live with him and with each other in a fellowship of covenant love and loyalty.

First he made a covenant with Abraham and his descendants—binding himself to bless them and binding them to worship and serve him. Later when he brought Abraham's family out of Egypt, he renewed the covenant and gave them, along with the Law which showed what behavior would please and displease him, a system which had sacrifice at its heart, whereby sin might be put away and communion between him and them maintained.

When Israel fell into unfaithfulness, a recurring pattern of divine action emerged—judgment on all, followed by deliverance and renewal for a faithful remnant.

When Christ came to set up a new and richer form of covenant relationship by his priestly sacrifice of himself, Israel spurned his ministry. He was then, in his own person, the true Israel, the faithful remnant. In him God's Israel was reconstituted out of believers as such, and in it Jew and Gentile are together as fellow citizens, branches of one olive tree and brothers in one family. Thus reconciliation to both God and each other takes the place of the alienation that was there before. In heaven the church will remain one city, family, and flock together.

Have you ever thought of your church as having (among others) the function described in Ephesians 3:10: to show forth to the watching angels the "manifold wisdom of God"?

Lord, let us not shrink from being known and treated as your people.

Jesus came and stood among them, and said, "Peace be with you."
John 20:26

There are many deep and thrilling truths in the Bible about the church, but the deepest and best of all is that the church is the people of the presence: the company of those who (when they meet) find their Lord in their midst, just like when Jesus came and stood in the Upper Room.

After bringing the people out of Egypt to Sinai and giving them the essence of the Law, God said to Moses, "Let them make me a sanctuary, that I may dwell in their midst" (Exod. 25:8). It could not have been at all easy to construct in the wilderness the tabernacle and all the apparatus of sacrificial worship, but obviously God intended it to be a priority that the people should recognize his presence with them and keep the lines of fellowship with him clear in the ways that he told them to.

Moses realized how important God's presence with them was. For in his prayer after the golden calf incident he said, "If thy presence will not go with me, do not carry us up from here" (Exod. 33:15). But God's presence did go with his people and in due course the tabernacle was replaced by the temple at Jerusalem. In psalm after psalm godly men proclaim how much they love going to the temple because there they experience the presence of God. Then came "Jesus our Emmanuel," God with his people in person (Matt. 1:23); and Jesus promised his permanent presence in the midst of those who gathered in his name (Matt. 18:20). Accordingly, in Revelation the church is pictured as seven golden lampstands with Jesus in the midst (Rev. 1:12–16).

If 1 Corinthians 14:24–25 is not happening in our church at all, then perhaps Jesus is not in our midst as he ought to be.
Lord, make our church into the people of your presence. May we and others feel that you really are among us.

The family unit
The people of the peace

Jesus said to them again, "Peace be with you."
John 20:21

Jesus' first words to his disciples after his death and resurrection were not words of recrimination: "Why did you run away? Why did you let me down? You're a poor lot, I must say!" Instead they were words of love and mercy, reassuring words: "Peace to you!" Then he showed them his hands and his side. Why? Partly no doubt for identification purposes, for in his hands were the prints of the nails and in his side was the wound left by the spear.

But surely he had another reason for showing these things to them. He wanted to remind them of the cross and of what he had achieved for them there. He had died to make peace and now he'd come back to bring them that peace. It was peace with God first of all, but from that flows much more. Once a person knows that God has forgiven and accepted him and will keep him right to the end of his life and then receive him into heaven to be with his Lord forever, he can enjoy peace with himself (if God has forgiven you, you have to forgive yourself!), and he can also be at peace with his situation. This will lead to peace with his fellow men. The deepest cause of tension between people is their own inner lack of peace. We denigrate and crush others because we feel insecure and discontented ourselves. When Jesus gives peace within, our attitude to others changes completely.

When Jesus said, "Blessed are the peacemakers" (Matt. 5:9) he meant more than is often found in this statement. He meant: Blessed are those who seek by what they do, are, and say to bring the peace of Christ into a rent world at every level of its life. Jesus brings peace from God to us so that we may share it with others.

When people have let me down, do my first words to them (if I'm speaking to them at all!) tend to be words of recrimination or love? What reactions have either sorts of words produced?
Lord, am I/Is my church family guilty of saying " 'Peace, peace,' when there is no peace" (Jer. 6:14) or of being controversial when I/we should be conciliatory?

God has so adjusted the body. . . that the members may have the same care for one another.
1 Corinthians 12:24–25

As an outcrop and sample of the church universal, created in Christ by the Holy Spirit of God, the local church has its own proper life to live—a life lived on very different principles and for very different ends from the life of the world around. The church's life, we are told, must be one of *love*—a life of gratitude to God in which we seek to imitate our Savior by love towards all people, and particularly those who are both his brothers and sisters and ours.

Specifically, this life of love is to be a life of *fellowship* whereby we share (for that is what fellowship really means) the good things that God has given us individually. No Christian is self-sufficient; we all need each other and what God has given each other; we must learn, therefore, to express our love in the give-and-take of Christian fellowship. And this loving fellowship must take the form of *ministry* (*diakonia,* in Greek; service, in literal English). "Through love be servants of one another" (Gal. 5:13). In this basic sense the church's ministry is a vocation to which every Christian is called.

It is for this life of ministry, in which every part of the body is called to make its contribution (Eph. 4:16), that God gives *gifts.* Gifts and ministry are in this sense correlative; God gives each man his gift not primarily for himself but for others to be used for their good in the fellowship of the body's life (1 Cor. 12:7). The body image provides on each occasion the context of Paul's teaching about spiritual gifts.

Do we in our church fellowship have the same care for one another?
Lord, help us never to forget that we are a supernatural community with your supernatural life flowing through us and binding us together.

On that day many will say to me, "Lord, Lord, did we not prophesy in your name. . .?" And then will I declare to them, "I never knew you; depart from me, you evildoers."

Matthew 7:22–23

Man sees the church as an organized society with a fixed structure and roll of members. But this society can never be simply identified with the one holy catholic church of which the Bible speaks. The identity between the two is at best partial, indirect, and constantly varying in degree.

The church as God sees it, the company of believers in communion with him and each other, is necessarily invisible to men since Christ and the Holy Spirit and faith, the realities which make the church, are themselves invisible.

The church becomes visible as its members meet together in Christ's name to worship and hear God's Word. But the church visible is a mixed body. Some who belong, though orthodox, are not true believers—true members of the church as God knows it—and need to be converted. Visible church membership saves no one apart from faith in Christ.

If a visible organization as such could be the one church of God, then the only way to reunite a divided Christendom would be to work for a single international super-church. But in fact the church invisible, the true church, is one already. Its unity is given to it in Christ. The proper ecumenical task is not to create church unity by denominational coalescence but to recognize the unity that already exists and to give it worthy expression on the local level.

In what ways are the local churches where you live saying to one another and to the world, "We are one"?

Lord, forgive us for the message that we are conveying to the world through our failure to express and demonstrate that we are one.

The family unit
Not *a* church—*the* church

Greet Prisca and Aquila...Greet also the church in their house.
Romans 16:3,5

Paul speaks not merely of the whole body but also of local groups in an area, and even of a Christian household, as *the* church. No local church is ever called *a* church. For Paul does not regard the church universal as an aggregate of local churches (let alone denominations!); his thought is rather that whenever believers meet in Christ's name, they *are* the church in the place where they meet. "Where two or three are gathered in my name, there am I in the midst of them" (Matt. 18:20). Each particular gathering, however small, is the local manifestation of the church universal, embodying and displaying the spiritual realities of the church's supernatural life.

So Paul can apply the body metaphor, with only slight alteration, both to the local church and to the universal church; he emphasizes that the local church is the body in Christ and the universal church is one body under Christ (Eph. 4).

Have I realized that even in small gatherings all that applies to God's people generally applies equally to them? What difference should this make to any small groups I may attend?

Meditate on Peter's description of the church and its function: "You are a chosen race, a royal priesthood, a holy nation, God's own people, that you may declare the wonderful deeds of him who called you out of darkness into his marvelous light" (1 Pet. 2:9).

God said, "I will live in them and move among them, and I will be their God, and they shall be my people."

2 Corinthians 6:16

The church is not simply a New Testament phenomenon. The New Testament church is the historical continuation of Old Testament Israel. The basis of the church's life in both Testaments is the covenant which God made with Abraham. He expounded this covenant in Genesis chapter 17.

God announced the covenant relationship as a *corporate* one, extending to Abraham's family throughout the generations. Thus the covenant created a permanent community. Second, the relationship was one of *pledged beneficence* (active goodness) on God's part. It was God who would give Abraham's descendants the land of Canaan and redeem them from captivity in Egypt (Gen. 15:13-21). Third, the goal of the relationship was *fellowship* between God and his people. Fourth, the covenant was confirmed by the institution of a token—the *initiatory rite* of circumcision.

Later, through Moses, God gave his people a *law* for their lives and authorized forms of *worship*. Also he spoke to them repeatedly through his prophets of their glorious *hope* which was to be realized when the Messiah came.

Thus emerged the basic biblical notion of the church as the covenant people of God—the redeemed family, marked out as his by the covenant sign which they had received—actively worshipping and serving him according to his revealed will, living in fellowship with him and each other, walking by faith in his promises, and looking for the coming of the glorious messianic kingdom.

What are the two main biblical pictures of the covenant relationship between God and his people (overlord and vassal, husband and wife) intended to convey?
You are our (my) God and we are (I am one of) your people. How often do you say this to God?

You are. . . God's own people.
1 Peter 2:9

When Christ came, the Old Testament concept of the church was not destroyed but fulfilled. Christ, the mediator of the covenant, was the link between the Mosaic and the Christian dispensations. The New Testament depicts him as the true Israel, the servant of God in whom the nation's God-guided history is recapitulated and brought to completion, and also as the seed of Abraham in whom all the nations of the earth find blessing. Through his atoning death, which did away with the typical sacrificial services forever, believing Jews and Gentiles become in him the people of God on earth. Baptism, the New Testament initiatory sign corresponding to circumcision, represents primarily union with Christ in his death and resurrection—the sole way of entry into the church.

Thus, the New Testament church has Abraham as its father, Jerusalem as its mother and place of worship, and the Old Testament as its Bible.

The New Testament idea of the church is reached by superimposing upon the notion of the covenant people of God the further thought that the church is the company of those who share in the redemptive renewal of a sin-spoiled creation which began when Jesus rose from the dead. As the individual believer is a new creation in Christ, raised with him out of death into life, possessed and led by the life-giving Holy Spirit, so also is the church as a whole.

If someone asked you for the biblical basis of the above definition of the church, would you be able to turn quickly to the relevant passages? If not, familiarize yourself with them as soon as possible.
Lord, am I/Is my church doing enough to share in the redemptive renewal of those parts of the sin-spoiled creation with which we are linked or surrounded?

December 1 — **The head of the family** / The God who adopts

God sent forth his Son. . . to redeem those who were under the law, so that we might receive adoption as sons.

Galatians 4:4–5

Adoption, by its very nature, is an act of free kindness to the persons adopted. If you become a father by adopting a child, you do so because you choose to, not because you are bound to. Similarly, God adopts because he chooses to. He has no duty to do so. He need not have done anything about our sins save punish us as we deserved. But he loved us; he redeemed us, forgave us, took us as his sons, and gave himself to us as our Father.

Nor does his grace stop short with that initial act, any more than the love of human parents who adopt stops short with the completing of the legal process that makes the child theirs. The establishing of the child's status as a member of the family is only a beginning. The real task remains: to establish a filial relationship between your adopted child and yourself. It is this, above all, that you want to see. Accordingly you set yourself to win the child's love by loving it. You seek to excite affection by showing affection. And so it is with God. Throughout our life in this world, and to all eternity beyond, he will constantly be showing us in one way or another more and more of his love, and thereby increasing our love to him continually. The prospect before the adopted sons of God is an eternity of love.

Adoption into God's family is the highest privilege that the gospel offers. Do you agree? Think about the blessings available for all God's adopted children.
Praise God for each of these and go into the day bearing in mind who you are in God's eyes. For most of us this will mean living with greatly increased confidence!

Those whom he predestined he also called; and those whom he called he also justified; and those whom he justified he also glorified.
Romans 8:30

I hope it doesn't frighten you to think that before the world was made, God knew what was going to happen: he foresaw the fall; he knew that we were going to be the sinners that we are; he chose to save us as we are now saved; he chose to glorify us as one day we will be glorified; he chose us to be with him and to be like Jesus and to enjoy heaven through all eternity.

Predestination is not a doctrine meant to frighten anyone; it's a family secret for the children of God. Nor does it in any way cut across the universal terms of the gospel invitation (John 3:16; Rom. 10:13). No hearers of the gospel will be denied heaven except those who have refused to accept the Christ who was truly offered to them. But those who have heard and responded to the good news of Christ are like people who have been invited to walk through a doorway. On the outside of the door are the words: "Whosoever will may come." Once they have come in, they look back and see what is written on the inside of the door: "Chosen in him before the foundation of the world."

Now that they are in the family, they can be told the family secret—that the faith by which they trusted Christ was itself God's gift to them, just as God's Son, their Savior, was God's gift to them; and that God willed to give them this gift from eternity, having chosen them in Christ before the foundation of the world and then, in the course of time, fulfilled the purpose of that choice. In fact, their renewed hearts tell them this before any human instructions do.

"Why me?" we ask, not bitterly, but in the tone of a happy wife asking, "Why ever did he choose me?" or a happy husband saying, "Why did she ever accept me?" Why God chose any of us, I don't know, but I can't get over the fact that he chose me.

Am I embarrassed, incredulous, or "lost in wonder, love and praise" about the family secret?
Father, thank you that you chose me because you loved me, and loved me because you loved me. . .

*I will restore to you the years which the swarming locust has eaten. . . You shall eat in
plenty and be satisfied, and praise the name of the LORD your God, who has dealt
wondrously with you.*

Joel 2:25–26

If I found I had driven into a bog, I should know I had missed the road. But
this knowledge would not be much comfort if I then had to stand helpless
watching the car sink and vanish: the damage would be done and that
would be that. Is it the same when a Christian wakes up to the fact that he
has missed God's guidance and taken the wrong way? Is the damage irrevocable? Must he now be put off course for life?

Thank God, no. Our God is a God who not merely restores, but takes
our mistakes and follies into his plan for us and brings good out of them.
This is part of the wonder of his gracious sovereignty. The Jesus who restored Peter after his denial, and corrected his course more than once after
that, is our Savior today and he has not changed. God makes not only the
wrath of man turn to his praise but the misadventures of Christians too.

Not merely does God guide us by showing us the way so we may tread
it; he also wills to guide us more fundamentally by ensuring that, whatever
happens, whatever mistakes we make, we shall come home safely. Slippings
and strayings there will be, no doubt, but the everlasting arms are beneath
us; we shall be caught, rescued, restored.

Are you bogged down by the feeling that you are enjoying God's second-best because of some wrong turning you took earlier? Realize that it is needless and
groundless, as well as self-defeating, to go on feeling this way.
*Lord, cleanse me from the guilt and power of my sin. . . (whatever it was). I accept
your forgiveness and trust you to restore me and the situation completely, so that I
can experience now your best will for my life.*

When the flame went up toward heaven from the altar, the angel of the LORD ascended in the flame of the altar while Manoah and his wife looked on; and they fell on their faces to the ground.
Judges 13:20

Read the story of Manoah and his wife and the angel of the Lord in Judges chapter 13 and notice the characters of the two people. Manoah appears as a fussy, pompous sort of man as well as a very religious and correct one. His wife told him exactly what had happened but Manoah felt he had to check it out for himself. I suspect he resented the fact that the "man of God" had come to his wife instead of to him! Anyway, he prayed to the Lord asking him to send the man of God to them again. His prayer was answered but again the messenger appeared first to Manoah's wife! She called her husband and he came and said, (v. 11) "Are you the man who spoke to this woman?" (Not "my wife" but "this woman"—note the nuance!) When the angel of the Lord said that he was, Manoah with fulsome eastern courtesy continued (v. 12), "When your words come true, what is to be the boy's manner of life?" The divine messenger (for the angel of the Lord, whom Manoah took for a prophet, was actually a theophany) replied in effect: What I say to you now is exactly what I said earlier to your wife; why did you feel you needed me to say it again?

The dialogue continued and then Manoah, at the messenger's suggestion, offered a burnt offering to the Lord. When the flames went up to heaven and the divine visitor with them, Manoah realized that he had been in direct contact with God himself and panicked. Again his wife had the right word!

If you're a married man, may I ask whether you're willing to take advice from your wife? If not, you're very foolish indeed!

Am I willing to learn from every and any other person who can help me know myself or God better? Beware of thinking about any other Christian, "There's nothing he/she can teach me."
Lord, make me humble enough to learn from anyone. Forgive me for my superior attitude to . . .

Manoah said to his wife, "We shall surely die, for we have seen God." But his wife said to him, "If the LORD had meant to kill us, he would not have accepted a burnt offering and a cereal offering at our hands, or shown us all these things, or now announced to us such things as these."

Judges 13:22–23

There was an inkling of wisdom in Manoah's panic reaction. He knew that the God of Israel was a holy God and that sinful humans who looked on him could not expect to live. Remember how Isaiah expected to die when he saw God in the temple (Isa. 6)? Only atonement wrought by God himself can finally quench this fear. But the panic proves that Manoah, although he was so careful and fussy, did not know well the details of his religion. He had not yet grasped that God can be relied on. However his wife knew this. She understood that God does not go back on his plans; if he takes people up, he doesn't abandon them; if he binds himself by promise, he keeps his word. She told her husband that God would certainly not wipe them out after accepting their burnt offering and telling them about their coming child and the divine purpose for him. In effect she was saying to Manoah: God is not capricious—he's consistent! Calm down! Rejoice!

There are many situations in which we feel that God is destroying hopes that he himself gave us. That was how the disciples felt on the road to Emmaus. We trusted that Jesus would redeem Israel, they said. But now look what's happened. He's dead. Joseph must have had similar feelings when he was in prison in Egypt. What about all those visions of greatness that God gave him as a teenager? But we know how both stories ended. The hopes God had given were truly fulfilled, though not in the way that was first expected.

Panic reactions at times of stress and trauma will lead us infallibly to the wrong conclusions.

"God has forgotten us." "God is destroying us." What other panic reactions can you think of and what are the answers to them?
Lord, your love in times past forbids me to think you'll leave us to sink in troubles! Thank you for your faithfulness to your own purpose.

And the angel of the LORD appeared to the woman and said to her, "Behold, you are barren and have no children; but you shall conceive and bear a son. Therefore beware, and drink no wine or strong drink, and eat nothing unclean."
Judges 13:3–4

The angel of the Lord told Manoah's wife that she would have a son and that he would live as a Nazirite. That meant he was to be specially dedicated to God and to observe certain rules as signs of this fact. To be *teetotal* and never cut his hair were two of these rules. As well as telling Manoah's wife all this, the angel said that she too must observe certain rules: she must not touch alcohol nor eat ritually unclean food. This is the only time in the Bible that specific rules were given to a mother-to-be. Manoah's wife might well have asked why she had to observe them. If she had, the only answer would have been, "Because I say so."

God makes the rules. He is not obliged to explain the reasons for them. Our part is simply to keep them. God did not tell Manoah's wife why he gave her certain instructions any more than he explained to Gideon why he must reduce his big army to a little band in the way that he did. We may guess at reasons, but ultimately we're left with the thought of our gracious God's right to make rules.

If ever we find ourselves saying to God, "But God, you can't want me to do that—it's not reasonable," we will probably receive no answer except a repetition in our own conscience of what God has told us to do. It is often pride that asks God why and makes us disinclined to do what he says just because he says it. Adam and Eve questioned God's order and eventually disobeyed it; and Satan, who tempted them, will tempt us in the same way. Manoah's wife didn't ask for explanations; she obeyed God, and thus received the blessing he had planned for her.

Am I mature enough to obey Mary's instructions to the servants in John 2:5?
Lord, help me to trust your love even when you don't give me any reasons.

The angel of the Lord said to him, "Why do you ask my name, seeing it is wonderful?"

Judges 13:18

When Manoah asked the angel of the Lord what his name was, the answer was, from one standpoint, rather evasive; from another, it was an invitation to reflect, think, and worship. Manoah was right to say that they had seen God (Judg. 13:22); the angel of the Lord was God himself acting as his own messenger.

When we think of God as the God of wonders, we think of him calling this world into being out of nothing and of Jesus turning water into wine, feeding the four thousand and five thousand, healing the sick, and raising the dead. Certainly, the God who has at his command every moment all the power that brought creation into being is a God of miracles. In the Bible miracles surround the great moments of revelation to call attention to what is going on.

But the Bible is also full of other and greater wonders than works of dazzling power. The fact that God in love saves sinners is the greatest wonder of all.

In the story of Manoah, his wife, and the angel of the Lord (Judg. 13), the wonder of God's love comes out in all sorts of ways. Israel had sinned, God in judgment had sent the people into captivity, and now God takes the initiative and begins to act for their salvation and restoration.

How does he do this? He comes to a barren woman and tells her she's going to have a special child who will deliver his people. And in time, she does. Shades of Jesus? Yes—literally! So here we see the wonder not just of God's power, but also of his mercy, faithfulness, and love.

For encouragement: Anything God has promised you, he will do.
Lord, I believe your promise. . . and trust in your power, love, and faithfulness.

My God will supply every need of yours according to his riches in glory in Christ Jesus.
Philippians 4:19

How would God supply every need of the Philippian Christians? Partly, at least, by Christ's work through the Spirit of actualizing the gifts of Samaritanship among the Philippians themselves. When Christians speak to one another in Christ's name and practice care for others because they are Christians, Christ in person blesses through them (2 Thess. 3:6; Mark 9:41). As Christ says categorically of the practice of care that "as you did it to one of the least of these my brethren, you did it to me" (Matt. 25:40), so we may say just as categorically that when other Christians bring us understanding and encouragement and relief of need in any form at all, Christ himself ministers to us, bringing us these benefits through them (2 Cor. 13:3; Rom. 15:18).

From heaven Christ uses Christians as his mouth, his hands, his feet, even his smile; it is through us, his people, that he speaks and acts, meets, loves, and saves here and now in this world. This seems to be part of the meaning of Paul's picture of the church as Christ's body in which every believer is a member—a limb or organ moving at the direction of Christ the head.

A paradox to ponder and keep us from either complacency or going frantic: "God has no hands but our hands" and ". . . thousands at his bidding speed, and post o'er land and ocean without rest" (Milton).
Lord, I put myself and all my potential into your hands for this day with all its opportunities.

In every way you were enriched in him with all speech and all knowledge. . . so that
you are not lacking in any spiritual gift.

1 Corinthians 1:5,7

We are right to say that spiritual gifts come from the Spirit (1 Cor. 12:4–11). However we go on to think of them in terms either of giftedness (human ability to do things skillfully and well) or of supernatural novelty (power to speak in tongues, to heal, to receive messages straight from God to give to others, or whatever). We have not formed the habit of defining gifts in terms of Christ, the head of the body, and his present work from heaven in our midst. In this we are unscriptural.

Paul makes it clear that spiritual gifts are given in Christ; they are enrichments received from Christ. 1 Corinthians 12 assumes the Christ-orientated perspective that 1 Corinthians 1:4–7 established. It is vital that we should see this, or we shall be confusing natural with spiritual gifts to the end of our days.

Nowhere does Paul or any other New Testament writer define a spiritual gift for us. But Paul's assertion that the use of gifts *edifies* (1 Cor. 14:3–5,12,17,26; Eph. 4:12), shows what his idea of a gift was.

For Paul it is only through Christ, in Christ, and by learning of and responding to Christ, that anyone is ever edified. So spiritual gifts must be defined in terms of Christ as actualized powers of expressing, celebrating, displaying, and thus communicating Christ in one way or another, either by word or deed.

Do I/Does my church fellowship need to be reminded of this emphasis?
Lord Jesus, help me/us to see the spiritual gifts which you have given to show something of yourself.

By grace you have been saved through faith; and this is not your own doing, it is the gift of God.
Ephesians 2:8

In the New Testament, grace means God's love in action toward people who merited the opposite of love. Grace means God moving heaven and earth to save sinners who could not lift a finger to save themselves. Grace means God sending his only Son to descend into hell on the cross so that we guilty ones might be reconciled to God and received into heaven.

The New Testament knows both a *will* of grace and a *work* of grace. The former is God's eternal plan to save; the latter is God's "good work in you" (Phil. 1:6) whereby he calls people into living fellowship with Christ, raises them from death to life, seals them as his own by the gift of his Spirit, transforms them into Christ's image, and will finally raise their bodies in glory.

It was fashionable at one time among Protestant scholars to say that grace meant God's loving attitude as distinct from his loving work, but that is an unscriptural distinction. For example Paul writes: "By the *grace* of God I am what I am, and his *grace* toward me was not in vain. On the contrary, I worked harder than any of them, though it was not I, but the *grace* of God which is with me" (1 Cor. 15:10). The word grace in this verse clearly denotes God's loving work in Paul, whereby he made him first a Christian and then a minister.

What is the *purpose* of grace? To restore our relationship with God and lead us into the exercise of love, trust, delight, hope, and obedience Godward.

If someone were to ask you what biblical backing there was for the five-fold aspect of God's "good work in you" (second paragraph), would you be able to find the relevant Bible passages easily? If not, find and familiarize yourself with them now. *Praise God for every aspect of his grace toward you.*

*For our sake he made him to be sin who knew no sin, so that in him we might be-
come the righteousness of God.*

2 Corinthians 5:21

If we are Christians, we *have been* saved as God's gift of justification has
saved us from sin's *penalty*; we *are being* saved as we are kept daily from
falling under sin's *power*; and we *will be* fully and finally saved when we are
freed from sin's *presence* and from all its traces at Christ's coming. These are
the three aspects of our salvation; and there are three means by which we
are saved.

First, the sacrificial death of Christ was the means whereby God provided salvation. He gave "his life a ransom for many," shedding his blood,
"like that of a lamb without blemish or spot," for the remission of our sins
(Matt. 20:28; 1 Pet. 1:19; Heb. 9:22).

Second, faith alone, apart from works, is the means whereby we receive
salvation. Faith is an outgoing of the soul in belief and commitment toward
a three-fold object: the God of the Bible; the Christ of God, who is the
Christ of the Bible; and the teaching and promises of God, which are the
teaching and promises of the Bible. Faith receives the truth of God and
trusts the person—or rather, the three persons—of God. Repentance,
which means turning or changing one's mind, is the negative side of faith. It
is saying, "No" to the old godless ways in order to say, "Yes" to Christ henceforth.

Third, regeneration by the Holy Spirit is the means whereby God conveys salvation. As Jesus told Nicodemus, a person cannot see or enter the
kingdom of God (the realm of salvation) without being born again (John
3:3,5). The word "cannot" reveals that fallen human beings like ourselves
lack the power to turn to God and exercise faith unless the Holy Spirit
works in our hearts (John 6:44; Rom. 8:7–8; 1 Cor. 2:14).

Look up the references above and use the verses to express your thanks to God for
what he has done for you and given to you.
Pray that he will do the same for some others who are close to you.

The word of the LORD came to Abram in a vision, "Fear not, Abram, I am your shield; your reward shall be very great."
Genesis 15:1

Is God's promise of a reward a motivation, a spur to make the right choice? Strictly speaking, no. The Christian's reward is not directly earned; it is not a payment proportionate to services rendered; it is a Father's gift of generous grace to his children, far exceeding anything they deserved (Matt. 20:1–16).

Also, we must understand that the promised reward is not something of a different nature tacked on to the activity being rewarded; it is, rather, the activity itself—communion with God in worship and service—in its consummation. God's promise of reward may well be a great encouragement, but the motive must be love to God and neighbor.

C.S. Lewis compares our position as we move on in the Christian life to that of a schoolboy learning Greek. The enjoyment of Aeschylus and Sophocles to which he will one day come is the proper consummation of all his slogging at the grammar, just as the enjoyment of God is the proper consummation of discipleship here. But at first the boy cannot imagine this enjoyment at all. As his Greek improves, however, enjoyment of Greek literature begins to come, and he begins to be able to desire the reward that awaits him (more of the same at a more intense level). This capacity for desire is itself a preliminary reward. Meantime it is the increased enjoyment of the present which sends him back to work at Greek with increased energy and excitement.

If there is more dutifulness than love in my attitude to God, I probably haven't grasped his stupendous, sacrificial love for me.
Lord, as I read, meditate, and pray, help me to grasp your great love for me.

He has sent me to proclaim release to the captives.
Luke 4:18

Ignoring zealot hankerings after national deliverance from Rome, Christ declared that he had come to liberate the slaves of sin and Satan, to overthrow the prince of this world, the strong man, and to release his prisoners. Exorcisms and healings were part of this work of dispossession.

Paul expands the thought that Christ liberates believers here and now from destructive influences to which they were previously in bondage: from sin; from the power of darkness; from polytheistic superstition; from the Law as a system of salvation; and from the burden of Jewish ceremonialism. To all those, freedom from physical corruption and death will be added in due course.

This comprehensive freedom is the gift of Christ, creatively conveyed to believers by the indwelling Spirit. It is the royal freedom of God's adopted sons.

The obverse of Christ's gift of freedom is the Christian's freely accepted bond service to God, to Christ, to righteousness, and to all men for the sake of the gospel and the Savior.

The law of liberty is the law of love. Christian liberty is precisely freedom to love and serve and is therefore abused when it is made an excuse for loveless license or inconsiderateness.

Am I/Is my church having a liberating effect on the captives around?
Lord, show me if there is anyone to whom I need to be proclaiming release in your name.

*What is sown is perishable, what is raised is imperishable. . .It is sown a physical
body, it is raised a spiritual body.*
1 Corinthians 15:42,44

In raising believers, God completes their redemption by the gift not of their
old bodies somehow patched up but of new bodies for new people.
Through regeneration and sanctification God has already renewed them inwardly; now they receive bodies to match. The new body is linked with the
old, yet different from it, just as plants are linked with, yet different, from
the seeds from which they grew (1 Cor. 15:35–44). My present body—
"brother ass" as Francis of Assisi would have me call it—is like a student's
old jalopy; care for it as I will, it goes precariously and never very well, and
often lets me and my master down (very frustrating!). But my new body
will feel and behave like a Rolls-Royce, and then my service will no longer
be spoiled.

No doubt, like me, you both love your body because it is part of you and
get mad at the way it limits you. So we should. And it is good to know that
God's aim in giving us second-rate physical frames here is to prepare us for
managing better bodies hereafter. As C.S. Lewis says, they give you unim-
pressive horses to learn to ride on and only when you are ready for it are
you allowed an animal that will gallop and jump. When I think of Christians who are in one way or another physical wrecks, I could weep for joy
at the thought of the resurrection bodies God has in store for them—and all
Christians—on resurrection day.

What do we know about our bodies?
*Pray for those you know who struggle constantly with bodies which limit them from
doing all that they long to do for God. Perhaps God will give you faith to pray that
they will be given a bit more of a foretaste of their resurrection bodies here and now!*

Do not lay up for yourselves treasures on earth.
Matthew 6:19

Jesus confronts his disciples with a basic choice between laying up treasure on earth and laying up treasure in heaven (Matt. 6:19–24). It is human and natural to want to lay up treasure so Jesus tells his disciples, "Lay up for yourselves treasures in heaven," not on earth. Why should we not lay up treasure on earth? For three reasons.

First, laying up treasure on earth is *daft* because in the long run such treasure is of very little value. You can't keep it (moth and rust consume it), nor take it with you (think of the rich fool, Luke 12:16–21). It cannot satisfy you; you think it's going to bring you joy but it never does. When someone asked an immensely rich man whether his wealth had brought him joy, he replied, "No, nothing tastes now."

Second, laying up treasure on earth is *dangerous* because such treasure destroys spiritual awareness. If your eyes are filled with light and working properly, your body will be able to move easily and safely. If you can't see clearly, you will lack physical ease and poise. Similarly, if your heart is possessed by what this world and this life offers, you will not be able to see spiritual issues clearly, and when you read the Bible, its full meaning will escape you.

Third, laying up treasure on earth is *disastrous* because no one can serve two masters. Even double agents are working for one country or organization in a way that they are not working for the other. In the same way, we cannot serve God and possessions. And to have God pass the verdict that one has not served him is life's ultimate disaster.

Try rewriting the parable of the rich fool giving it a twentieth-century setting. *Why is covetousness idolatry (Col. 3:5)? Think about this and about your own attitudes in this matter in God's presence.*

The truth will make you free.
John 8:32

There are certain illusions to which Christians are particularly prone and from which they need to be set free.

First, we must not expect to see what God is up to all the time—to be able to read the Book of providence and understand the meaning of what is happening at every moment. The truth is that much of the time we have to learn to live with bafflement and say, "God has done (or allowed) this thing that I don't understand; he has ordained it and overrules it, and has a good purpose in it; if I'm faithful to him during theses days of bewilderment and hurt because of it, then I may hope to see sense in it—human sense, and divine sense too—later on." Our job for the present is to concentrate on being faithful.

Second, we must not expect that we shall always know the best course to take. I assume that we shall always be looking for that course, but we're going to make mistakes, and out of these mistakes will come a degree of wisdom which otherwise we would never have had. Those who never make mistakes never make anything. God regularly teaches us by letting us make mistakes and then helping us to correct them and adjust accordingly.

A third illusion is that we will always be shielded from "the slings and arrows of outrageous fortune." Again and again things will happen which will seem grossly unfair and we will be forced to cry out to God, as many writers of the Psalms did, from the depths. It is through such experiences that the deepest knowledge of God will come so God can prepare us for greatest usefulness.

We don't always know what God is doing; we won't always know the best course to take; we won't always be shielded from trouble. These are awesome and not very pleasant truths, but they are meant to set us free, by not taking ourselves too seriously, to receive the daily joys that God will give us regardless of our bafflement, mistakes, and troubles.

Am I deluding myself on these matters?
Lord, it's hard to part with our illusions; it makes us feel very insecure at first. Help us to go through this "shaking" so that we will have our feet set on firmer foundations from now on.

Be not rash with your mouth, nor let your heart be hasty to utter a word before God, for God is in heaven, and you upon earth; therefore let your words be few.
                                                                    Ecclesiastes 5:2

The writer of Ecclesiastes warns us against the thoughtless irreverence which he sees so much in God's world (5:1–7). Looking around God's world, fallen as it is, and seeing its miseries can lead to bitterness and hence to irreverence. So "guard your steps when you go to the house of God; to draw near to listen is better than to offer the sacrifice of fools; for they do not know that they are doing evil" (v. 1).

One of the marks of a fool is that he says things without thinking about them or fully meaning them; so he forgets what he has promised and therefore breaks his word. "Pay what you vow" (v. 4) is a rule both in business and in our relationship with God. In business, people displease their peers, superiors, and trading partners and perhaps miss promotion if they don't do what they say they will. God will be displeased too, if we "vow a vow" to him and then say it was a mistake. "It is better that you should not vow than that you should vow and not pay" (v. 5).

The writer goes on: "When dreams increase, empty words grow many; but do you fear God?" (v. 7). The word *fear* there suggests the sort of reverence which makes you watch what you say, knowing that God will expect you to stand by your words.

What a difference it would make to our prayer life if we really thought about everything we were going to say to God!

Do I tend to be a bottler-up or a pourer-out of words both to God and to others? How can I change for the better?
Father, Son, and Holy Spirit, help us as individuals and as a church family not to let freedom and spontaneity tip over into irreverence and shallowness, or to allow pattern and order to become rigidities and ruts, so that our groove becomes our grave.

I know your works: you are neither cold nor hot. Would that you were cold or hot!
Revelation 3:15

If we are not being renewed, we are called to repent of our guilt in this area. With only one of the seven churches (the Philadelphian congregation) was the Savior pleased (Rev. 1:4–3:22). The Ephesian church was condemned for having left its first love, the church at Sardis for being dead, and the church at Laodicea for being self-satisfied and self-deceived. "You say, I am rich, I have prospered, and I need nothing; not knowing that you are wretched, pitiable, poor, blind, and naked...Those whom I love, I reprove and chasten; so be zealous and repent" (Rev. 3:17,19). It is hard to doubt that this is the mind of Jesus with regard to many churches today.

Biblical theology knows no middle condition for churches or Christians between spiritual advance under God's blessing and spiritual decline under his displeasure. The root of spiritual decline is always human unfaithfulness in some form, and its fruit is always chastening judgment from God whose gracious plan and supernatural enabling are hereby slighted and dishonored.

Marks of decline include high tolerance of half heartedness, moral failure, and compromise; low expectations of holiness in oneself and others; willingness to remain Christian pigmies; apathy about the advancement of God's cause and his glory; and contentment, even complacency, with things as they are. Charles Finney once said, "Christians are more to blame for not being revived than sinners are for not being converted."

Do you agree with Charles Finney?
"From hardness of heart and contempt of thy word and commandment, good Lord deliver us."

Keep back thy servant also from presumptuous sins; let them not have dominion over me!

                                                                    Psalm 19:13

Very revealing were the words that drew down judgment on the ziggurat-makers of primeval Babylon: "Let us build ourselves a city, and a tower with its top in the heavens" (Gen. 11:4). It was not for their achievement but for their conceited purpose, their "we can do anything" attitude, that God struck them with linguistic confusion. The Greeks called this attitude *hubris*, man getting above himself; Augustine called it pride (Latin, *superbia*), the urge to get on top of everything, even God.

As a writer, part of my job is to case the world of scholarship, like a woman bargain-hunting, to find what would be worthwhile for the thoughtful layman to know. If I were to cut corners, skip my research, and rely on verbal skills to conceal the fact that I had nothing to say, I would be betraying my ministry and showing a presumptuous and conceited spirit.

Perhaps God has called you to preach or give talks and has given you "the gift of the gab." If so, you may well find yourself being tempted to rely on your competence, to get above yourself, to be proud and presumptuous. Some preachers, once they get used to public speaking, find that they can keep going with very little preparation and this inevitably results in less and less "vitamin content" in their messages. Perhaps people tell them that their fluency is a *charisma* and that their spontaneity has charm and so they kid themselves that they needn't bother with their homework and that their ministry is just as rich without it. But what we offer in God's name to God's people, we offer to God himself, so we must be delivered from presumptions and illusions and offer the very best (Deut. 17:1).

Am I camouflaging to myself, to others, or both, the fact that I am skimping the hard graft necessary to produce the best in any area for God?

Father, convict me if I am more clever than wise, facile than craftsmanlike.

Are we to continue in sin that grace may abound? By no means! How can we who died to sin still live in it?
Romans 6:1–2

How can a student who's been expelled from school, or whose school has been closed down, continue attending there? How can an employee remain in a firm that has folded? How can a wife continue living with her deceased husband? In the same way, how can we, whose former relationship to sin has been broken, still continue in it as we did before? We can't. We have died to sin and that makes it impossible for us to continue in it.

Paul elaborates further: "Do you not know that all of us who have been baptized into Christ Jesus were baptized into his death? We were buried therefore with him by baptism into death, so that as Christ was raised from the dead by the glory of the Father, we too might walk in newness of life" (Rom. 6:3–4). Baptism (going under the water and coming up again) symbolizes the end of the old life and the beginning of the new. We cannot go on sinning as we did before, because we have been baptized into Christ's death. That means "we have been united with him in a death like his" (Rom. 6:5) and that "our old self was crucified with him" (Rom. 6:6). The result is that the person I was, dominated by the sin-principle, is a thing of the past.

Out of this inward, spiritual death comes resurrection; we are raised with Christ to a new life. Personal identity continues: I'm still me and you are still you. But the basic springs of our disposition and character have altered; our attitudes are different; there has been a change of heart brought about by God, so that now it is our nature to live for God.

Read Romans 6:1–14 and put in your own words the gist of Paul's answer to his question.
Lord, help me absorb this teaching into my life and my mind so that it will be experienced as well as grasped intellectually.

He who has died is freed from sin.
Romans 6:7

People have sometimes misunderstood Paul's teaching in the first half of Romans chapter 6. They think he was affirming there that the renewing work of God, involving union with Christ in his death and resurrection, brings sinless perfection at once. But it's clear from the next two chapters that this is not what he is saying. His line of thought is this: It's just not possible for believers to continue in sin (that is, under sin's rule, sinning as they did before); the former dominion of sin is finished. Once it was natural for them to live under sin's dominion—indeed they could do nothing else—but now it's natural for them to live for God, seeking to obey and please him. This is the natural expression of their renewed nature.

It follows that if a Christian lapses into the old bad habits of sin, he is denying his own new nature and will make himself profoundly miserable in two ways. First, he will feel guilty because he knows he disobeyed God when he did not need to. Second, he will be unhappy because he is doing violence to his own new nature. He will feel that he fed on ashes and put a barrier between himself and God.

What must he do? First of all, he must humble himself, get down before the Lord, and admit that he's been a fool. He must repent—which is not a matter of merely feeling remorse but of "right about turn, and quick march" in the opposite direction. And he must seek and accept forgiveness (1 John 1:9).

Is there any continuing problem in my life for which I should humble myself before God, repent, and ask in faith and forgiveness?
Pray for yourself or someone else whom you think is miserable for the reasons suggested above.

The crowds were astonished at his teaching, for he taught them as one who had authority and not as their scribes.
Matthew 7:28–29

Jesus' teaching in Matthew chapters 6–7 is in the form of a sermon rather than a lecture: not only are ideas stated clearly, they are also applied— chapter 7 being particularly the chapter of application.

We can learn so much from Jesus, the great teacher. Sometimes he made statements which had air all around them, so to speak; statements which he did not explicitly link with what went before or followed afterwards; statements which on first hearing seemed unconnected or enigmatic. This was because he wanted his hearers to think about what he was saying, to "stretch" for the truth, to work out the deep-level connections for themselves. He knew that the mental effort involved would be good for them.

Sometime he would say something startling or paradoxical; or he would ask questions or tell stories.

He showed great analytical power in his capacity to construct arguments and reason things through. He also demonstrated vividness of imagination. He could see and communicate pictures and images that acted like depth-charges in his hearers, bringing into play their emotions and involving them in situations in a way that analytical reasoning could not do. Jesus was overwhelming in both these aspects of effective communication; he was in truth one hundred percent analytical and one hundred percent imaginative all the time.

Thus, he had any number of ways of making people listen and think. Those of us who aim to be good communicators of Christianity could have no better model than Christ himself.

How do I rate as a Christian communicator? What can I do about any areas of weakness?
Lord, teach us to be good communicators whether we have the opportunity to preach, to teach, or simply to chat with others.

Take my yoke upon you, and learn from me; for I am gentle and lowly in heart; and you will find rest for your souls.

Matthew 11:29

In the time of Christ, two oxen pulling a cart would have one big yoke across both their necks. Jesus tells us to be yoked with him and pull along with him—in other words learn to live as he lived. Why? "For I am. . .lowly in heart." Do you find it startling that anyone, let alone the Savior, should claim to be lowly (humble)? I would not blame you if you did.

I remember laughing fit to burst when a friend told me that, at the end of a talk she gave, an old lady had come up to her and said, "I'm *so* glad you spoke on humility. That's my strong point, you know!" Surely it is all too plain that it is self-refuting for any of us fallen creatures to claim humility, though we may recognize it in others. If we who believe are honest with ourselves, we shall always find within us remnants of self-assertive, self-absorbed, self-inflated pride, so that we get puffed up at the thought that we are doing God's will; and to that extent we are not humble, and our obedience is spoiled.

But when Jesus said that he was "gentle and lowly in heart" no pride or self-assertion was involved. The sinless, incarnate Son of God was simply stating a fact: that he, a fully human person, not burdened with a low self-image or anything like that, was wholly and utterly committed to God's plan and place and will and way for his life. We must realize that true humility means not striking an artificial pose or pretending that you are not what you are, but realistically accepting God's will, just as you accept his gifts, with the gladness of heart and the unself-consciousness that flow from concentrating on the one whom you serve.

What differences do you see between a low self-image and true humility? How do non-Christians and the non-Christian media rate humility?

Lord, humility seems to be another of those by-product qualities. Help me to grow in commitment to your will and leave you to produce the fruit of true humility in my life and attitudes.

Not that I have already obtained this or am already perfect; but I press on to make it on my own.
Philippians 3:12

A veteran psychologist defined human maturity as emotional maturity. He analyzed emotional maturity in these terms: 1. Having the ability to deal constructively with reality; 2. Having the capacity to adapt to change; 3. Having a relative (real degree of) freedom from the symptoms produced by tensions and anxieties; 4. Having the capacity to find more satisfaction in giving than receiving; 5. Having the capacity to relate to other people with consistency, helpfulness, and mutual satisfaction; 6. Having the capacity to sublimate and redirect anger to constructive ends.

Each of these abilities or capacities could be classified under one of the following words: acceptance, love, or creativity. And the Bible has a great deal to say about each of these. It seems to me, indeed, that this definition of mental health meshes very directly with what the Bible reveals as being both God's will for human beings and the true fulfillment of human nature.

However, we must not stop short there because moral standards do not come within the purview of psychologists, and we need to say explicitly that there is no maturity without morality. Jesus, God's perfect example of human maturity, displayed perfectly not only acceptance, creativity, and love (i.e., emotional maturity), but also pure-hearted righteousness (i.e., ethical maturity).

We are called to grow more Christlike in both the emotional and the ethical areas. Paul, having said that he was not already perfect (sinless perfection is reserved for the life to come), urges us "to press on toward the goal for the prize of the upward call of God in Christ Jesus" since this is the way to mature and move closer to the ideal (Phil. 3:14–15).

Examine yourself in light of the above.
Lord Jesus, teach me and help me to grow more and more into human maturity.

The Word became flesh and dwelt among us, full of grace and truth.
John 1:14

The really staggering Christian claim is that Jesus of Nazareth was God made man: that the second person of the Godhead became the "second man" (1 Cor. 15:47), the second representative head of the race, determining human destiny; and that he took humanity without loss of deity, so that Jesus of Nazareth was as truly and fully divine as he was human.

Here are two mysteries for the price of one—the plurality of persons within the unity of God, and the union of Godhead and manhood in the person of Jesus. It is here, in the thing that happened at the first Christmas, that the most profound unfathomable depths of the Christian revelation lie. God became man; the divine Son became a Jew; the Almighty appeared on earth as a helpless human baby, unable to do more than lie and stare and wriggle and make noises, needing to be fed and changed and taught to talk like any other child. And there was no illusion or deception in this: the babyhood of the Son of God was a reality. The more you think about it, the more staggering it gets. Nothing in fiction is so fantastic as this truth of the incarnation.

This is the real stumbling-block in Christianity. It is here that Jews, Moslems, Unitarians, Jehovah's Witnesses, and others have come to grief. It is from misbelief or at least inadequate belief about the incarnation that difficulties at other points in the gospel story usually spring (i.e., the virgin birth, miracles, atonement, and resurrection). But once the incarnation is grasped as a reality, these other difficulties dissolve.

Lord, I marvel again at your willingness to be a vulnerable, helpless, dependent baby for our sakes.
Am I willing to put myself into vulnerable positions for love of God/others?

Behold, we are going up to Jerusalem; and the Son of man will be delivered to the chief priests and scribes, and they will condemn him to death, and deliver him to the Gentiles to be mocked and scourged and crucified, and he will be raised on the third day.
Matthew 20:18–19

Some people say that the relationship of Jesus with his heavenly Father was so close that it was a matter of vision rather than of faith. But I believe that it was both.

There were times, certainly, when the Father spoke directly to the Son. It's plain, for example, that when Jesus said, "The Father who sent me has himself given me commandment what to say and what to speak" (John 12:49), he was referring to direct communion between himself and God, such as the prophets had known.

But it's also plain, I believe, that Jesus gleaned his understanding of his own calling as the Messiah, God's appointed Savior-king, through reading and allowing God to speak to him through the Old Testament Scriptures. And surely the right term to use for that is faith. I, by faith, embrace what I understand of the mind and will of my heavenly Father as he teaches me through his written Word.

We see the perfection of faith in Jesus' last journey to Jerusalem; in his allowing himself to be arrested; in his refusal to ask the Father to send twelve legions of angels to protect him; and in his quiet going to the cross. Why did he put his head into the lion's mouth, as it were? Because he was confident that in this he was doing his Father's will in bearing the world's sin, and that his Father would raise him from death. And this confident faith, as we know, was triumphantly vindicated.

Look back and try to discern the stepping stones of faith which lie behind you and think about those which seem to lie ahead.
Lord, we need the gift of faith in our own lives and in the life of our church so that we may discover, from your Word and one another, your mind and will.

Jesus, delivered up according to the definite plan and foreknowledge of God, you crucified and killed by the hands of lawless men.

Acts 2:23

Why did the Father will the death of his only beloved Son, and in so painful and shameful a form? Because the Father had "laid on him the iniquity of us all" (Isa. 53:6). Jesus' death was *vicarious* (undergone in our place) and *atoning* (securing remission of sins for us and reconciliation to God). It was a *sacrificial* death, fulfilling the principle of atonement taught in connection with the Old Testament sacrifices: "without the shedding of blood there is no forgiveness of sins" (Heb. 9:22; Lev. 17:11).

As the "last Adam," the second man in history to act on mankind's behalf, Jesus died a *representative* death. As a sacrificial victim who put away our sins by undergoing the death penalty that was our due, Jesus died as our *substitute*. By removing God's wrath against us for sin, his death was an act of *propitiation* (Rom. 3:25; 1 John 2:2; 4:10—"expiation," signifying that which puts away sin, is only half the meaning). By saving us from slavery to ungodliness and divine retribution for sin, Jesus' death was an act of *redemption* (Gal. 3:13; Eph. 1:7; 1 Pet. 1:18–19). By mediating and making peace between us and God, it was an act of *reconciliation* (Rom. 5:10–11). It opened the door to our *justification* (pardon and acceptance) and our *adoption* (becoming God's sons and heirs—Rom. 5:1,9; Gal. 4:4–5).

This happy relationship with our Maker, based on and sealed by blood atonement, is the "New Covenant" of which Jesus spoke in the Upper Room (1 Cor. 11:25; Matt. 26:28).

"It's God they ought to crucify" (Sydney Carter: Song). Why?
Meditate on the stupendous fact that it was God they did crucify—and for you.

Christ. . .suffered for you, leaving you an example, that you should follow in his steps.
1 Peter 2:21

---

1 Peter 2:18–25 is one of the many places in the New Testament where a magnificent statement of doctrine slips in quite incidentally to make an ethical point. Verses 22–25 are a rich though compressed review of God's plan of salvation. Peter dwells on Christ's role as God's suffering servant in language that echoes Isaiah chapter 53. He calls attention to Jesus' total innocence and his patience under provocation and pain. He then explains that his innocent suffering was actually a work of vicarious sin-bearing; he reminds his readers that God purposed through this to bring them into a new life in which they said goodbye to sin and lived henceforth by God's Law; and finally he brings before them the fact that they have already turned from their life of sinful wanderings to the living Christ (God's vindication of Jesus through resurrection and exaltation is assumed, though not mentioned), so that Christ has now become their shepherd and overseer—their leader and protector.

What Peter wants his readers to learn from all this is that to follow in the steps of our Savior through suffering is in fact an honor for us—just as it is something which delights God and wins his approval. Following Christ's example in the New Testament means loving and serving others and enduring maltreatment while one does so.

What would be the natural reaction to the suffering described in these verses? What would be the supernatural reaction—the one shown by Jesus? How can I deal with my natural reactions? How can I react supernaturally?
Lord, I cannot deny that my natural response to this situation is. . .But I want to react in your way. Help me.

He looked around at them with anger, grieved at their hardness of heart.
Mark 3:5

Jesus went into the synagogue on the Sabbath and saw a man with a crippled hand. He knew that the Pharisees were watching to see what he would do, and he felt angry that they were only out to put him in the wrong. They did not care a scrap for the handicapped man, nor did they want to see the power and love of God brought to bear on him.

There were other instances where Jesus showed anger or sternness. He "sternly charged" the leper whom he had healed not to tell anyone about it (Mark 1:43) because he foresaw the problems of being pursued by a huge crowd of thoughtless people who were interested only in seeing miracles and not in his teaching. But the leper disobeyed and so made things very hard for Jesus.

Jesus showed anger again when the disciples tried to send away the mothers and their children (Mark 10:13–16). He was indignant and distressed at the way the disciples were thwarting his loving purposes and giving the impression that he did not have time for ordinary people.

He showed anger once more when he drove "out those who sold and those who bought in the temple" (Mark 11:15–17). God's house of prayer was being made into a den of thieves and God was not being glorified—hence Jesus' angry words and deeds. Commenting on this, Warfield wrote: "A man who cannot be angry, cannot be merciful." The person who cannot be angry at things which thwart God's purposes and God's love toward people is living too far away from his fellow men ever to feel anything positive towards them.

Finally, at Lazarus' grave Jesus showed not just sympathy and deep distress for the mourners (John 11:33–35), but also a sense of angry outrage at the monstrosity of death in God's world. This is the meaning of "deeply moved" in John 11:38.

For meditation/application: "Be angry but do not sin; do not let the sun go down on your anger" (Eph. 4:26). When is anger righteous?
Jesus, help me to be angry like you.

Jesus, full of the Holy Spirit, returned from the Jordan, and was led by the Spirit for forty days in the wilderness, tempted by the devil.
Luke 4:1–2

Right at the beginning of Jesus' ministry he was taken into the wilderness to be tempted by the devil, and we read of him showing Satan his resolve to do the will of God at all costs.

I may be wrong, but I think that the way the devil tempted Jesus was not by appearing and identifying himself ("this is your temptor speaking. . ."), but by injecting ideas into his mind. Jesus found himself beset by these strong ideas: "Command this stone to become bread. . . Worship me (Satan) . . . Throw yourself down" (Luke 4:3,7,9). The moment Jesus asked himself where these ideas came from, he knew and rejected them.

The devil was saying to him in effect: "This is how you could have the world as your kingdom. Give the people what they want—food, to start with. Play my game and appeal to the instincts which people under my rule recognize. Dazzle them with a show of personal invulnerability. Then they'll eat out of your hand." But all that was the opposite of God's plan.

Jesus told Satan (it is often good sense to talk out loud to the devil) that neither he nor the people to whom he would minister were going to live on bread alone; they were going to live by the Word of God. He would not worship Satan or look to Satan for any gift because the Bible states that God alone is to be worshipped and trusted. Nor would he presumptuously put his heavenly Father to the test, which was what he would have done by throwing himself down from a pinnacle of the temple. Satan had misapplied Scripture (Ps. 9:11–12) in suggesting that God's promise of protection was an invitation to suicidal action.

Jesus is our example of mature discipleship in recognizing the devil's temptations as they cut across God's Word, in rejecting the satanic suggestions, and in asserting that he would go God's way and live by Scripture, whatever happens. Like Jesus, we can throw the Book at Satan; while doing so, we should pray that Jesus himself will drive him back.

How much of the Book do I know well enough to be able to throw at the devil? *Lord, I pray for complete receptivity to your Word so that it will sink in and stay in—ready for use when needed.*

As... you received Christ Jesus the Lord, so live in him, rooted and built up in him and established in the faith, just as you were taught, abounding in thanksgiving.
Colossians 2:6

Read Colossians 2:6–19 and see what Paul says about the adequacy of Christ. The key verses are 6–8, which also sum up the message of Colossians. Let Jesus Christ be everything to you, Paul says. Live in him; acknowledge him as the ground in which you are rooted and the one who builds you up in the church; the one for whom you should constantly give God thanks because of the wealth he has brought you.

Paul's directive follows from his doctrine of who and what Christ is. Christ is and must be pre-eminent. In Christ God has renewed our hearts (inward circumcision and burial in baptism). Having found us spiritually dead, he brought us to life with Christ through faith (risen in baptism and forgiven). Through the cross he cancelled our death-sentence which the broken Law demanded and overthrew all the forces of cosmic evil. For those who have eyes to see, Christ's cross (which looked like a humiliating defeat) was actually his march of triumph in which he led his foes captive, in the manner of a Roman general after a successful campaign.

Paul's central point is that nobody needs more than Christ gives. For a Christian to turn to Judaizing ritualism, angel-worship, and the murky world of visions is not gain but loss. Christ alone makes the church, his body, live and grow spiritually. Christians must hold fast to the head and not seek spiritual enrichment from other sources; it's not there to be had and to seek it is to lose touch with Christ. Paul is attacking the particular errors of the Colossian theosophists but modern occultism and superstition fall equally under his apostolic ban.

Do you agree that nobody needs more than Christ gives?
Lord, lead me not into the temptation of trying to improve on your adequacy, and deliver me from the evil of taking it for granted.

Sources

June 1	Taped message	July 18	"Life in Christ" in *Bible Characters and Doctrines*
June 2	"Life in Christ" in *Bible Characters and Doctrines*	July 19	Ibid.
June 3	"My Path of Prayer" in *My Path of Prayer*	July 20	"My Path of Prayer" in *My Path of Prayer*
June 4	Taped message	July 21	Taped message
June 5	Ibid.	July 22	"On Knowing God" in *Our Sovereign God*
June 6	"Life in Christ" in *Bible Characters and Doctrines*	July 23	Ibid.
June 7	"My Path of Prayer" in *My Path of Prayer*	July 24	*Evangelism and the Sovereignty of God*
June 8	Taped message	July 25	"The Gospel: Its Content and Communication" in *Gospel and Culture*
June 9	Ibid.		
June 10	Ibid.		
June 11	Ibid.	July 26	Taped message
June 12	Ibid.	July 27	Ibid.
June 13	Ibid.	July 28	Ibid.
June 14	Ibid.	July 29	*Keep in Step with the Spirit*
June 15	*We Believe*	July 30	*Evangelism and the Sovereignty of God*
June 16	*God Has Spoken*		
June 17	Ibid.	July 31	"Christianity and Non-Christian Religions" in *Christianity Today*
June 18	*Beyond the Battle for the Bible*		
June 19	*God Has Spoken*		
June 20	*Fundamentalism and the Word of God*	August 1	*Knowing God*
June 21	"A Lamp in a Dark Place" in *Can We Trust the Bible?*	August 2	Ibid.
		August 3	"The Origin and History of Fundamentalism" in *The Word of God and Fundamentalism*
June 22	"Conscience, Choice and Character" in *Law, Morality and the Bible*	August 4	*Knowing God*
June 23	"Predestination and Sanctification" in *Tenth*	August 5	Ibid.
		August 6	"The Message is Unchanged" in *Alliance Witness*
June 24	*Keep in Step with the Spirit*	August 7	"Predestination and Sanctification" in *Tenth*
June 25	Taped message		
June 26	Ibid.	August 8	"Knowing Notions or Knowing God?" in *Pastoral Renewal*
June 27	"Conscience, Choice and Character" in *Law, Morality and the Bible*		
June 28	Ibid.	August 9	*God Has Spoken*
June 29	Ibid.	August 10	Ibid.
June 30	Ibid.	August 11	Ibid.
		August 12	Ibid.
July 1	Taped message	August 13	Ibid.
July 2	Ibid.	August 14	Ibid.
July 3	Ibid.	August 15	*Knowing God*
July 4	Ibid.	August 16	Taped message
July 5	Ibid.	August 17	Ibid.
July 6	*Knowing God*	August 18	Ibid.
July 7	Ibid.	August 19	Ibid.
July 8	Taped message	August 20	Ibid.
July 9	Ibid.	August 21	Ibid.
July 10	Ibid.	August 22	Ibid.
July 11	*Keep in Step with the Spirit*	August 23	"Jesus Christ the Lord" in *The Lord Christ*
July 12	Taped message		
July 13	"Joy" in *Discovery Papers*	August 24	"Life in Christ" in *Bible Characters and Doctrines*
July 14	Ibid.		
July 15	*Tomorrow's Worship*	August 25	"The Message is Unchanged" in *Alliance Witness*
July 16	*Knowing God*		
July 17	Taped message	August 26	*The Plan of God*

August 27	*Fundamentalism and the Word of God*
August 28	Taped message
August 29	"With All Thy Mind" in *Inter-Varsity*
August 30	Taped message
August 31	Ibid.
September 1	"Meeting God: Some Thoughts on Isaiah 6" in *Special Collection Journal*
September 2	Ibid.
September 3	Ibid.
September 4	Ibid.
September 5	Ibid.
September 6	"An Infinitely Extended Rice Pudding" in *Viewpoint*
September 7	*Knowing God*
September 8	Ibid.
September 9	*Keep in Step with the Spirit*
September 10	Taped message
September 11	"Three Studies in Biblical Evangelism" in *St. Andrews 73 Report on Conference on Evangelism in Scotland*
September 12	*Keep in Step with the Spirit*
September 13	"Life in Christ" in *Bible Characters and Doctrines*
September 14	"Body Life" in *Tenth*
September 15	*Evangelism and the Sovereignty of God*
September 16	"Body Life" in *Tenth*
September 17	*Keep in Step with the Spirit*
September 18	Taped message
September 19	Ibid.
September 20	*The Plan of God*
September 21	*Keep in Step with the Spirit*
September 22	*Knowing God*
September 23	Taped message
September 24	*We Believe*
September 25	*Knowing God*
September 26	Taped message
September 27	*God Has Spoken*
September 28	Taped message
September 29	"All Men Will Not Be Saved" in *Banner of Truth*
September 30	Taped message
October 1	Ibid.
October 2	Ibid.
October 3	"My Path of Prayer" in *My Path of Prayer*
October 4	Taped message
October 5	Ibid.
October 6	Ibid.
October 7	Ibid.
October 8	Ibid.
October 9	Ibid.
October 10	Ibid.
October 11	*Knowing God*
October 12	"The Message is Unchanged" in *Alliance Witness*
October 13	*Knowing God*
October 14	"Life in Christ" in *Bible Characters and Doctrines*
October 15	*God Has Spoken*
October 16	*The Plan of God*
October 17	*Keep in Step with the Spirit*
October 18	"To All Who Will Come" in *Our Saviour God*
October 19	"The Message is Unchanged" in *Alliance Witness*
October 20	"Sacrifice and Satisfaction" in *Our Saviour God*
October 21	Taped message
October 22	Ibid.
October 23	Ibid.
October 24	Ibid.
October 25	Ibid.
October 26	"Blind Spots" in *Discipulus*
October 27	Ibid.
October 28	Taped message
October 29	Ibid.
October 30	Ibid.
October 31	Ibid.
November 1	Ibid.
November 2	*Keep in Step with the Spirit*
November 3	"Conscience, Choice and Character" in *Law, Morality and the Bible*
November 4	*Knowing God*
November 5	"Poor Health May Be the Best Remedy" in *Christianity Today*
November 6	*Knowing God*
November 7	"Conscience, Choice and Character" in *Law, Morality and the Bible*
November 8	"A Lamp in a Dark Place" in *Can We Trust the Bible?*
November 9	*God Has Spoken*
November 10	Ibid.
November 11	"Life in Christ" in *Bible Characters and Doctrines*
November 12	Ibid.
November 13	"A Lamp in a Dark Place" in *Can We Trust the Bible?*
November 14	*God Has Spoken*
November 15	"Why is Authority a Dirty Word?" in *Spectrum*
November 16	"Life in Christ" in *Bible Characters and Doctrines*
November 17	"The Puritans and the Lord's Day" in *Servants of the Word*
November 18	"Situations and Principles" in *Law, Morality and the Bible*
November 19	"Life in Christ" in *Bible Characters and Doctrines*

Bibliography

"All Men Will Not Be Saved." In *Banner of Truth* 41(March 1965). Edinburgh, Scotland: The Banner of Truth Trust Publishers, 1965.

"Are Pain and Suffering Direct Results of Evil?" In *Moral Questions*, edited by Frank Colquhoun. East Sussex, England: Falcon Books, 1977.

"Atheism." In *Inter-Varsity* (Special Introductory Issue 1964). Leicester, England: Inter-Varsity Press, 1964.

Beyond the Battle for the Bible. Westchester, Illinois: Good News Publishers/Crossway Books, 1980.

"Blind Spots." In *Discipulus* (Advent 1954). Bristol, England: Trinity College.

"Body Life." In *Tenth* (July 1981). Philadelphia: 10th Presbyterian Church, 1981.

"Christianity and Non-Christian Religions." In *Christianity Today* (December 21, 1959). Carol Stream, Illinois: Christianity Today, 1959.

"Conscience, Choice and Character." In *Law, Morality and the Bible*, edited by Kay and Veenhan. Downers Grove, Illinois: InterVarsity Press, 1978.

"Death: Life's One and Only Certainty." In *Eternity* (March 1965). Philadelphia: Eternity, 1965.

Evangelism and the Sovereignty of God. Downers Grove, Illinois: InterVarsity Press. ©1961 by Inter-Varsity Fellowship, Leicester, England.

"Feet in the Clouds." In *Regent Quarterly Bulletin* (Spring 1984). Vancouver, B.C.: Regent College, 1984.

Fundamentalism and the Word of God. Grand Rapids, Michigan: Eerdman's Printing Company, 1958.

God Has Spoken. Downer's Grove, Illinois: InterVarsity Press, 1979.

"God's Word—Changed Lives." In *Canadian Report* (September 1983). Abbotsford, B.C.: Campus Crusade, 1983.

"The Gospel: Its Content and Communication." In *Gospel and Culture*, edited by J. Stott, R. Coote. Pasadena, California: William Carey Press. ©1979 by The Lausanne Committee for World Evangelization.

"The Holy Spirit and Authority." In *The Almond Branch* (1962). Bristol, England: Trinity College.

"The Holy Spirit and the Local Congregation." In *Churchman* LXXVIII.2 (June 1964). London, England: Church Society, 1964.

"An Infinitely Extended Rice Pudding." In *Viewpoint* 28. London, England: Inter-Schools Christian Fellowship. n.d.

"Introductory Essay to John Owen's The Death of Death in the Death of Christ." In *Banner of Truth* (1959). Edinburgh, Scotland: The Banner of Truth Trust Publishers, 1959.

"Isn't One Religion as Good as Another?" In *Hard Questions*, edited by Frank Colquhoun. East Sussex, England: Falcon Books, 1967.

I Want to Be a Christian. Wheaton, Illinois: Tyndale House Publishers, Inc., 1977.

"Jesus Christ the Lord." In *The Lord Christ*, edited by John R.W. Stott. London, England: Collins Publishers, 1977.

"Joy." In *Discovery Papers* (February 20, 1977). Palo Alto, California: Peninsula Bible Church, 1977.

Keep in Step with the Spirit. Old Tappan, New Jersey: Fleming H. Revell Company, 1984.

Knowing God. Downers Grove, Illinois: InterVarsity Press, 1973.

"Knowing Notions or Knowing God?" In *Pastoral Renewal* 6.9 (March 1982). Ann Arbor, Michigan: Pastoral Renewal, 1982.

"A Lamp in a Dark Place." In *Can We Trust the Bible?*, edited by Earl Radmacher. Wheaton, Illinois: Tyndale House Publishers, 1979.

"Life in Christ." In *Bible Characters and Doctrines*, Vol. 11. London, England: Scripture Union, 1974.

"Lord, Send Revival." In *The Bulletin of Westminster Theological Seminary* (Winter 1983). Philadelphia: Westminster Theological Seminary, 1983.

"Meeting God: Some Thoughts on Isaiah 6." In *Special Collection Journal* (Winter 1984). Berkeley, California: Spiritual Counterfeits Project, 1984.

"The Message is Unchanged." In The Alliance Witness (June 23, 1982). Nyack, New York: The Alliance Witness, 1982.

"The Nature of the Church." In *Basic Christian Doctrines*, edited by C.F.H. Henry. New York: Holt, Rinehart & Winston, 1962.

"On Knowing God." In *Our Sovereign God*, edited by James M. Boice. Grand Rapids, Michigan: Baker Book House, 1977.

"The Origin and History of Fundamentalism." In *The Word of God and Fundamentalism*, edited by T. Hewitt. London, England: Church Book Room, 1960.

"My Path of Prayer." In *My Path of Prayer*, edited by David Hanes. Sussex, England: Henry E. Walter Ltd., 1981.

The Plan of God. London, England: Evangelical Press, 1962.

"Poor Health May Be the Best Remedy." In *Christianity Today* (May 21, 1982). Carol Stream, Illinois: *Christianity Today*, 1982.

"Predestination and Sanctification." In *Tenth* (July 1983). Philadelphia: 10th Presbyterian Church, 1983.

"The Puritans and the Lord's Day." In *Servants of the Word*, n.p., 1957.

"Regeneration." In *Baker's Dictionary of Theology*, edited by C.F.H. Henry, Grand Rapids, Michigan: Baker Book House, 1959. Rev. to *Evangelical Dictionary of Theology*, edited by Walter Elwell. Grand Rapids, Michigan: Baker Book House, 1984.

"Sacrifice and Satisfaction." in *Our Saviour God*, edited by James M. Boice. Grand Rapids, Michigan: Baker Book House, 1981.

"Situations and Principles." In *Law, Morality and the Bible*, edited by Kay and Veenhan. Downers Grove, Illinois: InterVarsity Press, 1978.

"Steps to the Renewal of the Christian People." In *Summons to Faith and Renewal: Christian Renewal in a Post-Christian World*, edited by Peter Williamson and Kevin Perrotta. Ann Arbor, Michigan: Servant Publications, 1983.

"Three Studies in Biblical Evangelism." In *St. Andrews 73 Report on Conference on Evangelism in Scotland*, n.p.

"To All Who Will Come." In *Our Saviour God*, edited by James M. Boice. Grand Rapids, Michigan: Baker Book House, 1981.

"Training for Christian Service." In *The Evangelical Christian* (September 1961). Toronto, Ontario: Evangelical Publishers, 1961.

"Walking to Emmaüs with the Great Physician." In *Christianity Today* (April 10, 1981). Carol Stream, Illinois: Christianity Today, 1981.

"The Way of Salvation." In *Bibliotheca Sacra* nos. 515-18 (Part I, July 1972–April 1973). Dallas, Texas: Dallas Theological Seminary, 1972.

We Believe. Surrey, England: The Nurses Christian Fellowship, 1972.

"What Did the Cross Achieve?" In *Tyndale Bulletin* 25 (1974). Leicester, England: Inter-Varsity Press, 1974.

"What is Evangelism?" In *Theological Perspectives on Church Growth*, edited by Harvie M. Conn. Phillipsburg, New Jersey: Presbyterian & Reformed Publishing Company. ©1976 by Den Dulk Foundation.

"Why is Authority a Dirty Word?" In *Spectrum* (May 1977). London, England: Spectrum, 1977.

"With All Thy Mind." In *Inter-Varsity* (1959). Leicester, England: Inter-Varsity Press, 1959.

Printed in the United States
by Baker & Taylor Publisher Services